LINCOLN'S
QUEST
FOR UNION

LINCOLN'S QUEST FOR UNION

Public and Private Meanings

CHARLES B. STROZIER

Basic Books, Inc., Publishers

NEW YORK

Special acknowledgment goes to the Illinois State Historical Library for permission to quote from the Robert Todd Lincoln collection.

Photographs credited to *Ostendorf Collection* on pages 16, 36, 80, 93, 130, 133, 168 and 226 are courtesy of Lloyd Ostendorf, Dayton, Ohio.

The photograph on page 136 is from *Lincoln in Photographs: An Album of Every Known Pose,* by Charles Hamilton and Lloyd Ostendorf. Copyright © 1963 by the University of Oklahoma Press.

Library of Congress Cataloging in Publication Data

Strozier, Charles B.
  Lincoln's quest for union.

  Includes bibliographical references and index.
  1. Lincoln, Abraham, 1809–1865.   2.   Presidents—
United States—Biography.   I.   Title.
E457.S897   973.7'092'4   [B]   81–68406
ISBN 0-465-04119-1   AACR2

For Carol

CONTENTS

LIST OF
ILLUSTRATIONS

PREFACE

INCOLN'S story fades into legend. As a result, we are probably better informed about the trivial anecdotes and more confused about the significant events of his formative years than about those of any other figure in American history. Most of us know—or think we know—a good deal more about his rail splitting or his absentmindedness than we do about the shape of his personality, especially the sources of his periodic, paralyzing bouts of depression; what gave meaning to his relationship with his wife and his children (and what difference it makes); and what made him a uniquely fitted leader for a nation rent by discord. In suggesting some tentative answers to these and related questions, I have drawn upon a considerable body of documentary evidence. Throughout my approach is avowedly psychohistorical: that is, I have attempted to apply concepts from psychoanalytic theory critically and unobtrusively to bring the evidence alive in some new ways.

No one can tell the completely "true" story of any piece of the past. In the case of Lincoln it is particularly difficult to sort out fact from legend. For his childhood, there are no contemporary records, except indirect and relatively insignificant documents such as bills of sale. Both of Lincoln's parents were illiterate, so the tapestry of letters one often finds in educated families is absent. Myth-makers have found great material in Lincoln's early years because of the paucity of evidence about them and because of the idealizing needs of a country newly reunited after a terrible civil war.

The years of youth and maturity, though better documented, also have been caught up in exaggeration and legend. None of us can remain totally free from the legends of Abraham Lincoln, for they are too deeply embedded in the American consciousness. We learn them too early. The story comes to us as a fairy tale and we in turn embellish it with unconscious fantasy. Often as adults we turn against such idealized images of our childhood. A figure like Lincoln easily attracts debunkers who search relentlessly for warts that will turn heroes into antiheroes. Psychologically, however, debunking and idealizing represent two sides of our ambivalent attitude toward parental figures. Both are rooted in the needs and confusions of childhood and carry the burden of irrational distortion.

Probably every biographer identifies with his subject to some extent and is likely to distort the subject if he fails to acknowledge this. In this book I make no naive claim of being above this dilemma. The "real" Lincoln remains obscure to me. However, I have been acutely sensitive to the issue of my own involvement with Lincoln. I have analyzed my dreams of him and noted rather precisely the way he fits into my fantasies. I have tried to gain insight into the point of convergence between his life and my own. Such self-examination is not frivolous self-absorption but an attempt to go beyond mere idealization or debunking to the critical subjectivity that defines the working method of psychohistory.[1]

To a large extent this book is theoretically eclectic. There is nothing to be gained in psychohistory by forcing historical materials into any Procrustean bed. I have tried to become familiar with the essence of psychoanalytic theory since Freud and to use it to shape my questions of the sources. Many competing "schools," for example, have shed light on the intricacies of the mourning process. I have tried to read widely and deeply in this literature. Nevertheless, as a close student of Heinz Kohut and as a product of the Chicago Institute for Psychoanalysis, I owe a special intellectual debt to psychoanalytic self psychology. In the early chapters of this book Kohut's influence is more implicit than explicit. Toward the end, however, my essential ideas come from "seeing" the material in terms of self psychology.

Chapter 8 is especially problematic. It is highly theoretical and necessarily tentative. It leads into the subject with a theme in Lincoln's house divided speech, but the goal is to understand psychologically the crisis of the 1850s to which Lincoln responded. The perspective shifts from the close examination of the man to the times. The analysis is complicated, and the reader may find it overly ambitious and provocative. Some use there of psychoanalytic terminology is inevitable. For those whose interests focus solely on Lincoln, it might be wise to skip chapter 8. For the rest, take a deep breath.

For the most part this book relies on sources familiar to historians. There is no way anyone could read everything that has been written on Lincoln, nor would anyone of intelligence want to. Most is trivial or legendary or derivative. One learns after some time in the Lincoln field which books are reliable, and these are dutifully mentioned in my notes. But the essential source for the book is Lincoln himself, his letters, speeches, poetry, and miscellaneous writing that make up *The Collected Works*. I have also consulted the letters, diaries, and comments of those contemporaries who knew or worked with Lincoln. This book is biography, not social history, but I have tried to paint as rich a picture as possible of Lincoln's world.

One Lincoln document I use extensively deserves special mention. On the brink of his election as President, Lincoln wrote a very brief autobiographical sketch. This document lacks the expansive quality of Gandhi's *My Experiments with Truth*, the bombastic fervor of Hitler's *Mein Kampf*, or the relentlessly introspective vigor of Freud's *The Interpretation of Dreams*. Still, it is important for an understanding of Lincoln. In it, he looked back on his childhood, youth, and rise to prominence at that critical juncture before accomplishing his major work. Certainly political ambition motivated his reflections. Few people outside of Illinois knew much about him, and in those days it was regarded as unseemly for a candidate to campaign in his own behalf. His story, as prepared for John L. Scripps in the early summer of 1860, brought before the public the politically relevant facts of his life. But the effort of recalling his past also brought forth a number of psychologically significant memories filtered through a half century of experience. Telling that story was not an easy chore for Lincoln, whom his law partner, William Herndon, once characterized as "the most shut-mouthed man" he had ever known. "There was something about his origin he never cared to dwell on," Herndon wrote.[2] In talking with Lincoln, Scripps at first faced considerable difficulty in getting him to communicate "the homely facts of his youth." Lincoln protested to Scripps that it was "a great piece of folly to attempt to make anything out of my early life. It can all be condensed into a simple sentence, and that sentence you will find in Gray's Elegy, 'The short and simple annals of the poor.' That's my life, and that's all you or anyone else can make out of it."[3]

Anyone working on Lincoln has to deal with William Herndon. The devoted law partner decided from the moment of Lincoln's death that he would spend the rest of his life researching and writing a biography. He spent many years jotting down his own thoughts and collecting the thoughts of others. But the book itself languished. Herndon, in need of money, allowed Ward Hill Lamon and his ghost writer, Chauncey Black, to use, for a fee, his materials for their 1872 *Life*. Herndon's book did finally appear in 1889, but only with the help of a competent young journalist, Jesse Weik. What emerged from this collaboration was an extensive correspondence between the two coauthors and the most controversial book ever written on Lincoln. Bound in "three ridiculous little volumes," as Herndon's biographer, David Donald, comments, Herndon's *Lincoln* "has been absorbed into the stream of American folklore. It is usually safe to wager that any well-known anecdote about Lincoln derives from Herndon's writings."[4]

But there is more than folklore to Herndon's *Lincoln*. Herndon knew Lincoln longer and saw him in more varied public, private, and work situations than did any other man or woman except for Lincoln's wife, Mary, who left no such full record. Herndon had a rich fund of experience on which to draw, and in his own curious way he was committed to the truth. He created virtually every important myth about Lincoln, and yet his book made him our most important source on the pre-Presidential man. The key to truth or falsehood in Herndon lies in attention to his own sources and understanding a few important characteristics of his personality. He was an outgoing, flamboyant, young man who seemed to become instantly and uncritically loyal to Lincoln when he joined him as a law partner in 1844. Herndon jealously rivaled Mary for Lincoln's attention. The proud owner of an impressive library, he was well read and informed on current intellectual developments. He served actively in Whig, and later Republican, circles, and even won election for one term as Springfield's mayor. He was a highly competent lawyer whom Lincoln was able to entrust with an equal share of the business and, during Lincoln's frequent spells of campaigning, all of it.

Yet Herndon, when he later attempted to analyze Lincoln, lacked a sense of humor and seemed constitutionally deficient in compassion or empathy. His mind was always rushing forward, frantically searching for a new idea before digesting the last one. He loved to pile on adjectives with breathless haste. Lincoln was thus "tough-solid-knotty-gnarly, more or less like his body."[5] Dashes also expressed the flurry and confusion in Herndon's mind: "The *whole* of the man objectively and subjectively, should be truthfully and fully, without suppression, suggestion—or evasion—or other form of falsehood, stated—generously written out."[6]

Herndon never consciously lied. In fact he attempted (at times with a kind of naive passion) to tell the truth. David Donald was struck by the fact that no letter or manuscript of Herndon's "reveals a desire or willingness to tell an untruth about Lincoln."[7] This is in marked contrast to Lincoln's secretaries, John G. Nicolay and John Hay, for example, who deliberately skewed their story of Lincoln to keep Robert Lincoln happy, for he controlled the papers on which their book was based. However, Herndon was a terrible historian, a gullible listener, and a pretentious generalizer. When he relied on someone else as a source—that is, when he acted as a historian organizing and interpreting the evidence rather than providing it from personal experience—he was usually wrong. Thus most of Herndon's portrait of Lincoln that falls outside their period of extended contact (1837 to 1861) can be discarded.

There are also problems with what Herndon reports about Lincoln in the years when he knew him in Springfield. Paul Angle, who wrote a preface to Herndon's republished book in 1930, felt that "when Herndon relates a fact of his own observation, it may generally be accepted without question. . . ."[8] It is easy by this criterion to discard the highly dramatic story of Lincoln as a defaulting groom in 1841, for it is based on the erroneous testimony of Elizabeth Edwards forty-odd years afterward. But even on those years when he was closest to Lincoln, Herndon often got things muddled, his memory sometimes blurred, and his own idealization of Lincoln helped give a mythical edge to his story. For example, he claimed to know some surprising things about Lincoln's sexual activities.[9] Most of these statements require corroboration before they can even tentatively be accepted. Finally, Herndon tended to overstate his own importance and, on many issues, to misunderstand Lincoln's subtle irony.

A different kind of problem is presented by Herndon's portrait of Mary and Lincoln's domestic life. Herndon's view of Mary was distinctly uncharitable and he characterized Lincoln's home life as a "domestic hell." We know from other sources that Mary always detested Herndon for his vulgarity and drunkenness and, perhaps, because she cherished an exclusive love for Lincoln that Herndon's abject devotion seemed to threaten. The fact that Herndon never entered the Lincoln home might cast some doubt on his account of their domestic relations. However, Herndon worked daily with Lincoln not four blocks from that home, saw him interact with his children at the offices on Sunday, and was himself a member of the same small (perhaps "tight" would be more accurate) Springfield community as Lincoln for his entire adult life. Therefore, his views on Lincoln's domestic life, though indirect, merit serious, if cautious, consideration.

The material Herndon collected for his book presents even more complex problems than his personal memories of events. After Lincoln's death, he wrote to everyone he could who had known Lincoln and asked them to write down their memories. He also interviewed former acquaintances throughout Kentucky, Indiana, and central Illinois and, with the illiterate, wrote down what they told him. This was one of the first extensive oral history projects in American history and, until technology facilitated interviewing, one of the most important. These fascinating materials have never really been adequately used. Ward Hill

Lamon and Chauncey Black, lacking sympathy for Lincoln, insensitive to nuance, and unable to evaluate this material critically, abused the material in their 1872 *Life*. The same can be said for most writers, including Herndon himself, until Carl Sandburg, whose 1920s *Abraham Lincoln* was sympathetic and sensitive but, alas, not very critical. In fact, Sandburg's lyrical success turned subsequent writers against the Herndon material altogether. Sandburg wrote poetry, not history.

Around the time of Sandburg, Albert Beveridge, a relentless researcher, presented a marvelously detailed picture of Lincoln's early days and log cabin life. His description, to my mind, remains the best available for detail and accuracy. But Beveridge's account has its limitations. He viewed Thomas Lincoln harshly, was disgusted with rural life in general, and seemed to be ambivalent about Lincoln himself. Beveridge's most significant failing was that he had no sensitivity to important psychological issues. Thus his only comment on the effect of the death of Lincoln's mother restricts the possibility of interpretation: "Abraham was now nine years old, and there is no evidence that his emotions were unlike those of other children of similar age and in that situation."[10]

The two important biographers of the last generation—Benjamin P. Thomas and Stephen Oates—used the Herndon documents sparingly. There is, of course, need for extreme caution in using this material. Memories fade and, with Lincoln, many factors in play after 1865 distorted dimly recalled antebellum scenes. By then any early association, even a fantasized one, with the martyred President was treasured. One can make a good case that the best approach to these documents is to use in them only what can be corroborated elsewhere in the written record.

That approach, however, shortchanges the value of Herndon's vast records. Oral history is now regarded with much more respect than before. Roy Basler, who helped turn subsequent writers away from the Herndon material with his comments on Sandburg in 1935,[11] has recently changed his mind. "When I was writing *The Lincoln Legend*," he said in 1979, "I was a young man and saw the people Herndon talked to as old fools. I'm now

almost a half century older and read this material differently."
Basler also noted that, although it is unlikely the interpretation of
Lincoln's war years would change much, the complete story of
Lincoln's childhood and youth—indeed, the whole story before
1860—has yet to be written.[12]

ACKNOWLEDGMENTS

IRST books require undue encouragement from friends and colleagues. It is unlikely I can adequately thank everyone who has contributed to whatever insight this book brings to the study of Lincoln. Five people especially have read repeated drafts of emerging, often awkward, chapters and then reviewed the completed manuscript with care. Without their sustained interest over many years, I could never have completed the task. Often they disagreed with my conclusions, sometimes passionately. But each in different ways helped me make my points infinitely more clear.

Some eight years ago Geoffrey C. Ward, editor of *American Heritage* and himself an authority on Lincoln, read the first version of what is now chapter 2. His written comments nearly equaled the length of my short paper. He insisted I was onto something that needed elaboration. Subsequently, as a book began to emerge, he read every word, added innumerable insights, corrected errors, and, in many conversations, nudged me along. No footnote can document that kind of assistance.

As work proceeded, I began an extended conversation with a colleague in history at Sangamon State University, Christopher N. Breiseth (now Dean of Deep Springs College in California). He got it all before it even made sense to me. He listened and provoked and read and listened some more. He always asked the crucial question, and he shared unsparingly his ideas from his own area of scholarship—Lincoln and race. Often his casual asides became my orienting ideas. Chapter 7, as I remember, began in a noisy cafeteria over spilled coffee.

Sometime in the mid-1970s, Richard Current, one of a handful of recognized authorities on Lincoln, got interested in my work. His role in shaping inchoate ideas was incomparable. He seldom left a page without rewriting whole sections of murky prose.

Along the way, he taught me what good writing is all about and the incredible difference it makes to find the right word. He also never hesitated to share his own knowledge and to let me know decisively when I was off base.

Roy Basler, the editor of Lincoln's *Collected Works* and a distinguished scholar, also proved to be an enormously helpful reader. More than most, Roy disagreed with many of my conclusions. But his caveats directed me toward greater clarity. I always assumed that anyone of Roy Basler's stature who took that much time to disagree affirmed something essentially valuable in my work. He was especially helpful with what are now chapters 1, 2, 3, 4, and 9.

I was also the beneficiary of Stephen B. Oates's careful reading of the manuscript at various stages, including at the end, when he fitted it into a crushing deadline on his biography of Martin Luther King, Jr. Oates's 1977 book on Lincoln, *With Malice toward None,* is now justly the standard biography. He contributed numerous helpful suggestions and qualifications, almost all of which I unabashedly folded into the text. Oates's disagreement with me is on the subject of Lincoln and race. But if we all agreed on what the sources said to us, how could we ever justify all these books?

I also benefited in many ways from the help of Bruce Mazlish of the Massachusetts Institute of Technology, who has followed this book closely for the last four years. His comments were always instructive. He constantly prodded me to be clear and free of jargon. He also arranged two presentations of my work, at M.I.T. and at the Group for Applied Psychoanalysis at Harvard, experiences that forced me to think again about many issues.

A number of other friends and colleagues went through the final manuscript with care and devotion. Tom Kohut offered a wide range of helpful comments. Jack Nolan improved the style immeasurably. John Y. Simon (who also read drafts of two earlier chapters) caught some egregious errors in the final version and offered kind words of support. Lawrence J. Friedman also read two earlier chapters and made extensive comments on the completed manuscript that proved helpful. Harold Holzer caught

numerous errors, large and small, but most of all gave encouragement at a time when it was sorely needed. Lary Shiner read the
manuscript carefully and then prodded me to conclude. Marilyn
Immel listened to pieces of my Lincoln work for years and read
the final manuscript in a quizzical but supportive way. Judy
Everson and Mike Lennon improved the text at many points.
Both also helped me find a title. Linnea Larson read it all with
care and offered particularly useful comments on chapter 8.

Most of my students' eyes glazed over whenever I started in on
Lincoln again. But two—Mark Johnson and Cliff Wilson—listened carefully and read the final manuscript critically. The rest
endured.

Many others have read parts of this book during its long birth.
All have helped a great deal. These include (not in any special
order): Mark Neely, Gabot Boritt, Robert Brugger, Stanley H.
Cath, Norman Naimark, Ernest Wolf, Fred Weinstein, James E.
Hurt, Frank J. Williams, Daniel Offer, Neil Harris, George Fred-
rickson, George B. Forgie, Cullom Davis, William Gilmore,
Becky Veach, Ralph Stone, Richard Johnston, and Kathleen
Dalton.

From 1974 to 1977 I directed a project funded by the National
Endowment for the Humanities to develop interpretive materials
for the Lincoln sites in Springfield. That project proved an education in itself. Most of the scholars who served as advisers for
that project already have been thanked for their later involvement
in my own work. But I also want to extend my sincere thanks to
Don Fehrenbacher, who taught me a great deal about Lincoln. I
also want to thank Gern Stern, our producer, whose search for
Lincoln paralleled my own. One important result of the project
was to make me intimately familiar with the physical sites of the
Lincoln story. An understanding of those sites could only have
come from the sustained help and friendship of many people in
Springfield, who helped me come to know Lincoln: Sally and
Paul Schanbacher, Carolyn and Bob Oxtoby, Edith and Jim
Myers, Al Banton, Molly Becker, and Calista Herndon.

In 1973, I presented some of my Lincoln work to the Seattle
Psychoanalytic Institute, which proved useful. I would also like

to thank my classmates (and Jerome Kavka) at the Chicago Institute for Psychoanalysis who listened once to four hours of Lincoln—and had much to contribute. Mel Prosen, my coleader of the psychohistory seminar and associate chairman of the Department of Psychiatry at Rush Medical School in Chicago, has heard much of Lincoln and graciously shared his intimate knowledge of psychoanalytic theory.

Thanks for critical forums are also extended to the Illinois Adolescent Society, the Illinois State Historical Society, and the Department of Psychiatry at Michael Reese Hospital in Chicago. Two quite different formal settings—the Center for Psychosocial Studies in Chicago and the National Endowment for the Humanities' summer seminar in psychohistory at Brandeis University—gave me the benefit of John Demos's insightful comments. I also want to thank the other members of the National Endowment summer seminar for their thoughts on chapter 8.

Many libraries and their always helpful staffs have assisted me. But one—the Illinois State Historical Library in Springfield—deserves very special mention. James T. Hickey shared his extensive knowledge of Lincoln and allowed me to read the letters of Robert Todd Lincoln. Cheryl Schnirring fetched documents cheerfully. Roger Bridges always had a kind word. Dan Holt helped in diverse ways. Laurel Bowen guided me through many confusions. I also want to thank many—especially John Patterson—in the Illinois Department of Conservation for help at many points. Ruth Friedman, a graduate student at Sangamon State, generously shared some of her research on the eighth judicial circuit. Another student, Terry Otten, shared his work and helped introduce me to the records from Jacksonville State Hospital.

Two research assistants at quite different stages of this book deserve special mention. In the beginning, Becky Veach tracked down countless references and gathered materials. Then, at the end as I was completing the final draft and finishing off footnotes, Melinda Kwedar proved invaluable.

With all this expert advice, I wish I could disclaim responsibility for errors of fact and interpretation that remain. But, alas, for better or worse, it is all my fault.

Acknowledgments

There's an old saw among Lincoln students—a decidedly male bunch—that their wives have to go to bed every night with Abraham Lincoln. For that, and much more, I thank Carol.

CHARLES B. STROZIER
Springfield, Illinois
July 14, 1981

LINCOLN'S
QUEST
FOR UNION

Chapter 1

Childhood on the Frontier

I have found that people who know that they are preferred or favoured by their mother[s] give evidence in their lives of a peculiar self-reliance and an unshakeable optimism which often seem like heroic attributes and bring actual success to their possessors.

SIGMUND FREUD
The Interpretation of Dreams

OD bless my mother," Lincoln told his law partner, William Herndon, in 1850. "All that I am or ever hope to be I owe to her." This simple, direct, and perhaps eternal human sentiment had particular poignancy for Lincoln because he believed his mother was illegitimate. This statement to Herndon was one of the few times Lincoln mentioned his mother. He and Herndon were riding in a buggy to court in Menard County to handle a suit that raised the issue of hereditary traits. Lincoln said his mother, Nancy, was the illegitimate daughter of Lucy Hanks and a well-bred Virginia farmer or planter. From this Virginian, Herndon remembered Lincoln saying, came all the traits—his power of analysis, logic, mental activity, and ambition—that distinguished him from the Hanks family. He even appeared to believe that "illegitimate children are oftentimes sturdier and brighter than those born in lawful wedlock. . . ." Having unburdened himself, Lincoln became quiet and was "sad and absorbed." The buggy moved on but not a word was spoken. "He drew round him a barrier which I feared to penetrate. His words and melancholy tone made a deep impression on me. It was an experience I can never forget."[1]

There are a variety of ways to interpret Herndon's account of this experience. One is to dismiss it as improbable. To do so, however, is to reject Herndon as a source in the one area where all thoughtful observers agree his word is valid: where he recounts an actual experience he had with Lincoln. The episode, of course, proves nothing about Lincoln's genealogy. It only suggests that Lincoln doubted his mother's legitimacy. A more interesting question to ask is which mother Lincoln had in mind, for he deeply loved his stepmother, Sarah Lincoln, and yet undoubtedly had a residue of feelings for his biological mother, Nancy Hanks Lincoln. This question would seem an open one if Lincoln had only credited his "angel mother" for all that he was. Lincoln, however, went beyond that somewhat stereotyped praise to dwell on the issue that really concerned him—his mother's legitimacy. No one, not even any of the people Herndon interviewed in Kentucky or Indiana, ever questioned Sarah Lincoln's legitimacy. Many questioned the legitimacy of Nancy Lincoln. Furthermore, in the autobiography, Lincoln described Nancy as his "mother" and Sarah, though she "proved to be a good and kind mother," as his "stepmother." Lincoln also told his friend Leonard Swett that he had only faint recollections of his mother, for she was so young when she died, but, Swett concluded, "he spoke most kindly of her and of his stepmother, and of her [Sarah's] care for him in providing for his wants."[2] The distinctions in these statements are quite clear. Lincoln's mother was Nancy. "Mother," however, implied a quality of caretaking (mothering) that Lincoln attributed to the kind and gentle Sarah. Sarah could thus be a "mother" and yet clearly be distinguished in Lincoln's mind as stepmother. Lincoln used words carefully.

The issue of Nancy Hanks's illegitimacy may seem trivial, but few aspects of the Lincoln story have been more exhaustively investigated. During the 1920s two formidable genealogists—Louis A. Warren and William E. Barton—debated the Hanks ancestry.[3]

They tramped through graveyards, combed Virginia and Kentucky archives, and pulled together every scrap of relevant and irrelevant information. Ideally, this kind of basic research produces general agreement on the facts; in this case, however, passionate disagreement resulted. Both Warren and Barton were serious, honest, diligent, informed; yet they came to opposite conclusions. Warren felt he had demonstrated the legitimacy of Nancy Hanks; Barton persuaded himself of the opposite. Nor is the issue in this debate one of sentimentality versus realism. Many rigorous scholars accept Warren, while Barton's research influenced the misty-eyed Carl Sandburg:

The mother of Nancy was nineteen years old when she made this trip [from Virginia to Kentucky] leaving Nancy's father, who had not married her, back in Virginia. She could croon in the moist evening twilight to the shining face in the sweet bundle. "Hush thee, hush thee, thy father's a gentleman." She could toss the bundle into the air against a far, hazy line of blue mountains, catch it in her two hands as it came down, let it snuggle to her breast, and feed, while she asked, "Here we come—where from?"[4]

There is little to be gained by rehearsing the endlessly complex details that support each side of the argument over the legitimacy of Lincoln's mother. All of the "hard" evidence needed to settle such a discussion is absent. Nevertheless, as Herndon's biographer David Donald has pointed out, no marriage license has come to light to show that Lucy was wed before the birth of her daughter; the Kentucky and Illinois settlers whom Herndon interviewed agreed on the illegitimacy of Nancy; and Lincoln in his autobiography said his mother was "of the name of Hanks" (Lucy's maiden name). On the other side of the argument, the position of Louis Warren is quite strong and Donald feels "there is room for honest difference of opinion." Still, as Donald concludes, there seems to be a "slight preponderance of testimony favoring the Herndon theory of illegitimacy."[5] Both major biographers of the past generation—Benjamin P. Thomas and Stephen B. Oates—skirt the issue entirely, pointing out that the only thing we know with reasonable certainty is that Lincoln believed his mother was illegitimate.[6] Neither of these biographers, nor any earlier writer, has attempted to develop the significance of this psychological fact.

Illegitimacy has never been an easily accepted part of American family life. Our religious and social traditions carry a heavy weight for those who are, or believe they are, born out of wedlock. The precise meaning of illegitimacy, however, has varied enormously over time for different individuals in various parts of the country. Blacks in slavery, for example, out of necessity developed a much more accommodating attitude toward bastard children than their hypocritical white masters who often sired these children.[7] And in white society itself there was a great deal of difference between the sentimentalized domesticity of the urban middle class and the raw reality of life on the frontier. The "cult of domesticity" in the first half of the nineteenth century extolled the virtues of a benevolent, wise father, as idealized in the figure of George Washington, and a devoted, present, capable mother, as described in Catharine Beecher's *Treatise on Domestic Economy*.[8] There were, of course, variations in this picture, and recent work on the history of women has noted several competing "styles" of domestic adaptation during the period.[9] Still, idealized family life in the antebellum days glorified paternal values of moral authority and maternal values of acquiescent warmth and devotion to the hearth. A generation of American statesmen credited their angel mothers—exalted, pure, pious—for all they became. The ideal carried with it an implicit condemnation of illegitimacy.

Lincoln's experience with and attitudes toward illegitimacy departed sharply from this middle-class, urban ideal. For the Lincoln family, and probably for the frontier community at large, illegitimacy formed an integral and accepted part of life. Charles Friend, who had grown up with Lincoln in Kentucky, told Herndon, "In this county all bastard children are taught to call their mothers 'aunt' . . . ,"[10] which is what Nancy apparently called her mother, Lucy.[11] For a number of years after the move to Indiana, Nancy's illegitimate first cousin, Dennis Hanks, lived with the family; Sophie Hanks, who resided in the area, was one of six illegitimate children of a Sarah or Polly Hanks;[12] and even Lincoln seemed to doubt his own paternity. At least there is *some* evidence that the painstakingly honest Herndon *thought* Lincoln implied as much. "From what Lincoln has casually and indirectly said," Herndon wrote Ward Hill Lamon on February 25, 1870, "I was convinced that his illegitimacy was thrown up to him when a boy."[13] When Lamon balked at this information, he drew forth Herndon's wrathful reply: "If I thought Mr. Lincoln an illegitimate I should state it. . . . He was born into the social world with a curse on him, a millstone tied to his neck. . . ."[14] In 1886 Herndon spelled out his elaborate theory in a long letter to his coauthor, Jesse W. Weik: Thomas Lincoln was sterile; he married the pregnant Nancy because his first love, Sarah Bush, had rejected him; Nancy had been made pregnant by Abraham Enloe, who continued to live in Kentucky and who later fathered two more children by Nancy (including Abraham); sometime in 1815 Thomas found Nancy and Enloe together, and a terrible fight resulted in which Thomas bit off Enloe's nose; Thomas then left Kentucky for Indiana; and Nancy never again became pregnant, nor did Thomas's second wife, his first love, the widowed Sarah Bush Johnston.[15] There is not much evidence to recommend Herndon's theory. William E. Barton and Louis A. Warren have effectively discredited the Enloe thesis and, as David Donald caustically remarks, except for the caveat that no one's paternity can be proved absolutely, the notion of Lincoln's illegitimacy is "utterly groundless."[16]

Herndon seemed to feel that Lincoln carried "a millstone tied to his neck" with the knowledge of his mother's illegitimacy and whatever murky misgivings he carried about his own paternity. But here Herndon went beyond reporting, which he did well, and turned to interpretation, which he usually botched. Rather than shame, Lincoln felt a secret pride in his clouded past. On the confessional buggy ride, after telling Herndon of Nancy's illegitimacy, Lincoln continued: "Did you ever notice that bastards are generally smarter, shrewder, and more intellectual than others? Is it because it is stolen?"[17] The distant and mysterious "Virginia planter" thus gave Lincoln a genetic explanation for the profound differences between him and his crude, illiterate, low-born family. "He told me," Herndon reported at another point, "that his relations were *lascivious, lecherous*, not to be trusted."[18] The workings of fantasy seldom follow the rules of logic. Thus, Lincoln failed to question his implicit distinction between his angelic, genetically "high-born" but illegitimate mother and the rest of his crude, lascivious, and lecherous—but legitimate—relations (except for Dennis Hanks). It seems that, as a child, Lincoln had worked out a rather elaborate genetic myth that both explained and nourished his separateness from his family and environment.

Little else is known about Lincoln's mother. Because she is so obscure, Nancy has inspired poetry that has become, for better or worse, part of the record. "She believed in God," wrote Sandburg, "in the Bible, in mankind, in the past and future, in babies, people, animals, flowers, fishes, in foundations and roofs, in time and the eternities outside of time; she was a believer, keeping in silence behind her gray eyes more beliefs than she spoke."[19] Lincoln's own account of Nancy in the autobiography is sparse indeed. "Getting back into Kentucky, and having reached his twenty-eighth year, he [Thomas] married Nancy Hanks—mother of the present subject—in the year 1806." Lincoln added simply that his mother was from Virginia and that relatives of hers "of the name of Hanks, and of other names, now reside in Coles, in Macon, and in Adams counties, Illinois, and also in Iowa."[20] The accounts of Nancy by those who knew her differ in detail but are remarkably consistent in tone and overall impression. "She was a tall slender woman," wrote John Hanks, "dark-skinned, black hair and eyes, her face was sharp and angular, forehead big. She was beyond all doubts an intellectual woman, rather extraordinary if anything."[21] A neighbor in Indiana, William Woods, who knew Nancy for a year and a half before her death in 1818, also noted how "very smart, intelligent, and intellectual" Nancy was.[22] Dennis Hanks, probably the best source, confirmed the picture painted by others who knew her but added some important details:

Mrs. Lincoln, Abraham's mother, was five feet eight inches high, spare made, affectionate—the most affectionate I ever saw—never knew her to be out of temper, and thought strong of it. She seemed to be immovably calm; she was keen, shrewd, smart, and I do say highly intellectual by nature. Her memory was strong, her perception was quick, judgment was acute almost. She was spiritually and ideally inclined, not dull, not

[8]

material, not heavy in thought, feeling, or action. Her hair was dark hair, eyes bluish green—keen and loving. Her weight was one hundred thirty.[23]

There is no question that Nancy could only sign a mark for her name. But she seemed to have a quality of mind that distinguished her in the frontier settings in which she lived. Lincoln himself, interestingly enough, told Herndon that his mother was "an intellectual woman, sensitive and somewhat sad."[24] Many of the contemporary observers whom Herndon interviewed also called her "intellectual." All this has influenced people like Sandburg who would have her reading the Bible to young Abraham.[25] That seems unlikely though not impossible. Many children on the frontier learned to read but not to write. Even some slaves, who almost never wrote anything, learned to read. This quiet, strong woman who never had any opportunity to get an education absorbed readily and thoroughly the oral culture of her environment, a culture that was based much more than today's on the Bible.[26] A smart, receptive person on the frontier could "know" the Bible and still sign with a mark. Nancy must have shared this knowledge with her special son, who in turn was deeply influenced by Biblical phrasing, style, and content. He was also, in his style of intellectuality and creativity, much more a listener and speaker than a reader and writer. Most of his important and memorable prose was written to be read aloud.

Nancy's character can never be fully known. Contemporary observers tended to remember distantly that "Nancy Hanks was as above Thomas Lincoln as an angel is above mud."[27] There is so little to go on that "her face and figure waver through the mists of time and rumor."[28] For Dennis Hanks she was warmly affectionate, never out of temper, and immovably calm. Another theme in the sources notes Nancy's "habitual sadness"[29] and stresses the "primitive Baptist doctrine of fatalism in which she gloried."[30] She was definitely a Baptist, and Baptists then, and sometimes now, were indeed "primitive" in the sense of firm belief in the Bible and basic moral principles. However, such fundamentalism does not necessarily carry with it sadness; on the contrary, it may foster the quiet peace of someone in touch with God.

[9]

It would seem that Nancy was a remarkably intelligent woman who responded warmly and empathically to Lincoln during his earliest years, nourishing him with rich emotional supplies into his late infancy. This is the psychological message one gets from people like Dennis or John Hanks, and it was implied in Lincoln's own memory of his mother when he told Herndon of her angelic quality. Certainly, one suspects that Lincoln's adult strengths—his flexibility, empathy, humor, and creativity—derived from a close, loving relationship with his mother.[31]

But ambivalence affects any relationship. As a young man (twenty-nine years of age) Lincoln wrote a humorous letter to his good friend and maternal figure, Mrs. Orville Browning, on April Fool's Day, 1838. The letter mocks his recent unsuccessful courtship of Mary Owens, whom he could not behold without "thinking of my mother; and this, not from her withered features, for her skin was too full of fat, to permit its contracting in to wrinkles; but from her want of teeth, weather-beaten appearance in general, and from a kind of notion that ran in my head, that *nothing* could have commenced at the size of infancy, and reached her present bulk in less than thirty-five or forty years."[32] In this letter Lincoln used the image of his mother as a kind of baseline for ugliness. It is true, of course, that Lincoln called Sarah Lincoln "mother," as he was later to refer to Mary after they had children. But unconsciously "mother" for Lincoln also had to mean Nancy. Perhaps she was that ugly. Certainly the only form of dentistry in those days was extraction, and on her deathbed she may have looked suddenly old and withered to her young son. The endurance of this image in Lincoln suggests it carried some sense of childhood disappointment with his mother. In a part of himself he seemed not to trust her.

Lincoln's father was slightly less obscure than his mother, but he too is the source of endless controversy. The major questions center generally on his competence and possible impotence. These were causally related for Herndon: Thomas was hopelessly incompetent because at some point for some reason he lost his potency. Herndon was at his worst in handling the primary sources on this question, but he did not invent the story out of whole cloth. Dennis Hanks reported that Thomas and Nancy had no other children after Abraham's birth. The cause was said to be "a private matter."[33] (Hanks was wrong about dates here, for there was a third child, Thomas, born in 1811 or 1812; he died within a few days.) Herndon variously gathered reports that Thomas had castrated himself, had one testicle the size of a pea, had two testicles the size of peas, had always been sterile, or had the mumps and then became sterile.[34] Herndon pondered to himself: "But you say that Thomas Lincoln went in swimming and that people saw his manhood was taken out; grant it, and yet no witness fixes the date."[35] Herndon never wavered from the idea that Thomas at some point became sterile. In 1886 he told his co-worker Jesse Weik to be sure to confirm this issue with Dennis Hanks: "When you see him, ask him, in a roundabout way, if Thomas Lincoln was not castrated because of the mumps when young. Dennis told me this often and repeated it."[36] For Herndon, Thomas Lincoln's sterility became a crucial factor in his theory of Abraham's illegitimacy as well as a useful explanation for the physiological basis of Thomas's "utter laziness and want of energy." The problem, Herndon wrote, "is due to the fact of fixing."[37]

All the talk to Herndon of Thomas's emasculated or sterile condition carried a decidedly derogatory view of Thomas. A neighbor of Thomas's, Nat Grigsby, told Herndon that Thomas was not "a lazy man, but . . . a piddler, always doing but doing nothing great, was happy, lived easy and contented."[38] This image of Thomas as lazy and inert long held sway in the literature. Josiah G. Holland, who published his book on Lincoln in 1866 after a conversation with Herndon, first introduced the theme of the shiftless, irresponsible Thomas whom Lincoln thoroughly disliked.[39] Ward Hill Lamon, in his 1872 ghost-written *Life*—also based on the Herndon documents—so disliked Thomas that he wrote of his own "great pleasure" when he could leave him behind in the biography.[40] In 1889 Herndon and Weik arrived at their own characterization of Thomas as "roving and shiftless," "proverbially slow of movement, mentally and physically; was careless, inert and dull." Thomas could never pay for the parcels of land he purchased, because he never "fell in with the routine of labor."[41] Various writers echoed the main lines of this view of Thomas, especially Albert Beveridge, whose 1928 book on Lincoln characterized Thomas as "improvident," "slow," and "plodding," "a carpenter of sorts" who farmed in a "desultory way." He could sign his name, according to Beveridge, but preferred to use his mark, even on important documents.[42]

Research in the early twentieth century, however, uncovered some new information on Thomas Lincoln. He always owned one or more horses after he was twenty-one and generally enjoyed credit with no unpaid accounts. An Indiana tax book for 1814 ranked him fifteenth out of ninety-eight in terms of property values for those listed in the local county records. Thomas left Kentucky because of difficulties over title to his land, but many of his contemporaries also suffered from insecurity over land tenure. In post-revolutionary Kentucky, unscrupulous lawyers and speculators exploited the original settlers. In Thomas's case, faulty surveys and title disputes reduced holdings of 238 acres to 200.[43] Thomas bought several pieces of property in Illinois after 1830, though he had to sell some of these to cover his debts. Thomas was a respected member of the various communities in which he lived. The cabins he built were adequate for his needs. He was a responsible neighbor, a trustworthy citizen, and, with some exceptions as he aged, a good farmer and carpenter. He helped construct local churches and seemed to participate in other community activities.[44] Dennis Hanks noted that Thomas "didn't drink an' cuss none." He was definitely illiterate, able to write only his name, but then educational deficiencies were the rule, not the exception, on the American frontier. Thomas was also a devoted husband to his two wives. He always got along well with Sarah's children, especially John D. Johnston. Dennis Hanks remained a close friend of Thomas's through his later years. And, finally, Thomas was a perfectly good father to his own children by any criteria relevant for early-nineteenth-century frontier life. Sarah testified to his determination to see his talented son acquire skills he himself lacked. The two quarreled at times, but nothing suggests an open antagonism. Thomas occasionally whipped young Lincoln but hardly brutalized him. Apparently, Thomas was able to handle easily enough the competitive thrust of his son.

Louis A. Warren concluded in 1926 that "We must now bury the traditional Thomas Lincoln in the 'stagnant, putrid pool' discovered by William Herndon, and introduce to future biographers the historical Thomas Lincoln of Hardin County...."[45] Paul Angle, in his 1930 edition of Herndon's *Life of Lincoln*, reflected this view of Thomas when he felt obliged to interject an entire paragraph on the "real" Thomas following Herndon's disparaging characterization.[46] Benjamin Thomas agreed with Angle's revised picture of Thomas Lincoln, though he noted: "In the father, Thomas, there seemed to be a falling off in the general level of Abraham's ancestry."[47] Most recently, Stephen B. Oates has summarized what is now the standard view of Thomas Lincoln: "Although myths were to flourish about Thomas as a lazy ne'er-do-well, he was actually a hardworking carpenter and farmer who won the respect of his neighbors. He stayed sober, accumulated land, paid his taxes, sat on juries, and served on the county slave patrol."[48]

The revisionist work on Thomas Lincoln has effectively stripped away the myths surrounding the despicable figure created by the early commentators. Thomas was not in fact improvident, slow, terribly lazy, incompetent, dull, or dumb. He was interesting enough, among other things, to attract two apparently outstanding women to be mothers to his children. The revisionist research, however, has been fundamentally misplaced. It has assumed that a grasp of what Thomas was actually like will clarify our understanding of his infinitely more important son. Ironically, Lincoln's mental picture of his father was a good deal closer to Herndon's characterization than observers have wanted to acknowledge. There is little congruence between the three-dimensional figure of the "real" Thomas and Lincoln's psychological conception of him. All the evidence suggests that Lincoln retained some residual admiration and love for his father but basically grew up with an abiding sense of disappointment with and alienation from him. He struggled mightily with his inner picture of his father, a picture shaped by the distortions of unconscious wishes and fantasies.

The concrete evidence that Lincoln loved his father and dutifully molded his character after him is scant, though not altogether absent. There is no evidence that Lincoln ever openly rebelled against him. As an adolescent, he worked hard at the farming and diverse needs of survival on the frontier. He stayed with the family through its long move to Illinois in 1830 and helped it survive the devastating winter of 1830/31 on the banks of the Sangamon River near Decatur. As an adult, Lincoln often provided financial assistance to his father. Lincoln even named his fourth son "Thomas," which at least suggests some degree of affection. In personality, there seems to be a certain line of continuity between father and son. Each had a rich sense of humor and was remembered by neighbors for his friendliness. Both were physically strong and able wrestlers. Both seemed moderate in their habits. At one critical juncture in his own life, Lincoln referred to his old father's saying, "If you make a bad bargain, hug it the tighter."[49] William E. Barton, in 1929, noted that "some of the qualities which made Abraham Lincoln great, his patience, his good humor, his kindliness, his love of fun, he inherited from his father."[50] Such a genial picture of Thomas is questionable, but to the extent that it is true, Lincoln's most memorable personality traits derived in part from his positive identification with his father. It may also be that the source for Lincoln's adult interest in the law, and particularly his frequent handling of land cases, lay in Thomas's difficulty in establishing clear title to his land.

But Lincoln's own picture of his father was painted in many hues. Most of the hard evidence indicates that in Lincoln's mind Thomas *was* an illiterate, irresponsible ne'er-do-well; a man who chased rainbows but never managed to find any pots of gold; a typical low-born product of the frontier which Lincoln worked hard to escape and to which, once he had escaped, he never returned. Nowhere does Lincoln ever say anything good about Thomas—a reticence that contrasts strikingly with his openly expressed idealization of Nancy and his deep affection for Sarah. Benjamin Thomas came up with an interesting (if strained) interpretation of this aloofness: it reflected Lincoln's "fundamental honesty"; he disliked his father and therefore remained aloof, the only "honest" position to assume.[51]

In fact, Lincoln made clear his negative feeling toward his father, who never quite came up to his own standards. Thus Lincoln, in his 1860 autobiographical statement, described Thomas as a "wandering laboring boy" who grew up "literally without education. He never did more in the way of writing than to bunglingly sign his own name."[52] Some twelve years earlier, in response to a question from a relative, Lincoln also stressed his father's ignorance: "Owing to my father being left an orphan at the age of six years, in poverty, and in a new country, he became a wholly uneducated man; which I suppose is the reason why I know so little of our family history. I believe I can say nothing more that would at all interest you."[53] It seemed to pain Lincoln to realize how dull his father was, which tells more about Lincoln's driving ambition than it does about Thomas's character.[54] As a boy, Lincoln had aspirations beyond his grasp.

Lincoln's style of intellectuality and his interest in books created frequent conflict with his father. Dennis Hanks noted that Thomas sometimes had "to slash him for neglecting his work by reading."[55] His inquisitiveness also irritated Thomas: "When strangers would ride along and up to his father's fence, Abe always, through pride and to tease his father, would be sure to ask the stranger the first question, for which his father would sometimes knock him a rod."[56] This teasing seemed calculated to displace Thomas, who could only respond with anger. Sarah, however, who was undoubtedly more understanding of Thomas, provides a different perspective. "As a usual thing, Mr. Lincoln never made Abe quit reading to do anything if he could avoid it. He would do it himself first." Thomas was sensitive to his own educational deficiencies and wanted "his boy Abraham to learn, and he encouraged him to do it in all ways he could."[57] Lincoln, one suspects, understood these ambitions in his father and played on them. He was "rude and forward" as Dennis noted, teasing, testing, provoking his father by continuing to read when he knew he should be working. Up to a point, Thomas tolerated, even encouraged, his son's independence, but young Lincoln often seemed to push him too far. Then came a whipping, and in Dennis Hanks's phrase, Lincoln would drop "a kind of silent unwelcome tear."[58]

Standing beside the old Lincoln home are Lincoln's second cousins, Dennis (*left*) and John Hanks. Dennis married Lincoln's stepsister, Elizabeth. Both Dennis and John Hanks were important, if controversial, contributors to the oral historical record on Lincoln. *Ostendorf Collection*

The homes Thomas built for his family, as they moved west from Kentucky to Indiana and finally to Illinois, were simple log cabins. The cabin in which Lincoln was born had an earthen floor and a roof made of slabs held in place by poles or stones. A small opening in each of the side walls, perhaps covered by greased paper, let in light. Two broad pieces of wood fastened together were hung by hinges to an opening high enough for a man to pass through. A stone fireplace with a chimney of sticks and clay stood at one end of the single room. Everything in the simple structure was made of wood since there was no iron available.[59] The family crowded into the cabin with its one large bed when the children were young; later a smaller bed would serve the children. "The sense of modesty was embryonic," noted Beveridge of log cabins in general, "and men took off their clothes before women without a thought by either of any impropriety."[60]

The first cabin Thomas built in Indiana in the fall of 1816 was a simple lean-to that kept out the wild animals, some of the rain, and hardly any cold. The next spring he built an enclosed structure of rough rather than hewed logs with no window and with a roof that was not yet finished when winter came.[61] This crude building, about four miles from Gentryville, stood on a round hill or "knob."[62] For his growing family Thomas created some additional space by putting in a loft. Sarah Lincoln, who arrived as Thomas's second wife in 1819, commented later that this was "a good log cabin, tolerably comfortable. . . . Abe slept upstairs, went up on pins stuck in the logs, like a ladder."[63] Years later Thomas built a larger, two-room cabin, which the family never lived in because they left to seek a new home in Illinois. By then Lincoln was a young man.

As we think back to this period in American history, so distant in experience if not in time, it is easy either to romanticize the simple joys of the rugged outdoor life or to shrink back in disgust at the dirt, the smells, the hardships. The allocation of social/sexual roles on the frontier followed the "natural" order of things. Thomas cleared the land, farmed during the season, did all the heavy work with animals and worked as a carpenter in the off-season. Nancy, and later Sarah, took responsibility for all the chores inside and near the house: cooking, gardening, cleaning, child rearing. As Tocqueville was to note somewhat later, special attitudes in America gave women independence and self-reliance in carrying out duties that elsewhere were part of an overall pattern of degradation and inferiority. There were hardships, to be sure, but a pervasive equality defined the style of life.[64] Children, too, could acquire certain qualities from the strenuous frontier life—if, however, they were not numbed by the experience. In Lincoln's case, the frontier, it seems, gave him certain strengths such as self-reliance, patience, and understanding. Survival itself demanded them. Yet Lincoln never retained any attachment to the log cabins of his childhood; indeed, he strove relentlessly to rise socially into the comfortable, even genteel, upper middle class. That he later exploited his humble origins for political purposes should not obscure his essential impulse to escape his own past. As an ironic twist, the cabin in which he may have been born rests now within a marble temple in Kentucky. Thus do we idealize our heroes.

Nancy bore three children in rapid succession. Sarah, her first-born, came in 1807, and Abraham, born in 1809, grew up with her. Eventually, in 1828, she died as a young woman in child-birth. Two or three years after Abraham's birth (there is no way to be more precise) his brother Thomas arrived and "died in infancy," as Lincoln was to say.[65] The baby was buried in a small grave within sight of the cabin. Later, after his father died in 1851, Lincoln filled in his genealogy in the front of the family Bible. For some reason he forgot to enter the birth of the short-lived boy.[66] After 1811 or 1812 (whenever Thomas was born) Nancy bore no more children, though she lived until 1818. Nancy's childbearing pattern departed from that of the typical frontier woman, who bore a child every two years or so. We do not know whether the limited size of Nancy's family was due to Thomas's alleged sterility, some physical problem of Nancy's, marital indifference, or control. But the pattern of few children apparently influenced Lincoln; he and Mary rigorously controlled the size of their family.

The Lincolns stayed only briefly at Abraham's birth site near

Hodgenville, then moved some two miles to Knob-Creek. Here Lincoln lived until he was seven, growing rapidly, absorbing the culture of his environment. He and his sister attended for short periods two "A-B-C schools" kept by Zachariah Riney and Caleb Hazel. Of his education Lincoln had a somewhat deprecatory view (which tended to put his self-made success in a better light): "There were some schools, so called," he told Jesse Fell. "But no qualification was ever required of a teacher, beyond *'readin, writin, and cipherin,'* to the Rule of Three. If a straggler supposed to understand Latin, happened to sojourn in the neighborhood, he was looked upon as a wizzard. There was absolutely nothing to excite ambition for education."[67]

In 1816 Thomas decided to move to Indiana. "This removal," Lincoln commented, "was partly on account of slavery; but chiefly on account of the difficulty in land titles in Kentucky."[68] Thomas genuinely opposed slavery and had broken from his local Baptist church during a debate over that institution. The antislavery group Thomas was associated with established a separatist church, "which not only renounced human bondage but eschewed all written creeds and official church organizations, relying on the Bible as the sole rule of faith."[69] In 1816, Thomas and Nancy Lincoln joined the separatist church and prayed with its antislavery ministers. However, the more important reason for the move to Indiana was, as Lincoln himself said, the confusion over land titles.[70] Dennis Hanks said it was untrue that the existence of slavery in Kentucky had anything to do with the move to Indiana. He felt Thomas wanted to better his material condition by buying land at $1.25 per acre.[71]

So the Lincolns moved west after packing up their few belongings in an old wagon. At first life went well in Indiana. Lincoln, "though very young, was large of his age, and had an axe put into his hands at once. . . ."[72] The household soon expanded with the addition of Thomas and Elizabeth Sparrow, two of Nancy's relatives, and Dennis Hanks, the illegitimate eighteen-year-old son of another aunt. Lincoln and Sarah occasionally attended more A-B-C or "blab" schools, the sum total of which "did not amount to one year." Lincoln went to school, he said, "by littles," but what he acquired he held onto with pride. "He was never in a college or academy as a student," Lincoln wrote of himself, "and never inside of a college or academy building til since he had a law-license." After he left home in 1831 he studied English grammar and later, as a United States Congressman from 1847 to 1849, began to read and master the six books of Euclid. He regretted his "want of education," but the pride of the self-made man shines through when the Presidential candidate, who was soon to write some of this country's best prose, noted how "imperfectly" he knew English grammar and that "What he has in the way of education, he has picked up."[73]

While living in Kentucky, which he left at seven years of age, Lincoln apparently could not read,[74] but very soon he got "hungry for books, reading everything he could lay his hands on." He was, Dennis Hanks reported, "a constant and I may say stubborn reader."[75] His "library" included the King James Bible, Noah Webster's old spelling book, the *Life of Henry Clay*, *Robinson Crusoe*, Parson Weems's *Life of Washington*, Aesop's *Fables*, and Bunyan's *Pilgrim's Progress*.[76] In Indiana, Lincoln encountered a number of very good grammar books, as well as *Arabian Nights*, David Ramsey's *Life of Washington*, and William Grimshaw's *History of the United States*.[77] John Hanks, his cousin and neighbor in Kentucky, reported young Lincoln's devotion to reading and noted that he had made a kind of bookshelf out of two pins on the wall with a clapboard on them. "Lincoln got it of Crawford, told Crawford and paid it in pulling fodder by two or three day's work."[78] Lincoln's stepmother, Sarah, described him as "the best boy I ever saw. He read all the books he could lay his hands on."[79] Sarah added that he read the Bible some, "though not as much as said," and turned eagerly to newspapers, especially in the later 1820s.

He read diligently, studied in the daytime, didn't after night much, went to bed early, got up early, and then read, ate his breakfast, got to work in the field with the men. Abe read all the books he could lay his hands on. And when he came across a passage that struck him, he would write it down on boards if he had no paper and keep it there til he did get paper, then he would rewrite it, look at it, repeat. He had a copy book, a kind of scrapbook, in which he put down all things and then preserved them. He ciphered on boards when he had no paper or no slate, and when the board would get too black, he would shave it off with a drawing knife, and go on again. When he had paper, he put his lines down on it.[80]

John Romine, a childhood acquaintance and early employer, remembered how Lincoln was always reading and thinking. In fact, Romine, who wanted his chores done, used to get mad at Lincoln and thought he was awfully lazy. "He would laugh and talk—crack his jokes and tell stories all the time; didn't love work half as much as his pay. He said to me one day that his father taught him to work; but he never taught him to love it."[81] This delightful memory expresses the ambivalence of the frontier toward any learning and suggests how determined Lincoln must have been to acquire knowledge (and at the same time to gently tease his self-righteous employer). Lincoln's early fascination for newspapers absorbed much of his intellectual curiosity and in turn helped feed his interest in politics. According to Herndon, "Politics were his life, newspapers his food, and his great ambition his motive power." Nevertheless, he admitted that Lincoln sometimes dipped into Herndon's own remarkable library, which may have been one of the best private collections in Illinois in the 1840s and 1850s.[82]

Lincoln listened with the same energy that sparked his interest in books. As a child, he occasionally went to church, and when he did, he listened closely to the sermon. At home, later, to the delight of the children, he would mount a stump or log and humorously repeat the sermon almost word for word.[83] Sarah noted how young Abe "was a silent and attentive observer" who never spoke or asked questions until the person he was listening to left. Then he had to understand everything, "even to the smallest thing, minutely and exactly; he would repeat it over to himself again and again, sometimes in one form and then in another, and when it was fixed in his mind to suit him, he became easy and he never lost that fact or his understanding of it." The intensity here is remarkable. Lincoln seemed driven, and his listening, like his reading, had a certain compulsive quality to it. Not to grasp something was impossible. Indeed, "Sometimes he seemed perturbed to give expression to his ideas and go mad, almost, at one who couldn't explain plainly what he wanted to convey."[84] Herndon later encountered the same intensity in the adult Lincoln, whom he once described as "persistent, fearless and tireless in thinking."[85] Herndon would greet Lincoln on the street, for example, but Lincoln, lost in thought, would appear not even to notice his friend. Some hours later, he might say: "Billy, what did you say to me on the other side of the square this morning as we passed?"[86]

In the fall of 1818 there were tears to shed. Lincoln's mother, Nancy, and Thomas and Elizabeth Sparrow, died of the "milk sickness," a disease cows periodically caught from poisonous roots and then transmitted through their milk. The deaths left Thomas Lincoln alone to care for his nine-year-old son and eleven-year-old daughter. Within a year he married Mrs. Sarah Bush Johnston of Elizabeth-Town, Kentucky, a widow with three children: Elizabeth, twelve, John D., ten, and Matilda, eight. Now the Lincoln household was much larger than ever before: two adults, three boys (counting Dennis Hanks), and three girls. The parents and girls occupied two beds on the first floor and the boys slept in the loft. There is some suggestion of temptation and sexual excitement in this household menagerie, for within a year the twenty-one-year-old Dennis Hanks married Elizabeth Johnston and moved to a cabin a short distance away.[87]

Lincoln also seemed to feel some of the same pressures. Sarah's daughter Matilda was responsible for taking lunch to Lincoln when he went deep into the woods to cut trees. As Matilda later reported to Herndon, when he was eighteen and she sixteen tongues apparently began to wag in the neighborhood about the two running wild and alone in the forest together. Sarah ordered Matilda to prepare Lincoln's dinner *before* he left for his day's work. All worked well, except that in time Matilda grew tired of the restraint. She decided secretly to follow Lincoln into the woods for a "good long chat and a wild romp." Matilda sneaked up behind Lincoln and jumped on his back to surprise him. In the resulting fall Lincoln's ax cut a gaping wound in Matilda's thigh near an artery. Both were frightened. Lincoln tore off the "tail of his undergarment" to staunch the wound. The issue then became what to tell Sarah. Matilda was inclined to lie but Lincoln urged

[22]

her to tell the truth. "Tell the whole truth, 'Tilda, and trust your good mother for the rest."[88] This ruthless honesty is ostensibly the point of the story; Herndon thus labeled it in his notes, "Honest Abe—A Story of Lincoln's Youth." However, the sexual play and excitement between adolescent siblings unrelated by blood, living in a one-room cabin, seem the deeper meaning of the anecdote.

Sarah was a gentle woman who helped young Lincoln adjust to the painful loss of Nancy. Dennis reported that Sarah "had been raised in Elizabeth-Town in somewhat a high life," but adapted easily to the rugged life near Little Pigeon Creek in Indiana. The year or so between Nancy's death and Sarah's arrival was difficult for the Lincoln household. The speed with which Thomas found a second wife suggests his loneliness. Dennis reported that, when Sarah arrived, "Abe and his sister were wild, ragged and dirty . . . she soaped, rubbed and washed the children clean, so that they looked pretty, neat, well, and clean. She sewed and mended their clothes, and the children once more looked human as their own good mother left them."[89] On Friday, September 8, 1865, Herndon visited Sarah and recorded her memories of Lincoln. Her account is honest and informative, warm and yet free of sentimentality. "His mind and mine, what little I had," she said, "seemed to run together, more in the same channel." Herndon recalled that as he was leaving, "she arose, took me by the hand, wept, and bade me good-bye, saying: 'I shall never see you again, and if you see Mrs. Abraham Lincoln and family, tell them I send them my best and tenderest love. Good-bye, my good son's friend, farewell.' "[90]

Lincoln loved his stepmother.[91] As a lawyer in Springfield, he occasionally visited Sarah, who lived about ninety miles away, near Charleston, Illinois. "I saw him every year or two," she told Herndon.[92] The most emotional visit to his stepmother was the one Lincoln made just before leaving Springfield for Washington in 1861. According to Ward Hill Lamon, who made the trip with him, "The meeting between him and the old lady was of a most affectionate and tender character. She fondled him as her own 'Abe,' and he her as his own mother."[93] Joshua Speed, Lincoln's close friend in the late 1830s and early 1840s, later spoke of Lin-

Lincoln's stepmother in her old age. She was "good and kind" to Lincoln, who lost his own mother when he was nine years old. *Courtesy of the Illinois State Historical Library*

coln's great fondness for Sarah.[94] Lincoln's wife, Mary, echoed this sentiment in a letter of December 19, 1867, to Sarah: "In memory of the dearly loved one, who always remembered you with so much affection, will you not do me the favor of accepting these few trifles?"[95] In Sandburg's evocative terms, Sarah became "one of the rich, silent forces" in Lincoln's life.[96]

It is usually difficult to identify the central events of childhood. Even in clinical psychoanalysis, as Freud discovered, what is remembered as experience may have originated entirely in fantasy.[97] Even when "real," early memories function primarily as condensed representations of psychological relationships.[98] In

[24]

this sense, life indeed seems to be a stage—or, perhaps, a dream. But some events, particularly if they occur early enough, do seem capable of significantly distorting all else that follows. Early parent loss is such an event.[99] The problem with the theoretical literature on this subject is its failure to identify any clear *necessary and sufficient outcomes* for a child who loses a parent. One may hypothesize a desperate and continuing need for mirroring self-objects as a basic psychological drive motivating behavior following childhood parent loss (to use Heinz Kohut's language), but one often encounters the same need in a person whose parents have both been alive and well throughout his childhood. Furthermore, there may be a loss without death, for example, divorce or serious illness, that may or may not have similar effects as death, or there may be relative emotional health despite childhood traumas that should make the best of us schizophrenic. When all is said and done, however, there is one universal observation about childhood parent loss that anyone would agree with: it is a significant event that may be central in shaping development. One can only know for sure by a close examination of the facts in each case.

In his autobiography, Lincoln tells a curious story of killing a wild turkey just before his eighth birthday.[100] The story, in parentheses, goes:

(A few days before the completion of his eighth year, in the absence of his father, a flock of wild turkeys approached the new log cabin, and A. with a rifle gun, standing inside, shot through a crack, and killed one of them. He has never since pulled a trigger on any larger game.)[101]

The turkey story follows a brief description of the move to Indiana in 1816, when Thomas settled "in an unbroken forest" and Lincoln "had an axe put in his hands at once." But then the first sentence after the turkey story relates both the death of his mother and his father's remarriage: "In the autumn of 1818, his mother died; and a year afterwards his father married Mrs. Sally Johnston. . . ." Such a juxtaposition of memories suggests an association between the wild turkey and his dead mother. Both are helpless and both die. The odd insertion of the turkey scene in parentheses between the description of Indiana and the report of

Nancy's death seems a symbolic way of communicating unconscious feelings about his mother's death. The most important detail in the turkey story is Lincoln's responsibility for killing the bird. This apparently left deep remorse—guilt in our terms—and makes it impossible for Lincoln to pull "a trigger on any larger game." This guilt, one suspects, has been displaced from his mother onto the wild bird. Thus it seems he felt somehow responsible for causing his mother's death.

It would appear from the story that renounced infantile sexual longings toward the mother prompted the sense of guilt Lincoln felt after her death. This sexual theme enters the story by proxy, for Lincoln killed the turkey "in the absence of his father" and with a "rifle gun" that probably belonged to his father and that, according to Dennis Hanks, may have been loaded by his mother.[102] If we take the appropriation of the father's gun as a wish—and the story itself seems dreamlike—then the meaning of the condensed memories expressed in the story becomes more apparent. Lincoln wished his father away because he wanted to possess the mother. He could only realize the wish, however, by appropriating the magical power of the father's gun as he struggled to beat out his father in competition for the mother. At some point, he must have felt victorious in that struggle, but the gun he appropriated proved more deadly than anticipated, for with it he killed the helpless turkey. Punishment must be extracted: "He has never since pulled a trigger on any larger game." In the confusion of mourning his mother's death, Lincoln thus seemed to construct an unconscious explanation for her loss that "explained" her death in terms of punishment for his own earlier forbidden sexual wishes. As punishment for his love, she died.[103]

One indirect, if curiously confirming, piece of evidence for this interpretation is Lincoln's lifelong sympathy for animals. Such a sentiment was hardly the norm for the frontier. By his report he was reluctant to hunt large game. He also seemed to have had bad experiences with animals; when he was ten he was kicked in the head by a horse and, in his words, "apparently killed for a time."[104] Several reports later testified he was sensitive "almost to a fault" about animals. Mary S. Vineyard (whom Lincoln courted as Mary Owens) reported Lincoln's story of helping the mired shoat (young pig) because "the poor thing seemed to say so wistfully: There now! my last hope is gone."[105] J. D. Wickizer reported Lincoln's furious anger on finding an old sow once eating her young ones. Lincoln heard the squeals of the little pigs and leaped out of his buggy to break up such an "unnatural" scene.[106] There was also the time Lincoln helped his frightened little dog across an icy bridge on the trip from Indiana to Illinois in 1830. The grateful dog, when safe on dry land, "cut up such antics as no dog ever did before."[107] This otherwise innocuous story became a staple Lincoln tale and, apparently, something of a family legend.

But such things are seldom simple. Dennis Hanks reported hunting often with Lincoln in Indiana, and Sarah Lincoln noted that Lincoln disliked hunting but "sometimes went coon hunting and turkey hunting at nights."[108] Lincoln himself reported the "ludicrous" incident of sewing up the eyes of some hogs. It was 1831 and Lincoln was working for Denton Offutt who thought of the scheme to make his thirty hogs more manageable. Lincoln did the actual sewing and seemed glad to report that the whole idea was a complete failure.[109] Nor were animals free from Lincoln's absorbing rivalry with his father. Lincoln often repeated for Herndon the odd story of the way he and John Johnston handled Thomas's cussed little yellow dog who always gave away their attempts to sneak out late and go coon hunting. One night they took the dog with them and sewed around it the skin of a dead coon. The terrified dog ran for home, but his powerful scent attracted a host of neighborhood dogs who proceeded to kill him. "Father was much incensed at his death," Lincoln reported to Herndon.[110]

The turkey scene from his autobiography suggests in highly condensed form Lincoln's particular oedipal tensions as they emerged in connection with his mother's death: a competitive sense of regretful victory over his father; a deep and abiding love for his mother that was powerfully libidinal; guilt for feeling forbidden sexual desires which became, in the irrational but psychologically comprehensible mind of the child confronted with

[27]

parent loss, responsibility for death; and, finally, an unconscious connection between loving and killing that was to severely affect Lincoln's intimate relations as an adult. The rumpled, even dirty appearance of nine-year-old Abraham and eleven-year-old Sarah after their mother's death and the disarray of the home suggest not only the severe impact of the loss but also that Nancy was being profoundly if crudely mourned. The arrival of the "new" mother, Sarah Lincoln, with her gentle, loving, understanding qualities, may have cut short Lincoln's mourning process, encapsulating his guilt and areas of conflict behind a defensive wall. This is, of course, speculation, but just as Sarah meliorated the pain of Nancy's death for Lincoln, she may have aggravated his unconscious guilt for having caused her death; and as she provided desperately needed continuity to allow Lincoln's further development, she may also have helped create a major discontinuity for young Lincoln that took him a lifetime to work through.

If such an approach to one story deeply embedded in the autobiography seems fanciful, there is other evidence that the wrenching loss of Nancy was the critical point in Lincoln's childhood. In the fall of 1844 Lincoln, then a rising young Whig lawyer/politician, took a campaign swing through Indiana in behalf of Henry Clay. On the way he visited "the neighborhood in that state in which I was raised, where my mother and only sister were buried. . . ." The visit "aroused feelings in me which were certainly poetry," Lincoln told a newspaper editor at the time, "though whether my expression of those feelings is poetry is quite another question."[111] Lincoln wrote two lyrical poems after the trip, both of which express the exquisite pain he felt on visiting his "childhood's home." The dating of the poems, their internal structure, and even whether they should be considered one rather long poem are unclear. The answer to these confusions may lie in the dreamlike quality that his childhood memories seem to have aroused in Lincoln.[112]

> *My childhood's home I see again,*
> *And sadden with the view;*
> *And still, as memory crowds my brain,*
> *There's pleasure in it too.*

Childhood on the Frontier

O Memory! Thou midway world
'Twixt earth and paradise,
Where things decayed and loved ones lost
In dreamy shadows rise,

Out of these "dreamy shadows" from the past Lincoln retrospectively isolated several emotionally laden memories. One was

When first my father settled here,
'Twas then the frontier line:
The panther's scream, filled with fear
And bears preyed on the swine.

A stroke of disaster seemed imminent in the move to Indiana, a "panther's scream" filling the night with fear. This part of Indiana in 1816 was, in fact, wild country full of animals. Albert Beveridge, using twelve different accounts of settlers and travelers, described the "raccoon, squirrel, opossum, skunk, deer, bear, wolf, wildcat, panther."

Wild turkeys ran through underbrush filled with grouse and quail; wild ducks and geese flew overhead. Incredible numbers of pigeons hid the sun, darkening the air like a thick passing cloud, and, when settling for the night, broke down stout branches of trees. Swarms of mosquitoes rose from dank, stagnant pools and noisome swamps; large black and poisonous yellow flies abounded. Innumerable frogs rasped the stillness.[113]

Psychologically, however, Lincoln's fear of the panther's scream and of the bear preying on the swine suggests that he may well have experienced the move from Kentucky as a painful separation and even trembled as a child in anticipatory anxiety at what awaited him in Indiana. Death occurs in these few lines when helpless animals are destroyed by wild and brutal bears and panthers. This, indeed, is the theme of the entire poem, though it takes an ironic twist at the end.[114]

But the poem even more clearly suggests that, at some point, Lincoln invested certain relatively incidental memories from before his mother's death with the predictive power of what was to come. The animals may or may not have been frightening at the point of his moving to Indiana. Probably there was some fear,

though nothing beyond a young boy's normal dread of the unknown, of strange and potentially dangerous sounds. After
Nancy's death, however, and Lincoln's apparent association between her and helpless wild animals, these earlier memories assumed new significance as Lincoln worked over his confused,
conflicted feelings during mourning.

Death is also the central theme of the earlier canto (or separate
poem) that begins "My childhood's home I see again." Here he
describes the memories and sights of his youth that were so poi-
gnantly real. "Now twenty years have passed away" since he last
saw his playmates from childhood. "And half of all are dead."

> I hear the loved survivors tell
> How nought from death could save,
> Till every sound appears a knell,
> And every spot a grave.
>
> I range the fields with pensive tread,
> And pace the hollow rooms,
> And feel (companions of the dead)
> I'm living in the tombs.

The feelings of seeing his mother's grave and his childhood home
flooded Lincoln with memories of her death and everyone else's
from that era. He felt a "companion of the dead" and thus separated from the present and reunited with the past through his
own death. Such depersonalization at seeing his "childhood's
home" suggests incomplete mourning and a repressed encapsula-
tion of everything associated with his mother. This was to play an
important role in shaping his personality.

Chapter 2

Young Man Lincoln

I tell you, Speed, our *forebodings*, for which you and I are
rather peculiar, are all the worst sort of nonsense.
A. LINCOLN to Joshua Speed
February 25, 1842

S a young man in his twenties, from 1831 to
1837, Lincoln lived in New Salem, Illinois.
This small, bustling community with a buoyant
sense of its own importance had been staked out
as an entrepreneurial venture in 1829 to rival
Cincinnati and St. Louis. It included many arti-
sans, two physicians, one John Allen, a graduate of Dartmouth,
the loquacious Mentor Graham, and a slick businessman, William
Greene. At its founding in 1829 New Salem had as much apparent urban potential as the larger town of Springfield (which
contained five hundred people in 1830). Men—and women—
gathered in a debating society to discuss the range of human affairs within their horizons;[1] and the moody figure of Lincoln
reading on a woodpile, though regarded as unusual, was left
alone.[2] As it turned out, New Salem failed economically, and in
1836 the post office was moved to Petersburg, which became the
seat of the newly formed Menard County in 1839.[3]

Lincoln arrived in New Salem in July, 1831, having just taken a
load of produce down the Mississippi to New Orleans on Denton
Offutt's flatboat. He had left home some five months before.[4]
Lincoln's first job in the village was as a clerk to Offutt's store,

which he carried out affably but without commitment. He left this job in April, 1832, for service in the Black Hawk War. He was immediately elected captain by his company, an honor that for Lincoln was a source of enormous satisfaction.[5] When in May his term ended, he reenlisted for twenty more days in the service of Captain Elijah Iles, and then in June he signed on for thirty more days in Captain Jacob M. Early's company.[6] This extended service was not a result of military need; Lincoln later ridiculed his "bloody encounters" with mosquitoes[7] and told William Herndon that the only reason he served so long was that he had no other work.[8]

So Lincoln drifted back to New Salem. He toyed with the idea of "learning the black-smith trade" and considered the study of law, but he "rather thought he could not succeed at [the law] . . . without a better education."[9] Even before his first arrival in the village, he had announced his intention to run for office. Shortly after his return from the war, he sought election to the legislature. He lost the election, though he carried his own precinct—New Salem—by 277 to 7.[10] Surviving on odd jobs, he next stumbled onto the purchase of a store with William Berry. With the store he assumed a heavy mortgage and responsibilities. These he did not seem prepared to handle, and he got little help from Berry, who proceeded to drink himself to death. As Lincoln later commented, "Of course they [Lincoln and Berry] did nothing but get deeper and deeper in debt." In no time, "The store winked out."[11]

Lincoln also tried surveying during the New Salem period. John Calhoun, the county surveyor, had befriended him and recommended him as his assistant. As Lincoln described it: "He [Lincoln] accepted, procured a compass and chain, studied Flint, and Gibson a little, and went at it. This procured bread, and kept soul and body together."[12] In his attempt to master the necessary mathematics for surveying, Lincoln had enlisted the help of Mentor Graham. As Benjamin P. Thomas writes: "Often he and Graham stayed awake until midnight, interrupting their calculations only when Mrs. Graham ordered them out for a fresh supply of wood for the fire."[13] But this new venture was as ill-fated as the investment in the store. In order to begin surveying, Lincoln had purchased on credit from William Watkins a horse, saddle, and bridle for $57.86. Lincoln failed to make the payments for these items, and on April 26, 1834, Watkins got a judgment in the Sangamon County Circuit Court on Lincoln's personal possessions.[14] Though a competent surveyor,[15] Lincoln was hardly dedicated enough to become a successful one.

Lincoln also served as village postmaster, a position to which he was appointed on May 7, 1833. Though a Whig, he served during the Jackson administration because, in his own words, "the office . . . [was] too insignificant, to make his politics an objection."[16] The mail arrived once each week. Postage was determined by the number of pages and the distance the letter traveled. Thus a single sheet cost six cents for the first thirty miles, ten cents for thirty to eighty miles, and so on. There were no stamps or envelopes. Letters were simply folded and sealed, and the postage charge, written in the upper right hand corner, was paid by the person receiving the letter.[17] For Lincoln, the best part of being postmaster was the opportunity it gave him to read all the newspapers.[18] But during his tenure in office, which lasted until May 30, 1836, Lincoln was neither conscientious nor competent. On September 17, 1835, New Salem settler Matthew S. Marsh wrote his brother: "The Post Master is very careless about leaving his office open and unlocked during the day—half the time I go in and get my papers, etc., without anyone being there as was the case yesterday. The letter was only marked twenty-five [cents] and even if he had been there and known it was double, he would not have charged me any more."[19] Marsh may have been something of a busybody, but Lincoln also had trouble with George C. Spears, to whom he wrote on July 1, 1834: "At your request I send you a receipt for the postage on your paper. I am some what surprised at your request. I will however comply with it. The law requires News paper postage to be paid in advance and now that I have waited a full year you choose to wound my feelings by insinuating that unless you get a receipt I will probably make you pay it again."[20]

All of these New Salem activities of Lincoln's were necessarily part-time affairs. And they were supplemented by occasional stints at splitting rails, working at the mill, harvesting, and tending store for Samuel Hill. After December, 1834, Lincoln served as the local agent for the *Sangamo Journal* and regularly clerked at the polls on election days.[21] He even spent the better part of one winter working at Isaac Burner's still.[22] Between these diverse and not particularly demanding duties, he only gradually came to make creative use of his free time. Until 1834 he was too intimidated by his lack of education to begin the study of law.[23] Even after John T. Stuart encouraged him to start reading law, he did it selectively, though carefully.[24] He had access to the law books of H. E. Dummer and Stuart and could have delved into Stuart's fine personal library.[25] The books were available, but he was not ready for them.

Only after joining the legislature did Lincoln achieve any consistent success. He was elected in 1834, 1836, 1838, and 1840. Even his service in the legislature was a part-time activity. Each regular session met from late November in the year of election until February or March of the next year. Frequently there were special sessions, such as the one in the summer of 1837 to deal with the financial panic. Lincoln the legislator developed slowly. He gradually won respect from his colleagues in the ranks of the Whig minority, and in his last term he became minority leader. He was one of the nine legislators instrumental in moving the state capital from Vandalia to Springfield in 1837. As a legislator, Lincoln was always diligent and earnest but not always wise and responsible. Paul Simon, who has thoroughly investigated Lincoln's legislative career, chastises him for his ambiguous stand on education.[26] But Simon is most critical of Lincoln's unequivocal support of the Illinois Internal Improvement Act, which nearly ruined the state by burdening it with an overwhelming debt for the next four decades. The act began as a ridiculously optimistic venture to encourage economic development by a program of improvements costing $10,250,000. Hardly any improvements were actually made and most of the funds ended up in speculators' pockets. By 1857 the debt stood at $17,000,000; not until 1882 were the bonds finally paid off. Simon concludes quite sensibly that Lincoln learned a great deal about the operation of government and politics during his years in the legislature.[27] This education, however, nearly bankrupted the state.

During the New Salem period Lincoln was, in short, undirected and unfocused, charming and well liked by his neighbors, but singularly unsuccessful in most ventures he undertook. He had failed in a series of enterprises and had faced two law suits on account of his personal debts. He fell into surveying as he did splitting rails or delivering the mail or working at the still—by chance, as opportunmity beckoned and the need to survive demanded. Even in his most rewarding activity in these years, serving in the legislature, he felt his way cautiously and with some serious errors in judgment.

Lincoln's long, stumbling search for satisfying work with which to supplement his political career may in part have been simply a reflection of his lack of a formal education. But his experimentation may also have been part of a larger search for personal coherence and integrity, a search that theoretically makes sense in terms of psychoanalytic conceptualizations of identity. Sigmund Freud, as an old man, was asked what defines normality. He replied with the terseness characteristic of his old age: "Lieben und arbeiten" (to love and to work). Each person must discover for himself how to love and to work. An inability to love precludes working that is free from compulsive fastidiousness; and the commitment to professional activity that realizes one's potential and risks failure flows from a firm sense of sexual identity.[28] The youth is challenged from many directions. There is a forward movement that must meet the needs of society.[29] There are as well inner expectations that draw on enduring childhood issues of self-cohesion.[30] Work and career focus a large part of these concerns; love, social relating, and sexual identity constitute other important aspects of the emerging self.

Lincoln's earliest romantic involvement remains in doubt. It could have been with Ann Rutledge in New Salem. As Herndon told it, the famous affair was the "grand passion" of Lincoln's life, and Ann's death in 1835 cast a melancholy shadow over the rest of his days.[31] But Herndon never heard Lincoln talk about Ann, and Lincoln never mentioned her in anything he wrote (anything that has survived) or in anything he said to a reputable witness.

Mary Owens, to whom Lincoln proposed in 1837. Lincoln described her as ridicuously fat and "weather-beaten" in appearance. He also noted that he had been in love with her. *Ostendorf Collection*

James G. Randall, after sifting through all the evidence, came to the conclusion that the story should be left for the fiction writers.[32] Ann Rutledge may have been Lincoln's first love and her death may have prompted a severe depression on his part. But since there is no single thread of good evidence on the subject, the episode must be passed over quickly.

Lincoln's first documented romance appears to have been with Mary Owens, "an amiable, attractive Kentucky girl of considerable culture."[33] It was a curious affair, and the complicated way he dealt with her foreshadows his tortured courting of Mary Todd. Lincoln first met Miss Owens in 1833 when she visited her sister, Mrs. Bennett Abell, in New Salem. After she returned to the village in 1836, Lincoln began to court her. There never appeared to be much passion on either side; nevertheless, by May, 1837, the two were clearly discussing marriage. Lincoln was curiously ambiguous in the proposal he made in a letter: "Whatever woman may cast her lot with mine, should any ever do so, it is my intention to do all in my power to make her happy and contented; and there is nothing I can immagine [*sic*], that would make me more unhappy than to fail in the effort. I know I should be much happier with you than the way I am, provided I saw no signs of discontent in you. . . . What I have said I will most positively abide by, provided you wish it. My opinion is that you had better not do it."[34]

A little over three months later Lincoln broke off his relationship with Mary Owens in a confused fashion. He wrote: "I can not see you, or think of you, with entire indifference," a phrasing that cast his supposedly affectionate feeling into a double negative. He continued: "I want in all cases to do right, and most particularly so, in all cases with women." Doing right in this case, Lincoln suggested, probably meant leaving her alone. If that was her desire, he urged her simply not to answer the letter. Such a solution to their "romance" forced her to act and made Lincoln the passive recipient of her decision. He then made the same point again with greater emphasis: "Do not understand by this, that I wish to cut your acquaintance. I mean no such thing. What I do wish is, that our further acquaintance shall depend upon yourself. . . . If you feel yourself in any degree bound to me, I am now willing to release you, provided you wish it; while, on the other hand, I am willing, and even anxious to bind you faster, if I can be convinced that it will, in any considerable degree, add to your happiness."[35]

Lincoln, with apparent disregard for himself, desperately feared hurting Mary. At all costs he sought to make her happy, and if his actions hurt her he was hurt even more himself. He loved ambivalently, and at the point of marriage, with its potential of intimacy, he withdrew in a clumsy, if genuine, expression of sympathy for Mary's feelings. As she later wrote to Herndon, "Mr. Lincoln was deficient in those little links which make up the chain of a woman's happiness—at least it was so in my case."[36]

In a letter to Mrs. Orville Hickman Browning, the wife of a state senator from Quincy, Lincoln dismissed the love affairs in a most casual way. He recounted that he had first seen Mary in 1833 and had not been displeased; that in 1836 his friend, Mrs. Abell, had played matchmaker for a willing swain; but that when he saw Mary again he was aghast at how fat—"a fair match for Falstaff"—and ugly she was.[37] Yet Lincoln confessed his suffering and mortification at Mary's turning him down: "She whom I had taught myself to believe no body else would have, had actually rejected me with all my fancied greatness; and to cap the whole, I then, for the first time, began to suspect that I was really a little in love with her."[38]

In 1839 Lincoln first met and was captivated by the sprightly, well-educated, and charming Mary Todd. James C. Conkling, a young lawyer from the East and a graduate of Princeton, described this Mary as "the very creature of excitement."[39] Lincoln courted her vigorously and successfully throughout 1839 and 1840. Each of her three extant letters from these two years mentions him, and the third one dwells at some length on marriage.[40] Apparently, before the end of 1840 Lincoln and Mary were engaged.

Lincoln was then thirty-one. He had some useful experience as a lawyer behind him and was making a respectable income. He had made a mark in the legislature and was generally esteemed by friends and colleagues throughout Springfield. Still, he was something of a social upstart in Mary's snobbish circle, which centered on the home of Ninian and Elizabeth Edwards, the kind of people whom, in his first impression of Springfield in 1837, he had referred to as "flourishing about in carriages here."[41] His fiancée was probably the most desirable unmarried woman in Springfield. Yet suddenly, in a move that perplexed all his friends—and was to baffle historians and biographers—he broke off the engagement on January 1, 1841.

Herndon's fanciful account—to the effect that the wedding was scheduled for that date and that Lincoln failed to appear[42]—has been proven false by the masterful detective work of Ruth Painter Randall.[43] Randall notes that both Mary's guardian, Ninian Edwards, and her father opposed her marriage to young Lincoln.[44] Yet Lincoln loved her. Randall hypothesizes that in the end he respected the feelings of the Todd family: "How could he marry the girl when her family thought he would make her unhappy? He had so few things upon which to pride himself, but among these things was his integrity. Yet no course of action was open to a man with his torturing conscience that left that integrity unviolated."[45]

Randall's well-researched explanation is plausible and has become the standard account of the troubled courtship. As a documented chronology of events, the account is not likely to be surpassed. But the explanation of Lincoln's motivation is naive. Randall speaks of Lincoln and Mary's "appealing love story," one Herndon obscured with "belittling distortions and fabrications," but one that the nation can be proud of as an "American romance" in which an aristocratic girl and her "lover of log-cabin origin" triumph over family opposition.[46] This drama of Romeo and Juliet, American style, posits an external force to explain Lincoln's breaking the engagement. The snobbish Todds intimidated the fragile young man, though he eventually was to win the hand of his beloved.

Lincoln was uneasy in social situations during these years. As a newcomer, in 1837, he felt out of place in Springfield. Throughout his life he often joked about his homeliness and excessive height. He felt somewhat embarrassed by his humble origins, though in time he became aware of the political value of having been raised in a log cabin. Nevertheless, he was not easily intimidated by anyone, not even the lordly Todds.[47] His natural assumption of superiority and his vigorous ambition were always sources of great strength. John Hay, Lincoln's private secretary during the war, believed that it was "absurd to call him a modest man. No great man is ever modest. It was his intellectual arrogance and unconscious assumption of superiority that men like Chase and Sumner could never forgive."[48] For Herndon, Lincoln's ambition was "a little engine that knew no rest."[49] "The sober truth is that Lincoln was inordinately ambitious."[50] The first visible expression of this ambition occurred "in the year 1840 *exactly.*"[51] But Elizabeth Edwards, sister of Mary Todd and wife of Ninian Wirt Edwards, provided (in 1887) a different but also interesting explanation of the broken engagement. Mrs. Edwards, an important member of the family opposing the marriage, said Lincoln "doubted his ability and capacity to please and support a wife."[52]

Elizabeth Edwards dimly perceived Lincoln's excruciating ambivalence. For, as with Mary Owens, so too with Mary Todd, he broke off a fully developed romance just at the point of marriage and sexual union. In both relationships Lincoln feared intimacy with a woman. His natural exuberance and virility led him toward both encounters, but in both his ambivalence led to agonizing retreat before consummation. To explain this curious behavior, some have even argued that Lincoln had self-doubts that derived from a case of syphilis he supposedly contracted sometime in 1835 or 1836. This theory originated with Herndon, who said Lincoln wrote to a Dr. Drake in Cincinnati about his disease shortly after coming to Springfield.[53] But Milton Shutes, a doctor writing in 1957, carefully sifted all the evidence for syphilis and concluded that it is virtually certain that Lincoln never contracted the disease.[54] What Shutes guessed—assuming the validity of Herndon's story—is that Lincoln developed syphilophobia. In other words, the Drake letter, which has never been found (and may never have existed) underlined Lincoln's sexual conflicts, his fears of a contaminating injury to his penis. The letter, if found, would not prove prolific sexual vigor but only sexual confusion and ignorance.

Intimacy involves a merging of selves—both physical and emotional—in a union that can permit each partner to rise above his or her existential loneliness. In Erik Erikson's formulation, intimacy is "the capacity to commit [oneself] to concrete affiliations and partnerships and to develop the ethical strength to abide by such commitments, even though they may call for significant sacrifices and compromises."[55] The avoidance of situations which have the potential of close affiliation and sexual union "may lead to a deep sense of isolation and consequent self-absorption."[56] This general characterization fits well with what we know about Lincoln. He could not go beyond himself because he had not fully consolidated the bases of his sexual or work identity. He lacked an inner coherence or identity that would permit him to transcend himself and reach out to another. Loss of self for such young men offers only the potential of psychic disintegration and frightening regression.

The theoretical connection between a lack of identity and a fear of intimacy is therefore far more than an accidental occurrence. Lincoln, in the 1830s, sought a unity among the several roles he was juggling: store owner, surveyor, rail splitter, lawyer, politician. By 1841 the lawyer-politician in him seemed dominant; but it was a recent and tentative consolidation that was neither immutable nor at the time the basis of anything more apparent than moderate professional success. He also sought a heterosexual union that kept eluding him. His ego identity—his accrued confidence in an inner sameness and continuity—was fragile at best. For many less sensitive, it is all too easy to choose an identity from the available roles defined and outlined by parents, teachers, and social mores and expectations. But with Lincoln this was impossible, and its impossibility suggests an insight into a crucial aspect of greatness: the proud and obstinate refusal to wear the mask painted by others. In any event, intimacy and love are bound to be approached ambivalently for such a confused young man as Lincoln. Thus fear of intimacy and of the binding nature of sexual love contributed to Lincoln's identity confusion.

But Lincoln's inner conflicts over intimacy cannot be fully grasped by examining his courtship of Mary Todd. Of even greater significance is his relationship with Joshua Fry Speed, whose patient friendship during these crucial years first aggravated Lincoln's conflicts, then served as the vehicle for their resolution. Joshua Speed was an engaging young merchant, who moved from Kentucky to Springfield in 1835. Lincoln's relationship with Speed began on his own arrival in Springfield in 1837. Lincoln, only recently admitted to the bar, had neither relatives nor friends on hand to see him through or help him pay his debts. He was probably already acquainted with Joshua Speed and certainly familiar with Speed's store.[57] He went directly there and asked how much it would cost to buy the material for a bed. Speed made the calculation and told Lincoln it would cost a total of seventeen dollars. As Speed later reported to Herndon, Lincoln asked for the money on credit until Christmas but in such a sad tone as to elicit Speed's sympathy.

The tone of his voice was so melancholy that I felt for him. I looked up at him, and I thought then as I think now, that I never saw so gloomy, and melancholy a face. I said to him; "The contraction of so small a debt, seems to affect you so deeply, I think I can suggest a plan by which you will be able to attain your end, without incurring any debt. I have a very large room, and a very large double bed in it; which you are perfectly welcome to share with me if you choose." "Where is your room?" asked he. "Upstairs" said I, pointing to the stairs leading from the store

[41]

to my room. Without saying a word, he took his saddle-bags on his arm, went up stairs, set them down on the floor, came down again, and with a face beaming with pleasure and smiles exclaimed "Well Speed I'm moved."[58]

In 1838 Speed and Lincoln were joined in their room above the store by William Herndon, who later reported: "Lincoln, Speed, and I slept together for two or three years, i.e., slept in the same home, I being Speed's clerk; and Lincoln sleeping with Speed."[59] For a time Charles R. Hurst joined the dormitory, sleeping in a separate bed.[60] Life in the store centered on open and congenial discussion and was pervaded by a rough maleness that sharply distinguished it from the sophisticated and slightly effete atmosphere of the coterie that met in the Edwards's home.[61] According to Speed, discussion in the store revolved around Lincoln: "Mr. Lincoln was a social man, though he did not seek company; it sought him. After he made his home with me, on every winter's night at my store, by a big wood fire, no matter how inclement the weather, eight or ten choice spirits assembled, without distinction of party. It was a sort of social club without organization. They came there because they were sure to find Lincoln."[62]

Joshua Speed was the only intimate friend Lincoln ever had. Ward Hill Lamon, in his 1872 biography, was the first to make this point.[63] The only quarrel with this assertion later came from a jealous Herndon, who also wanted to be considered an intimate friend of Lincoln.[64] In fact the difference was complete. Lincoln liked Herndon but treated him condescendingly: he always called him "Billy" while Herndon called him "Mr. Lincoln." To Speed, Lincoln wrote: "You know my desire to befriend you is everlasting—that I will never cease, while I know how to do any thing."[65] Even Herndon had to admit Lincoln and Speed were unusually close.[66] Speed was an attractive young man, affable, kind, and easygoing. Ruth Painter Randall mentions his Byronic eyes and characterizes him as a rake,[67] though the sources do not bear this out.[68] On the contrary, Speed seems to have been as innocent of sex as Lincoln, and when he began seriously courting Fanny Henning, whom he later married, Speed reported: "strange to say something of the same feeling which I regarded as so foolish in him took possession of me and kept me very unhappy from the time of my engagement until I was married."[69]

It would appear, therefore, that Lincoln and Speed's close relationship centered on their similar and reinforcing conflicts. Their sleeping in the same bed for three and one-half years may have intensified their closeness and aggravated their conflicts. It is probable that such close male contact during the years of Lincoln's greatest heterosexual tension heightened the difficulty he found in securing intimacy with a woman. The period during which Lincoln slept with Speed began and ended with unconsummated female relationships, first with Mary Owens and then with Mary Todd. Speed provided an alternative relationship that neither threatened nor provoked Lincoln. Each of the two men found solace in discussing their forebodings about sexuality. Their intimate maleness substituted for the tantalizing but frightening closeness of women.

Such close male relationships were characteristic of early-nineteenth-century America and were quite common in an urban frontier town like Springfield, where there was a distinct shortage of eligible women.[70] In that pre-Freudian age, society legitimated such close male friendships, and it was not at all strange for men to sleep together in the same bed. This kind of sleeping arrangement grew out of economic necessity, and neither Speed nor Herndon found anything unusual in it. Inns at that time, with few rooms, simply separated the men from the women. Everyone crowded into all available space—for warmth as much as anything else.[71] Both before and after Lincoln met Speed it was a common experience for him to sleep with other males. William Greene of New Salem days told Herndon that he had worked with Lincoln in Offutt's store and had "slept in the same cott & when one turned over the other had to do likewise."[72] Later, on the judicial circuit that Lincoln and other lawyers rode for many months of every year, they regularly piled into crowded beds.[73] Spacious homes with individual chambers were extremely rare; the typical log cabin had only one room and one large bed and only when that room began to burst with children was a loft put in.

Social custom and individual biography, however, are not always congruent. Lincoln was sensitive to issues of male closeness in a way that distinguished him from his peers. Mrs. Elizabeth Crawford, whom Herndon talked with in early 1866, remembered much about Lincoln from his adolescent days in Indiana. She shared with Herndon the long story of the "Chronicles of Reuben," which Lincoln had composed and read aloud to his friends. It told of the marriage of two brothers, Reuben and Charles, with two girls and also of the homosexual marriage of a third brother, Billy, with Natty.

> *The girls he had tried on every side*
> *But none could he get to agree;*
> *All was in vain, he went home again*
> *And since that, he is married to Natty.*
>
> *So Billy and Natty agreed very well;*
> *And mamma's well pleased at the match.*
> *The egg it is laid but Natty's afraid,*
> *The shell is so soft that it never will hatch.*
> *But Betsey, she said: "you cursed baldhead,*
> *My suitor you never can be;*
> *Besides, your low crotch proclaims you a botch*
> *And that never can answer for me."*[74]

Though it was common for men to sleep together, there may have been significance for Lincoln in the fact that, at the point of his greatest sexual tension and conflict, he shared a bed with his closest friend. The broken engagement with Mary Todd *exactly* coincides with the separation of Lincoln and Speed. On that same fateful day, January 1, 1841, Speed sold his store,[75] and he and Lincoln separated, leaving their common bed.[76] This separation apparently threw Lincoln into a panic that shook his fragile sexual identity.[77] In this state his fear of intimacy with a woman was revived, and he broke his engagement with Mary. One point is worth stressing, namely, that Lincoln's conflicts and fears operated at an unconscious level. He was only dimly aware of his conflicts as he struggled to define his identity.

Abandoned by Speed and abandoning Mary, Lincoln fell into a severe depression. He was of course subject to depression throughout his life, but his most severe bout occurred in January,

1841. On January 20 he wrote his friend John T. Stuart: "I have, within the last few days, been making a most discreditable exhibition of myself in the way of hypochondriaism." Three days later, also to Stuart, Lincoln noted in a tone of negative grandiosity: "I am now the most miserable man living. If what I feel were equally distributed to the whole human family, there would not be one cheerful face on the earth."[78] He came to refer to January 1, 1841, as the "fatal first," the memory of which was painful for him to recall.[79] Speed and other friends worried over Lincoln's condition.[80] "We have been very much distressed, on Mr. Lincoln's account; hearing that he had two Cat fits and a Duck fit since we left," Martin McKee wrote to John J. Hardin on January 27.[81] Herndon wrote in retrospect: "Did you know that Mr. Lincoln was 'as crazy as a loon' in this city in 1841; that he did not sit, did not attend to the Legislature, but in part, if any (special session of 1841); that he was then deranged? Did you know that he was forcibly arrested by his special friends here at that time; that they had to remove all razors, knives, pistols, etc. from his room and presence, that he might not commit suicide?"[82] He was confined to his bed for a week and only gradually resumed his legislative duties.[83] During his depression he was tended by a kindly doctor, Anson G. Henry, who later wrote that Lincoln told him things he never said to anyone else.[84] Afterward Lincoln was always eager to help Henry,[85] and during his Presidency Lincoln encouraged Henry to make long visits to the White House.[86]

Lincoln slowly recovered, though as late as June, Mary Todd noted that she had not met him in the "gay world for months."[87] Speed remained in town until May and probably helped meliorate Lincoln's mood. Then Speed left for Kentucky to settle his family estate (his father had died). Lincoln, emotionally unfit to be alone, went on a long visit to Speed's home, where he was welcomed warmly as a member of the family.[88] In September Speed accompanied him back to Springfield and remained there until the end of 1841, although he was anxious to return to Louisville, where he had recently begun to court the lovely Fanny Henning.

Speed was full of self-doubts about marriage, just as Lincoln had been. Lincoln seemed almost to welcome the appearance of

Joshua Fry Speed, shown here with his wife Fanny Henning Speed and her sister Maria Louisa Henning in 1853, was Lincoln's only close male friend. They roomed together from 1837 to 1841. It was Speed's marriage to Fanny with her "heavenly *black eyes*" on February 15, 1842, that freed Lincoln to renew his courtship of Mary Todd. *Isaac Hilliard and the Speed Museum, Farmington*

his friend's dilemma, so similar to his own. After Speed's departure, Lincoln proffered advice in frequent letters (Speed's letters in reply have been lost). Lincoln wrote: "I know what the painful point with you is, at all times when you are unhappy. It is an apprehension that you do not love her as you should."[89] A month later: "I am now fully convinced, that you love her as ardently as

[46]

you are capable of loving. Your ever being happy in her presence, and your intense anxiety about her health, if there were nothing else, would place this beyond all dispute in my mind. I incline to think it probable, that your nerves will fail you occasionally for a while; but once you get them fairly graded now, that trouble is over forever."[90]

Lincoln projected his own attitudes and conflicted feelings onto Speed, through whom he vicariously reexperienced the drama he had twice played out in the previous decade. Lincoln related to Speed's difficulties in courtship with an intensity and involvement that suggests he saw Speed as a mirror of his own inner experience. "I now have no doubt," Lincoln told Speed, "that it is the peculiar misfortune of both you and me, to dream dreams of Elysium far exceeding all that any thing earthly can realize."[91] Both also felt the same anxieties. Lincoln encouraged Speed to ease his "nervous temperament" and simply let himself love Fanny: "Say candidly, were not those heavenly *black eyes*, the whole basis of all your early reasoning on the subject?"[92] Lincoln told him that his deep fears for Fanny's health should at least reassure him of the "truth" of his "affection for her." He even suggested: "The Almighty has sent your present affliction expressly for that object."[93] He concluded: "Why Speed, if you did not love her, although you might not wish her death, you would most calmly be resigned to it."[94] This juxtaposition of love and death suggests a morbid fascination with the destructive potentiality of sex.

At the news that Speed finally was wed, Lincoln experienced feelings that he revealed to Speed in a letter of February 25, 1842: "I received yours of the 12th. written the day you went down to William's place, some days since; but delayed answering it, till I should receive the promised one, of the 16th. which came last night. I opened the latter, with intense anxiety and trepidation— so much that although it turned out better than I expected, I have hardly yet, at the distance of ten hours, become calm." With clear relief Lincoln continued: "I tell you, Speed, our *forebodings*, for which you and I are rather peculiar, are all the worst sort of nonsense."[95]

This letter of February 25 might suggest that at thirty-three

[47]

Lincoln was a virgin and terrified of sexual intimacy. There is, however, evidence to the contrary. Lincoln himself told Speed on February 13 in a footnote to a letter: "I have been quite a man ever since you left."[96] This statement could refer to a sexual encounter. It could also express his good feelings at not being depressed, despite Speed's absence. Other evidence on this issue from the oral history record is clouded in fantasy and conjecture. John Hanks referred cryptically to the pretty women that "took Abe's eyes" as a youth, though Sarah Lincoln testified he was not very fond of girls as far as she could tell.[97] Herndon collected various outrageous (and second-hand) stories of Lincoln's escapades. For example, Herndon reported to Weik on January 5, 1889, a story reported to Herndon by Speed concerning Lincoln's visit to a prostitute. It is a preposterous story, however, that has Lincoln undressed and in bed with the woman before he asks how much she charged. On learning the fee was five dollars and aware that he had only three dollars, Lincoln got up and dressed but offered her the three dollars for her trouble. "Mr. Lincoln," she replied, "you are the most conscientious man I ever saw."[98] Somehow, one senses a Lincoln joke that got lost in translation.

If the documentary evidence, therefore, can only suggest Lincoln's virginity, it is more conclusive if the focus is on the issue of psychological conflict in Lincoln rather than his actual sexual experiences. The letter of February 25 suggests that when Speed at last actually consummated his relationship with Fanny—and the sky did not fall in—Lincoln was liberated from his fear of marriage. Speed experienced what Lincoln could only fantasize about. He served as a kind of emotional proxy for his conflicted friend. Speed thus proved therapeutic. Within months, Lincoln began secretly to meet with Mary Todd again, and on November 4, 1842, the two were wed. Meanwhile, there was one last expression of the old inner conflict. On October 5, 1842, a month before his marriage, Lincoln wrote Speed: "But I want to ask a closer question—'Are you now, in *feeling* as well as *judgment*, glad you are married as you are?' From any body but me, this would be an impudent question not to be tolerated, but I know you will pardon it in me. Please answer it quickly as I feel impatient to know."[99] Lincoln apparently was satisfied with Speed's answer.

As this personal drama unfolded Lincoln was well aware of the significance for him of his relationship with Speed. He had reported to Speed the "sleepless vigilance" with which he followed Speed's courting of Fanny.[100] When Speed thanked him for his help, Lincoln responded that he was not sure he deserved gratitude for his role, since he had been "drawn to it as by fate." He explained: "I always was superstitious; and as part of my superstition, I believe God made me one of the instruments of bringing your Fanny and you together, which union, I have no doubt He had fore-ordained."[101]

For the rest of his life Lincoln retained affectionate feelings for Speed. He considered naming his first son Joshua, but in the end he and Mary chose Robert.[102] He wrote Speed of problems with his children, something he never mentioned to anyone else.[103] In a letter in 1855, he unburdened himself to Speed on the complexities of his feelings about the political turmoil in the country.[104] As President, he appointed Speed's brother, James, to his cabinet. Occasionally the Lincolns and Speeds visited each other, though Mary apparently had little enthusiasm for such visits. In the White House Lincoln once warmly welcomed Speed and talked of old times.[105]

After February 25, 1842, however, Speed had begun to lose emotional significance for Lincoln. Lincoln's letters became fewer and more formal. When Lincoln took care of the legal aspects of the sale of Speed's Springfield store, the letters the two exchanged contained little except matters of business. Though, in 1843, Lincoln had considered naming his first son Joshua, in 1846 he delayed for eight months to inform Speed of Eddie's birth.[106] In 1848 the two even got angry with each other over a lost note that affected a case.[107] In the 1855 letter, in which Lincoln unburdened himself on politics, he sharply challenged Speed's ideas about slavery. Once Lincoln was through his own crisis of courtship, Speed had little to offer, and the friendship faded away.

Chapter 3

Fathers and Sons

I happen temporarily to occupy this big White House. I am a
living witness that any one of your children may look to come
here as my father's child has.

A. LINCOLN
August 22, 1864

HE issues of the self unite a host of complex
themes from the past. Joshua Speed—and, later,
Mary Todd—helped in Lincoln's search for
sexual identity. The human animal, however,
especially one as fiercely political as Lincoln, is
more than a bundle of sexual drives. In a sim-
plified (and therefore distorted) sense, Lincoln's young-adult
struggles with intimacy reflected the confusions of his childhood
relationship to his mother. But for a political man in nineteenth-
century America the vital issues of the public self clustered
around the relationship with the father. As Erikson has noted in
another context, to make sexuality available for mastery "a man
must confront his childhood and, above all, give an account of his
conflicts with his father."[1]

In the spring of 1831, while Lincoln was helping take a flatboat
of cargo to New Orleans with Denton Offutt, Thomas Lincoln
moved to Charleston, Illinois. Over the years Thomas made a
number of unfortunate land purchases, and he lived in poverty
and disappointment until his death in 1851. In these two decades

[50]

Lincoln occasionally visited his father and stepmother, though the record here is notably unreliable.

Sarah said Lincoln used to visit her "every year or two," but it is unclear whether she meant for the entire period after 1831 or, more likely, for the years following Thomas's death in 1851.[2] Usher F. Linder, a law associate, testified later that he first met Lincoln in Charleston when Lincoln was visiting his father's house.[3] A few other such visits are acceptably documented. For example, in 1841 Lincoln traveled to Charleston to close a land transaction with his father.[4] Occasionally he practiced law there, even though Charleston was not on the eighth circuit. The question is how often Lincoln took the trouble to travel the additional seven miles to Goosenest Prairie, where his father lived. Charles H. Coleman, who from fact and fiction put together an entire book on Lincoln in Coles County, assumed that whenever Lincoln was in Charleston he went to see his father.[5] It seems safer to assume the opposite: Lincoln generally avoided him.

No matter how often, or how seldom, Lincoln visited his father near Charleston, the record shows that his father never visited him in Springfield. Thomas and Sarah Lincoln did not attend Abraham and Mary's wedding, and none of the four children ever met their paternal grandfather. Apparently, in all her life Mary never laid eyes on him. It seems therefore that on his rare visits to his father Lincoln went grudgingly and without his wife or children. Undoubtedly, Mary's social snobbery reinforced Lincoln's emotional distance from his father. She probably would have welcomed such a backwoodsman in her elegant house at Eighth and Jackson no more readily than she did the drunken, obstreperous Herndon. Herndon once told Weik: "You wish to know if Mrs. Lincoln and the Todd aristocratic family did not scorn and detest the Hanks and the Lincoln family and in answer to which I yell—yes." If Thomas and Sarah Lincoln had ever appeared at her door, "I doubt whether Mrs. Lincoln would have admitted them."[6] Still, she did not create the hostility between Lincoln and his father. Furthermore, Lincoln clearly separated the antagonism he felt toward his father from his abiding affection for his stepmother. It is therefore reasonable to suppose that Lincoln traveled

[51]

to Goosenest, his parents' home near Charleston, in the 1830s and 1840s to see Sarah and that he merely put up with the presence of his father.

As Thomas aged he became less and less capable of supporting himself and his wife. Lincoln gradually assumed responsibility for his parents' financial security, but he did so with marked irritation and resentment. The forty acres Lincoln purchased for Thomas in October, 1841, was in fact a gift, for it allowed Thomas and Sarah full use of the property during their lifetime. (Certainly Lincoln himself had no intention of farming it. "*I have no farm, nor ever expect to have* . . . ,"[7] he told Speed in 1842.) Over the years he periodically assigned legal fees to Thomas and gave him the power to collect on some notes (Lincoln regularly loaned money to friends and associates).[8]

But Thomas's needs exceeded Lincoln's generosity. On December 7, 1848, John D. Johnston, Lincoln's stepbrother, requested in Thomas's behalf (Thomas, remember, was illiterate) a loan of twenty dollars to avoid the loss of his land. Johnston's letter, a curious document, reveals as much about Johnston as about Thomas. It begins with Thomas reporting: "I and the old womman is in best of health" and "soe is all of the relations at present." Then it notes with regret that Lincoln has failed to visit Goosenest on his way to Washington as Congressman-elect (though Lincoln and his family did manage a visit to the Todd's in Kentucky). Thomas complains: "as you faild to come a past, I am compeled to make a request by Letter to you for the loan of, Twenty Dollars, which sum I am compeled to razes, or my Land will be sold. . . ." Thomas finds it embarrassing to have to borrow such a small amount to avoid so great a calamity as the loss of his land. "I doe expect you will think strang at this request, for that much money & it was eaquely as strange, to me & John. . . ." Thomas tries to explain that he forgot an old judgment against him and thinks he paid it, but lost the receipt "if we ever had one." The "we" here seems to be Thomas and Johnston, whose affairs were intermingled. Possibly the debt was Johnston's, and Thomas was covering up for his wayward stepson. In any event, Thomas appears to anticipate Lincoln's anger at the request, for he immediately adds: "I now you cant apreciate the reluctance that I have made this request of you for money but I am compled to do so. . . ."[9]

To his father's abject plea, Lincoln replied with sarcasm and condescension. "My dear father: Your letter of the 7th was received night before last. I very cheerfully send you the twenty dollars, which sum you say is necessary to save your land from sale. It is singular that you should have forgotten a judgment against you; and it is more singular that the plaintiff should have let you forget it so long, particularly as I suppose you have always had property enough to satisfy a judgment of that amount."[10]

Just over two years later Thomas lay on his deathbed, and through John D. Johnston and a more distant relative, Harriet Hanks Chapman, he urged Lincoln to come and see him. Though the letters of Johnston and Chapman have not survived, it is apparent from Lincoln's reply on January 13, 1851, that Thomas knew he was dying and probably hoped for a final reconciliation with his estranged son. "Dear Brother," Lincoln responded to Johnston: "On the day before yesterday I received a letter from Harriet written at Greenup. She says she has just returned from your house; and that Father is very low, and will hardly recover. She also says you have written me two letters; and that although you do not expect me to come now, you wonder that I do not write. I received both your letters and although I have not answered them, it is not because I have forgotten them, or been uninterested about them—but because it appeared to me I could write nothing which could do any good." Lincoln's advice was to "procure a doctor, or any thing else for Father in his present sickness." He made two excuses for not coming: he was very busy, and Mary was "sick-abed."[11]

With the Illinois Supreme Court in session, this was indeed a busy season for Springfield lawyers. Still, Lincoln's presence was not required between January 13, the day of his letter, and January 17, the day of Thomas's death. In three cases, he was associated with other attorneys (in one case, Stephen T. Logan; in the others, William Herndon), who could have made the necessary court appearances or arguments. The only case that presented genuine difficulty, a case in which Lincoln alone represented the clients, came before the court on January 14.[12] But it was common practice for lawyers to substitute for one another in times of overwork or emergency. There was also the possibility of an extension or postponement of the case.[13] And, though there was as yet no railroad line between Springfield and Charleston, the trip could be made in a day by horse or buggy.

Lincoln's reference to his wife's illness is difficult to assess. Their second son Edward had died almost a year earlier, and Mary had collapsed in shock and for weeks remained in her room and wept. Soon she was pregnant again. Her third son, William Wallace, was born on December 21, 1850, more than three weeks before Lincoln wrote Johnston that he could not visit his father. Though Mary was still recovering from childbirth, there were no complications, and Lincoln told Johnston he supposed her condition was "not dangerous." He was accustomed to her desperate pleas for closeness and attention, and he could spend months away campaigning or riding the circuit when it suited his needs. What she faced in mid-January, 1851, was apparently one of her periodic bouts of depression, one associated this time with a minor physical illness. His use of this illness as an excuse for remaining in Springfield while his father was dying in Charleston appears, therefore, specious. He was trying desperately to justify his own inability to face his father's death.

Lincoln's letter to Johnston supports this interpretation. After explaining why he could not visit his father, Lincoln asked Johnston to "tell him [Thomas] to remember to call upon, and confide in, our great, and good, and merciful Maker; who will not turn away from him in any extremity. He notes the fall of a sparrow, and numbers the hairs of our heads; and He will not forget the dying man, who puts his trust in Him." Then Lincoln added a phrase that dramatically expressed his own conflict: "Say to him that if we could meet now, it is doubtful whether it would not be more painful than pleasant." Possibly Lincoln was accurately predicting his father's reaction, but, more likely, the pain would have been Lincoln's, not his father's. Psychologically, our deepest conflicts always manage to find expression, however confused, distorted, or disguised. In this letter Lincoln tried to convince himself that factors beyond his control—his busy schedule and his wife's illness—directed his behavior. But he realized the hollowness of these excuses, and so he turned to the absolving power of God. He simply could not bear the thought of meeting with his father on his deathbed.

If Lincoln had trouble dealing with his dying father, he was equally unable to handle the simplest of rituals our culture expects for the deceased. Lincoln did not attend his father's funeral, and he spent the rest of his life intermittently resolving to mark his father's grave in some appropriate way. Though he never got around to it, he did name his next child (his fourth son, born April 4, 1853) Thomas, after his father. There are many reasons for the naming of children, but in this case the timing suggests a kind of expiation or atonement for the guilt that Lincoln felt for the neglect of his father. In any event, in late January, 1861, during his final visit with his stepmother before leaving for Washington, Lincoln visited his father's grave, which was "unmarked and utterly neglected," and at least thought of ordering a stone marker for the site.[14] On December 19, 1867, Mary wrote to his stepmother: "My husband a few weeks before his death mentioned to me, that he intended *that* summer [i.e., 1865], paying proper respect to *his* father's grave, by a head and footstone, with his name & age & I propose very soon carrying out his intentions."[15] Mary, in her state of emotional disarray after the assassination, was even less capable than Lincoln of doing anything about the marker. The task was left to some local residents of Coles County, who finally erected a twelve-foot monument at the grave in 1880—twenty-nine years after Thomas's death.[16]

It is possible to see Lincoln's idealization of the nation's founders as an attempt to establish paternal surrogates. Certainly, his political and emotional investment in their personalities and documents proved to be a creative, healing force in a time of national breakdown.

In his idealization of the founders, Lincoln went along with a powerful trend in American culture. The "post-heroic generation," as the historian George B. Forgie has called it, defined itself collectively in the shadow of these figures. Parson Weems's *Life of Washington* painted an idealized and quite mythical picture of

[55]

the Father of His County,[17] and Americans continuously revered him and other founders. When the Whig leader Henry Clay sought authority for federal expenditures on internal improvements, he found it in the Constitution and in the policies of Washington.[18] Politicians North and South, from Daniel Webster to John C. Calhoun, talked of their special relationship to a mighty past.[19] Still, the post-heroic generation remained ambivalent toward the fathers, and the ambivalence provides a backdrop for Lincoln's own engagement with them.[20]

Lincoln intimated his feelings toward the fathers in a speech he gave in 1838 before the Young Men's Lyceum in Springfield. The panic of 1837 had created widespread social unrest and had intensified the growing discord over slavery. A spirit of mob violence prevailed in many areas of the country, as when, in the fall of 1837, a mob attacked the abolitionist press of Elijah P. Lovejoy in Alton, Illinois, and killed him when he attempted to defend it. In his speech, "The Perpetuation of Our Political Institutions," Lincoln dealt in a general way with the issues he felt the Alton lynching raised.[21]

Lincoln began with a lofty description of the riches and abundance of America. This "fairest portion of the earth," he said, possessed the world's best land, soil, and climate. But the country's most important assets were its political institutions, which provided more civil and religious liberty than any other in history. These institutions were gifts from "a *once* hardy, brave and patriotic, but *now* lamented and departed race of ancestors," noble souls who had built a "political edifice" of liberty and equal rights. Our sacred duty was to preserve the edifice and hand it down "unprofaned by the foot of an invader," "undecayed by the lapse of time," and "untorn by usurpation." This task was to be performed out of "gratitude to our fathers, justice to ourselves, duty to posterity, and love for our species in general."

According to Lincoln, these institutions faced three potential dangers: invasion by an outside enemy, internal rot, and overthrow by a native dictator. He eliminated the possibility of invasion ("All the armies of Europe, Asia and Africa combined, with all the treasures of the earth ... with a Buonaparte for a com-

mander, could not by force, take a drink from the Ohio"). He ignored the danger of rot (though he returned to the rotting metaphor in a curiously altered form at the end of the speech). So he
was left with the possible overthrow of the government by an
American dictator. "If destruction be our lot, we must ourselves
be its author and finisher." If we prepare the path for a dictator,
we will do it by "the increasing disregard for law which pervades
the country; the growing disposition to substitute the wild and
furious passions, in lieu of the sober judgment of Courts; and the
worse than savage mobs, for the executive ministers of justice." In
other words, the "wild and furious passions" of the mob threatened to undermine order and stability and thus to destroy the attachment of the people to their institutions. Once this happened,
Lincoln feared, the way would be open for a dictator to take over
and abolish the sacred institutions inherited from the fathers.

For Lincoln, the alternatives were stark—on the one hand democracy and, on the other, dictatorship. To him it seemed that
would-be dictators were always lurking in the shadows. "Is it un-
reasonable then to expect, that some man possessed of the loftiest
genius, coupled with ambition sufficient to push it to its utmost
stretch, will at some time, spring up among us?" Only our attachment to the government and laws would thwart such ambitions. This line of reasoning left Lincoln with a curious problem.
Our "hardy, brave, and patriotic" fathers had fashioned our free
institutions out of revolution and chaos—exactly the conditions
he now believed were conducive to the emergence of a dictatorship! Lincoln seemed to be saying that the accomplishment of the
founders was all the more remarkable in view of the tendency for
dictatorship to follow revolution. He concluded:

They [the fathers] were the pillars of the temple of liberty; and now,
that they have crumbled away, that temple must fall, unless we, their
descendents, supply their places with other pillars, hewn from the solid
quarry of sober reason. Passion has helped us; but can do no more. It
will in future be our enemy. Reason, cold, calculating, unimpassioned
reason, must furnish all the materials for our future support and defence.

The historian George Fredrickson argues that the young Lincoln was helping to define a conservative intellectual style in American politics that adamantly opposed the "trend toward general anarchy or majority tyranny." The Jacksonian spirit of unrestrained, romantic democracy strongly supported the expression of spontaneous popular feeling, as Fredrickson points out, and some Jacksonian theorists even defended in principle the rights of the mob. Other Americans, with a more traditional notion of order and community, "mounted a substantial counter-attack against the ideas and practices associated with the radical democratic impulse." Fredrickson sees Lincoln's Lyceum speech as a classic expression of this conservative response to the "mobocratic spirit" and as a statement of faith, "in regular and established ways of making decisions and resolving disputes." The speech, Fredrickson says, is not open to psychological interpretation, because "it was not at all unusual for a lawyer to deprecate genius or defend calculating reason against exalted passion. It was, as we have seen, an integral part of the juridical defense of a procedural community."[22]

Psychological interpretation, however, is not separate from but congruent with other approaches. No doubt Lincoln's call for order and reason, for "cold, calculating, unimpassioned reason," was intended as an antidote to the "mobocratic spirit" that he saw in evidence throughout the land. His passionate interest in order and reason ran like a thread throughout his life, influencing his conception of the political process, his choice of career, and his style of domesticity. Furthermore, Lincoln wrestled throughout his life with the issue of losing control, which may have symbolized death for him. In 1846 he described in poetry the terror of madness. He wrote of a childhood friend, Matthew Gentry, once of "genius bright. . . . Now locked for aye, in mental night, / A haggard mad-man wild." Lincoln described how Gentry maimed himself, fought his father, and tried to kill his mother. The terror spread. Neighbors came to tie down the "howling crazy man" who kicked and shrieked and "With burning eye-balls glared." Then came quiet, except for Gentry's plaintive and mournful song. Lincoln links this wail directly to death: "The funeral dirge,

[58]

it ever seemed / Of reason dead and gone." The poem ends with
an angry incantation of death itself:

> *O death! Thou awe-inspiring prince,*
> *That keepst the world in fear;*
> *Why dost thou tear more blest ones hence,*
> *And leave him ling'ring here?*[23]

It is striking that the vehement defense of the procedural community in the Lyceum speech came at a time in Lincoln's life
when he was personally most turbulent. Nor was the Lyceum
speech an isolated example of this theme in Lincoln's thought at
that period. On February 24, 1842—the same day he received
Speed's "promised" letter—Lincoln concluded a temperance address with an extraordinary apotheosis of control and rationality.
He himself never liked alcohol much, for it made him feel "flabby
and undone."[24] In the speech he called for humane treatment of
drunks as the best approach to ridding the world of alcoholism.
His rhetoric betrayed his metaphoric purpose, for he invoked an
"all conquering mind" that would someday control appetites and
subdue passion but would be itself sexualized and "consummated" in the act of control. "Happy day," he said, "when, all appetites controlled, all passions subdued, all matters subjected,
mind, all conquering *mind*, shall live and move the monarch of
the world. Glorious consummation! Hail fall of Fury! Reign of
Reason, all hail!"[25]

In the Lyceum speech Lincoln apparently identified himself
with the would-be dictator lurking in the shadows. For him, there
seemed to be a morbid attraction in this evil power who "thirsts
and burns for distinction" with an ambition that soars above the
ordinary drive for a "seat in Congress, a gubernatorial or a presidential chair." Such petty goals—even the Presidency—*"belong
not to the family of the lion, or the tribe of the eagle."* A "towering genius" like Alexander, Caesar, or Napoleon "disdains a
beaten path. It seeks regions hitherto unexplored. It sees *no distinction* in adding story to story to story, upon the monuments of
fame, erected to the memory of others. It *denies* that it is glory
enough to serve under any chief. It *scorns* to tread in the foot-

steps of *any* predecessor, however illustrious." The towering genius—and here Lincoln was chillingly prophetic—"thirsts and
burns for distinction; and, if possible, it will have it, whether at
the expense of emancipating slaves, or enslaving freemen."

Edmund Wilson first noted Lincoln's identification with the
towering genius of the Lyceum speech.[26] But Wilson failed to
grasp that the genius spoke for Lincoln's unacknowledged (or
unconscious) wishes. At twenty-eight, Lincoln had accomplished
very little to justify a self-conception that would rank him with
Alexander, Caesar, or Napoleon. His vigorous rationalism forced
him to be more honest than that with himself. The grandiose
wishes, which rose from his own murky inner needs, he dealt
with largely through repression, but repression only distorts and
does not destroy such urges. His desire to be the greatest and
most powerful leader of all time, to be the towering genius, appears in the speech as motivating someone else. This other figure
he feared because it spoke for his forbidden self; the wish, as
Freud has observed, is father to the fear. Lincoln shrank back
from his projective creation, the scary towering genius, with a
shiver of unacknowledged recognition.

Lincoln's wishful identification expressed both his childhood
sense of omnipotence and his youthful longing for political
power. At this stage he seemed to be torn between the impermis-
sibility of acknowledging the wish and the severe measures
needed to keep it under wraps. Thus in the Lyceum speech he
spent most of his time on the necessity of protecting our political
institutions against the kind of erosion that would permit the dictator to appear. This defensive posturing served Lincoln's psychological needs, for it allowed complete, if disguised, expression of his conflict: the repressed wish to be the towering genius
and the elaborate structures to defend against the wish. The more
he warned against the disruptive capabilities of the towering genius, the more he suggested a subjective investment in the need to
perpetuate our political institutions to protect against the genius.
For only the binding force of our institutions hold in check the
"unruly passions" of the mob. Unleashed, these "passions"
would destroy everything. Reason, "cold, calculating, unimpassioned reason," must prevail.

[60]

Fathers and Sons

The oedipal implications of the speech should not be ignored. The danger the towering genius poses is the destruction of the idealized fathers' glorious work, their "temple of liberty," which they have left for us to protect and maintain. By his identification with the towering genius, Lincoln makes himself the one to carry out just such a destruction, to become the jealous son displacing the ambivalently loved father and to wage a mythic battle against the collective, historical fathers. His language tends to support this view. The towering genius is vibrant, powerful, unfettered, above and beyond history itself, but the founders are now dead and their work is rotting, subject to the abuse of nature: "They [the founders] were a forest of giant oaks; but the all-resistless hurricane has swept over them, and left only, here and there, a lonely trunk, despoiled of its verdure, shorn of its foliage; unshading and unshaded; to murmur in a few more gentle breezes, and to combat with its mutilated limbs, a few more ruder storms, then to sink, and be no more." The imagery here suggests emasculation and castration at the hands of the aspiring son.

Thomas Lincoln, as we have seen, failed to live up to his son's expectations. In the Lyceum speech, Lincoln invested the founders and their work with all the grandeur so lamentably absent in his real father. His feeling for the "old fathers" and their famous documents was to continue unabated. In speech after speech he invoked the spirit of the "fathers" and their Declaration of Independence as the basis for the salvation and rejuvenation of the country. For example, in 1854 he told a Peoria audience:

Let us return it [slavery] to the position our fathers gave it; and there let it rest in peace. Let us re-adopt the Declaration of Independence, and with it, the practices, and policy, which harmonize with it. Let north and south—let all Americans—join in the great and good work. If we do this, we shall not only have saved it, as to make, and to keep it, forever worthy of the saving. We shall have so saved it, that the succeeding millions of free happy people, the world over shall rise up, and call us blessed, to the latest generations.[27]

During the debates with Stephen A. Douglas in 1858, Lincoln returned to this theme with almost monotonous regularity, stressing the wisdom of the "fathers" and the power of their documents to solve current political problems, especially the problem of slavery.

On February 27, 1860, at the Cooper Institute in New York City, Lincoln delivered one of his most important speeches before his Presidency. In it he sought to understand "the frame of Government under which we live" and how slavery fitted into it. He carefully examined the attitudes of the thirty-nine signers, "who were our fathers," to see what they expected to become of slavery. He also addressed the vital issue of federal versus local authority in the territories. He concluded: "*As those fathers marked it* [slavery], *so let it be again marked, as an evil not to be extended, but to be tolerated and protected only because of and so far as its actual presence among us makes that toleration and protection a necessity.*"[28] Four New York papers published the entire speech, and the *Tribune* remarked: "No man ever before made such an impression on his first appeal to a New York audience."[29] Later the Young Men's Republican Union, the sponsor of the speech, brought it out as a pamphlet.

As President of a war-torn nation, Lincoln could no longer rely on the redeeming power of the founders. He realized how his election had changed his understanding of history. As he told the Springfield citizens who came to say goodbye to him at the depot on February 11, 1861, "I now leave, not knowing when, or whether ever, I may return, with a task before me greater than that which rested upon Washington."[30] The Springfield *Journal* editor had "heard him speak upon a hundred different occasions" but had "never seen him so profoundly affected."[31] With dramatic suddenness Lincoln had assumed a position alongside the founders of the republic.

In the Gettysburg Address, November 19, 1863, Lincoln subtly indicated his awareness of the change.[32] He now invoked the familiar respect for the fathers who had "brought forth, upon this continent, a new nation, conceived in Liberty, and dedicated to the proposition that all men are created equal." Then he stated a momentous issue for himself and the nation: whether the Civil War, symbolized by the battlefield where he spoke, would put an end to this great experiment. He concluded that the deaths were not in vain and that the nation—under his leadership in a war for which he personally assumed responsibility—would have "a new birth of freedom," and "government of the people, by the people, for the people" would not "perish from the earth."

The war and its terrible carnage, as well as his own inner needs, created for Lincoln something of a psychological and moral crisis. There seemed no explanation for the suffering, the death, and destruction. In the past Lincoln had always related the great political issues of the day to the thought of the founders. But the war tore loose his own and the nation's moorings in the past. For security and for meaning, he now turned more and more to God.

Never religious in a conventional sense, Lincoln confessed on December 7, 1864: "I am not much of a judge of religion. . . ."[33] After the death of Eddie in 1850, Lincoln had become friendly with the Reverend James Smith of the First Presbyterian Church, but he never joined it. He seemed to believe in a deity, and he had, of course, a firm grounding in the Bible. According to Nicolay and Hay, it genuinely cheered him to know others prayed for him. During his forty-nine months in office he issued nine separate calls to public penitence, fasting, prayer, and thanksgiving.[34] Until the war, he had appeared to find ample basis for his evolving political positions in his own common sense and in the documents of the founders. Then he began to look elsewhere. "Through this dreadful national crisis," Harriett Beecher Stowe noted in 1864, "he has been forced by the very anguish of the struggle to look upward. . . ."[35] And up there was God, august, mysterious, majestic.

In his Second Inaugural Address, March 4, 1865, Lincoln dramatically illustrated the transformation of his thought. At the outset he established the South's responsibility for the war: "Both parties [North and South] deprecated war; but one of them would make war rather than let the nation survive; and the other would accept war rather than let it perish. And the war came." Lincoln then turned to the issue of slavery: "One eighth of the whole population were colored slaves, not distributed gen-

erally over the Union, but localized in the Southern part of it. . . .
All knew that this interest was, somehow, the cause of the war."
No one anticipated the magnitude or duration of the war that
came, Lincoln continued. "Both [North and South] read the
same Bible, and pray to the same God; and each invokes His aid
against the other." The prayers of both could not be answered,
and "neither has been answered fully."

The Almighty has His own purposes. "Woe unto the world because
of offences! for it must needs be that offences come; but woe to that man
by whom the offence cometh!" If we shall suppose that American Slavery is one of those offences which, in the providence of God, must needs
come, but which, having continued through His appointed time, He
now wills to remove, and that He gives to both North and South, this
terrible war, as the woe due to those by whom the offence came, shall we
discern therein any departure from those divine attributes which the be-
lievers in a Living God always ascribe to him? Fondly do we hope—fervently do we pray—that this mighty scourge of war may speedily pass
away. Yet, if God wills that it continue, until all the wealth piled by the
bond-man's two hundred and fifty years of unrequited toil shall be sunk,
and until every drop of blood drawn with the lash, shall be paid by another drawn with the sword, as was said three thousand years ago, so
still it must be said "the judgments of the Lord, are true and righteous
altogether."[36]

Here was a divine aim in the war. Here was a framework, an
explanation, for what seemed as senseless as it was interminable.
Here, too, was a feeling far different from the "cold, calculating,
unimpassioned reason" of the Lyceum speech some twenty-six
years earlier. He had warned strongly against the emergence of a
dictator who would surely take advantage of the ensuing chaos—
and only thinly disguised his own identification with that
"towering genius." Later, as the country moved toward war over
slavery, Lincoln became a passionate spokesman for a return to
the wisdom of the fathers and their successors like Henry Clay.
These men emerged in Lincoln's thought as our only source of
wisdom and guidance in perilous times. Then came the war, and
with it Lincoln assumed a place in history which he quickly realized put him on a par with the founders. Suddenly, those revered,

distant, idealized figures lost their psychological significance. Lincoln had been lifted by history to look directly into the eyes of his heroes. It was a startling experience. And his gaze drifted upward. Finally only God, and no man, could supply the meaning of human existence.

The first photograph of Mary Todd Lincoln, taken in 1846. She was twenty-seven years old and the mother of two small boys. She was devoted to her husband, whose political ambition she warmly embraced. *Library of Congress*

Chapter 4

M. T. L.

What changes—*time* brings to us all—I sometimes feel as if I had lived a century. *My life* is not dated by years.
MARY TODD LINCOLN
December 5, 1869

 ER earliest photograph dates from 1846. It shows an attractive young woman in her mid-twenties gazing expectantly at the camera. Full cheeks, though suggesting a tendency toward plumpness, only accentuate the softness and femininity. A high forehead blends with light brown hair wrapped in an unseen bun. The eyes and nose are regular, even pleasant. The mouth pulls together tightly above a rounded chin. A long graceful neck plunges into folds of obscuring Victorian fabric. Short arms rest uneasily, one of them propped against a chair, as the subject waits rigidly through a long exposure. The hands seem large for the body, and the fingers long.

Other sources add lifelike details to this stark black and white daguerreotype. "Her features were not regularly beautiful," recalled Mary's childhood friend, Mrs. Elizabeth L. Norris, "but she was certainly very pretty with her clear blue eyes, lovely complexion, and soft brown hair." She had a bright and intelligent face and "no Old Master ever modeled a more perfect arm and hand."[1] Mary took great pride in her soft complexion, graceful arms, and full buxom figure. In her early years the fashion

[67]

forbade much décolleté, but by the 1860s plunging necklines and bare shoulders were in style. Mary, a matronly forty, eagerly adopted the new mode. She was short (five feet, two inches) and seemed shorter beside a husband who was extraordinarily tall for the time (six feet, four inches). Yet she carried herself well and "was graceful in her movements,"[2] a fine and experienced dancer, familiar with the best technique and able to move easily across the floor.

This attractive woman had a complex personality. Vivacious, infectiously enthusiastic, delightfully witty, she could make a bishop forget his prayers, as her brother-in-law once said.[3] Her letters bustle with energy, haste, and excitement. Of an 1840 trip to Missouri, she wrote that she "remained a week, attended four parties, during the time, once [*sic*] was *particularly* distinguished for its brilliancy and *city like* doings, the house was very commodious, four rooms & two halls, thrown open for the reception of the guests, in two, dancing was carried on with *untiring vigor*, kept up until 3 o'clock."[4] She described the Virginia reel as "poetry of motion," yet confessed she was nearly exhausted at the *"desperate exertions"* of the dance. Then she referred to *"some letters"* (perhaps from Lincoln) that "were entirely *unlooked for.*"

Mary's letters of this period seem to burst from the page. The sentences run on with few paragraph breaks but with occasional dashes. Indiscriminate underlining gives a feeling of exaggerated drama. The diversity of topics testifies to the range of Mary's interests and the extent of her involvement in the world around her. She describes an incredibly busy schedule, with "scarce a leisure moment" to call her own. She delights in gossip: "I know you would be pleased with Matilda Edwards, a lovelier girl I never saw. *Mr. Speed's* ever changing heart I suspect is about offering *its young* affection at her shrine." The mention of Speed reminds her of *"Mr. Webb,* a widower of modest merit" and of her sister's "most agreeable party," with over a hundred guests. She refers to two married friends, then asks: "Why is it that married folks always become so serious?" She expresses ironic pleasure that another friend is about to commit the *"crime of matrimony."* (These references are the only suggestions of her engagement to

Lincoln, which is to be prematurely ended in two weeks.) Without a breath she moves abruptly into politics, noting her elation at the 1840 election of William Henry Harrison as President. Apparently she worked for Harrison during the campaign: "This fall I became quite a *politician*, rather an unladylike profession, yet at such a *crisis*, whose heart could remain untouched while the energies of all were called in question?"[5] Politics, love, marriage, friends, relatives, parties, and the weather all dance across the page.

At that time Mary had a capacity for self-reflection and ironic humor that gave depth to her somewhat superficial concerns with the swirl of social life around her. Would her real nature be satisfied with the excitement of continued parties? She doubts it. "I would such were not my nature, for mine I fancy is to be a quiet lot, and happy indeed will I be, if it is, only cast near those, I so *dearly love*, my feelings & hopes are all so sanguine that in this dull world of reality tis best to dispel our delusive day dreams so soon as possible."[6] She laughs at her own frailties and at her plumpness. She describes herself as the "same ruddy *pineknot*" but without quite the same "exuberance of flesh," though with "quite a sufficiency."[7] There is a certain reflective detachment in her descriptions of the most trivial occurrences. She provides concrete information (for example, how many guests were at the ball), describes the courtships of others as an outside observer might, and easily separates her own fantasies and dreams from the lives of those around her.

There was gaiety and brightness in young Mary Todd. She "was one of the brightest of all the circle in Springfield at that time [ca. 1840]," as her friend Mrs. John T. Stuart later commented. "She could entertain a roomful with her ready wit."[8] Her overly protective biographer Ruth Painter Randall says she had a "natural cheerfulness," which makes her gaiety sound almost genetic.[9] Mary cut quite a figure in Springfield. Once, when she and her friend Mercy Levering were cooped up at home by heavy rains, she finally could stand it no longer and decided to set out for town. With some wooden shingles she thought she could lay a movable track and thus advance over the mud. The two young women made it to town reasonably well but then had to confront the dismaying prospect of a return by the same tedious method. Instead of trying it, Mary enlisted a dray from a Hart to haul her home, though Mercy declined to accompany her. Mary's ride created a sensation. Here was Springfield's leading belle plopped unceremoniously in the rear of a lowly wagon. A socially conscious young Dr. E. H. Merryman took note of the event in a humorous poem, which begins:

> Up flew windows, out popped heads
> To see this lady gay
> In silken cloak and feathers white
> A riding on a dray.

The poem concludes with a rather cruel reference to Mary's plumpness:

> At length arrived at Edwards' gate
> Hart backed the usual way
> And taking out the iron pin
> He rolled her off the dray.[10]

There was a proud, stubborn streak in young Mary. She knew what it meant to ride in Hart's dray, just as she knew it infuriated her family for her to fall in love with the low-born and apparently hapless Abraham Lincoln. She pursued her unflagging interest in politics, even though she was aware it was "unladylike." In love, too, she stubbornly clung to the memory of Lincoln for a year and a half, even though he had broken their engagement. She wrote Mercy Levering in June, 1841, that she had been "much alone of late" and had been left to the solitude of her own thoughts and "some *lingering regrets* over the past, which time can alone overshadow with its healing balm."[11] If only Lincoln would return to her company "much, much happiness" would it afford her.[12] She remained quietly faithful all that summer, fall, and following winter, waiting patiently for him to wrestle his own inner demons to the ground. There is no indication he asked her to wait; on the contrary, he seemed unable to communicate anything to her until the spring of 1842. Perhaps she sensed time would heal the wounds. So she waited.

There is an old Todd family tale that when Lincoln first met Mary at a ball he said he would like to dance with her in the worst way. She reportedly commented later how accurate that was. Lincoln obviously could handle such repartee, but most of the other young men in Mary's life suffered severely from her occasional biting sarcasm. "Without designing to wound," Elizabeth Norris later recalled of Mary in Kentucky, "she now & then indulged in sarcastic, witty remarks that cut like a Damascus blade—but there was no malice in it—She was impulsive & made no attempt to conceal her feelings."[13] In the summer of 1842 Mary was apparently the prime mover, along with Julia Jayne and Lincoln, in writing the "Rebecca Letters," which ridiculed James Shields and nearly resulted in a duel between him and Lincoln.[14]

Sarcasm, of course, is the less gentle side of humor. It tells more about the insecurities and foibles of the joker than about the person taken as the butt of the jokes. In the case of young Mary her sarcasm was associated with a ferocious temper. Her rages were legion, though they were worse in the matron, Mrs. Lincoln, than in the young Mary Todd. Young Mary was impulsive, quixotic, nervous, and frenetic, a coiled bundle of energy under relatively good control but ready at any point to burst forth. At this point in her life her capacity for genuine warmth and sympathy for others, her self-reflection, and the effusive enthusiasm of ripe youth, partially hid the potential meanings of her rage. But several observers close to Mary later commented on the contrast between her happy, warm self and the rage beneath. "She was very highly strung," wrote her sister Emilie Todd Helm, "nervous, impulsive, excitable, having an emotional temperament much like an April day, sunning all over with laughter one moment, the next crying as if her heart would break."[15] Her face was an index to every passing emotion.[16]

Lincoln's cousin Dennis Hanks noted that Mary came from "blue blood, blue grass Kentucky stock."[17] She was indeed the scion of a distinguished Kentucky clan. Her father, Robert Smith Todd, was the owner of a fine house and a number of slaves and was a leader in Whig politics. Their house in Lexington was a center of informed political debate with guests that included Henry Clay. At thirteen, so the story goes, Mary rode out to Ashland, Clay's home just outside Lexington, to show him her new white pony.[18] And reportedly she was once romping through the house when her elderly grandmother cautioned, " 'Sit down Mary. Do be quiet. What on earth do you suppose will become of you if you go on this way?' 'Oh, I will be the wife of a President some day,' carelessly answered the petted child."[19]

Her father was born in 1791, the seventh of eleven children of the distinguished Levi Todd. Robert Todd entered Transylvania University at fourteen years of age, then clerked in an office, studied law under the tutelage of George M. Bibb, and was admitted to the bar in 1811. He soon excelled in business, politics, and Lexington public life. After opening a fancy retail store in 1817, he expanded into other retail enterprises and into the cotton manufacturing business, with a large packaging plant and a wholesale outlet. In 1835 he became the first president of the new Branch Bank of Kentucky. He also wielded political clout. He served repeatedly as the clerk of the Kentucky House of Representatives and in 1831, when Lexington was incorporated, he was elected to its first board of council. Though high-strung and impetuous, he was highly successful and widely admired for his wealth, power, and family background.[20]

In 1811 Robert married his second cousin, Eliza Parker. Her family was just as distinguished as his; she had relatives who had been friends of George Washington.[21] Settling down to a comfortable life, Robert and Eliza began to produce children with regularity: 1813 (Elizabeth), 1815 (Frances), 1817 (Levi), December 13, 1818 (Mary), 1820 (Robert), 1824 (Ann Maria), 1825 (George). Eliza died from complications following George's birth, and her death left an unhealed wound in seven-year-old Mary. She remained permanently vulnerable to separation and loss, and later, as her own children one by one died, she lost her psychological moorings in reality. The death of her mother had left Mary alone, unwanted, and something of a bother to her father, to the unmarried aunt who moved in, and to the overworked household slaves: Jane Saunders, the housekeeper; Chaney, the cook; Nelson, the body servant, coachman, and jack-of-all-trades; and "Mammy Sally" and Judy the nurse, the two who cared for the children.[22] "Mammy Sally" perhaps filled some of the void in Mary's life, but nothing Mary did could bring her father more tightly into her orbit. Within a year he seemingly rejected her when he took a second wife, Elizabeth Humphreys, who began dutifully to produce new babies for him, eight of them in thirteen years. He probably felt that by remarrying he was providing a better home for all his children. In any event, Mary's need for his attention and love precluded a sharing of affection with her second mother and those hateful new babies. Mary's resentment of her stepmother—and of her father—may have received some outside reinforcement, for Grandmother Parker, who lived next door, detested the second Mrs. Todd. Mary's situation intensified her willfulness and tendency to tantrums. In confused expressions of undirected rage she seemingly cried out for support, love, and nurturing from her father, her missing mother, and anyone else who might help her. Her calls went largely unheeded. As an adult, she attached herself to Lincoln with all the intensity resulting from these unfulfilled childhood longings. She adored him for his calm, fatherly presence, and nothing made her happier than when he called her his child-wife.

Mary's stepmother, "Betsy" Humphreys Todd, seems to have been incapable of responding to Mary's needs. Her unfeeling way is suggested by an incident that occurred in 1848, when Mary was staying in her father's house with her five-year-old Robert and her two-year-old Eddie, while Lincoln served as a Congressman in Washington. As Mary told her husband in a long, rambling letter, Robert had brought home a cat, to the immense delight of Eddie. "Ma came in, she you know dislikes the whole cat race." In a "very unfeeling way" the old woman ordered the nearest servant to throw the cat out. Eddie began screaming violently, but "she never appeared to mind his screams." Mary concluded: "Tis unusual for her *now a days*, to do any thing quite so striking, she is very obliging and accommodating, but if she thought any of us, were on her hands again I believe she would be *worse* than ever."[23]

Mary was writing Lincoln from her father's home late on a Saturday night. The children were finally asleep and she was alone, longing for her husband and writing him how "very sad" she felt at their separation. Such a setting was calculated to revive childhood wishes and memories. In her "dreamy" state Mary transferred to Lincoln her childhood longings for her father. The cat incident marked Betsy as an intruder and solidified Mary's relationship with her father-husband. It confirmed the wickedness of the stepmother and reinforced Mary's unconscious desire for her husband-father to make her his child-wife.

Mary adjusted in a complex way to the (for her) confused and unempathic family relationships that followed her mother's death. She grew up "without learning the essential lesson of self-restraint," as Ruth Painter Randall quaintly puts it.[24] Such a view makes the tantrum a problem of discipline and fails to appreciate the desperate search for inner cohesion and meaningful attention that is the psychological message of the incoherently screaming child. A relevant anecdote is the one that Elizabeth Norris, Mary's friend and roommate in the Todd home for several years, recalled of Mary as an early adolescent. Mary and Elizabeth wanted hoopskirts so as to look grown-up for church. Mary conceived a plan to make the hoops out of dried willows, but these spread the skirts awkwardly and unevenly. Still, Mary was determined to wear the hoops, and she sneaked out of the house to avoid her stepmother's censure. The hateful Betsy, catching sight of her from a window, insisted that she come back and take off the ridiculous outfit. In her room Mary burst into furious and futile tears.[25]

The hoops, it seems, symbolized maturity for Mary. The stepmother's harsh response failed to grant Mary independent initiative or to recognize her awkward but genuine expression of individuality. The scene reveals the sexual tension between Mary and Betsy. Mary had gone to great effort to make herself pretty, only to have Betsy tell her how ugly and stupid she looked. In this struggle Betsy emerged victorious, but in the process she only made it more difficult for Mary to develop her sexual identity.

The story of the willow hoops reflects Mary's resourcefulness and creativity. By the age of ten, when Elizabeth Norris first met her, Mary was "bright and talkative & warm hearted." She seemed "far advanced, over girls of her age, in education." Her school was the center of her psychological existence. The principal, Mr. Ward, was a harsh taskmaster, but Mary never came under his censure. Instead, she seemed to find solace in the rigorous schedule, "pouring over her books" by the light of a candle and often getting up before breakfast to complete her lessons. Cold though the winter days often were, Mary never complained. "I never saw any display of temper on her part," Norris recalled, "or heard her reprimanded."[26]

At fourteen, Mary progressed to Mme. Victorie Charlotte Leclere Mentelle's select school, just outside Lexington, to board there Mondays through Fridays for the next four years. The school emphasized the fine graces required of a lady—Mary became a superb dancer, for example—but it also provided an intellectually stimulating environment for a smart young girl. Mme. Mentelle required her charges to speak French while at school, and dancing lessons alternated with courses on the classics. Here Mary received a remarkable and quite atypical education for an antebellum southern belle. She became witty, articulate, and outspoken with both peers and adults. She learned to enjoy the finest French authors and could astound visiting Frenchmen with her Parisian accent.[27]

At nineteen, Mary had not yet completed her education. After spending the summer of 1837 in Springfield with her sister, Elizabeth Edwards, she returned to Lexington and spent the next two years studying under Dr. Ward, her earlier principal. Her work with him amounted to a kind of graduate study, and the results were impressive. She now was "forever reciting" poetry, to the delight and amusement of her friends. "Page after page of classic poetry she could recite and liked nothing better."[28] When she went back to Springfield in 1839 to live with her sister, the twenty-one-year-old Mary was an accomplished woman, fully prepared to assume a leading position in the Springfield coterie. Even her worst enemy of later years, William Herndon, could not help giving a favorable description of the young Mary. According to him, she was pleasant, polite, civil, graceful, intelligent, witty (though sometimes bitter), polished, well educated, a good linguist, a clever conversationalist, a little proud and sometimes haughty but a very shrewd girl.[29]

Lincoln called her "Molly" before the birth of their first son, Robert (1843). After that, she was "Mother" or occasionally "little-woman" or "Puss" or "child-wife."[30] She found security in his fatherly presence and remembered later that "he was never himself" when she was not perfectly well.[31] Lincoln enjoyed Mary's enthusiasm for fine clothes and seemed proud of her good looks. She in turn delighted in making herself pretty for him.[32] Her total love for him magnified his public and private virtues and minimized those of his political opponents. "Mr. Douglas," she once commented, "is a very little, little giant by the side of my tall Kentuckian, and intellectually my husband towers above Douglas just as he does physically."[33] When, in 1855 Lyman Trumbull defeated him for the Senate, there was a hint of double-dealing on Trumbull's part, but Lincoln soon accepted the inevitable and patched up fences with his former friend. Mary, however, refused ever again to speak with Lyman Trumbull or with his wife, who had been one of her best friends. Even the amicable Dr. Anson G. Henry could not mediate between Mary and Julia. "Mary and Julia have both made me their confidant telling me their grievances, and both think the other *all* to blame," Henry wrote his wife in February, 1861. "I am trying to make peace between them."[34]

Mary's first years of marriage were troubled by problems of financial insecurity, continuing tension with her Todd relatives, and the lack of a home she could call her own. She and her husband moved at first to the Globe Tavern, where they rented a room for four dollars a week. For Mary, raised in genteel comfort, it was an awful experience to begin married life in a single rented room. She was aggressively materialistic, and at the Globe she had to endure the constraints of possessing neither money to buy things nor space to display them. She soon came to hate boarding houses. She only lasted briefly at Mrs. Sprigg's in Washington in 1847. And after 1865 she continually lamented her cramped hotel quarters and the shame of not owning a house appropriate for a President's widow. Her post-1865 attempts to buy a house seem to have repeated the earlier experience when she and Lincoln carefully husbanded their resources to escape the confining atmosphere of the Globe.

Mary's father, Robert Todd, visited the Lincolns shortly after their marriage. Though impressed with his son-in-law (in a way the Edwardses had never been),[35] he apparently thought Mary lacked the comforts she required, for he began to give her $120 a year and continued to do so until his death in 1849. The money was more than enough to pay the wages of a maid. Mary's sister Elizabeth Edwards and Elizabeth's husband always objected to Lincoln, whom they thought never quite met Todd standards. Mary, ever loyal to Lincoln, held her own in this struggle. Nine months after her marriage she gave birth to Robert at the Globe Tavern rather than in the comfort of the Edwards home. Years later she recalled her "darling husband" bending over her with love and tenderness at the birth.[36]

Mary felt it impossible to remain at the Globe Tavern with a new baby. So while hoping to buy a house of their own, the Lincolns moved in 1843 to a rented one. Finally, in 1844, they bought their home at Eighth and Jackson for $1,500, paying $1,200 in cash and a transferred title to a lot valued at $300.[37] In this house Mary defined her own style of domesticity, one that was distinct but reflected the middle-class taste of the period. Her entire upbringing, as well as her personal needs, influenced her decision to devote body and soul to husband, children, home.

In their life together, as Randall describes it, Lincoln and Mary "knew drudgery, monotony, illnesses, clashes of nerves and viewpoints, scoldings, 'blues,' fears, disappointments, small disasters—all the elements that go into the daily exasperation of the average household." To this home, as to others, "the husband returned after the day's work to tell his wife all that had happened to him that day," and the wife told of babies learning to talk in "such a dear, funny combination of sounds" that both of the parents laughed. "There was love in the house on Eighth Street, there was fun and playfulness, there was the joy of children."[38] This rosy picture, though true as far as it goes, misses the significance, for Mary, of Lincoln's reserve. "You are aware," she wrote Josiah G. Holland in 1865, "that with all the President's deep feelings, he was *not* a demonstrative man, when he felt most deeply, he expressed the least."[39] In this statement she accurately identified an important aspect of Lincoln's personality. She also revealed an underlying note of resentment—that is, she believed in his love but needed much more attention and care than he seemed constitutionally able to give. He was absent physically for much of the time and, when home, was not always there in an emotional sense. Once, for example, he was reading before the fire and was so absorbed in his book that he let the fire get low. Mary asked him three times to build it up, but he did not hear her. Finally, in a rage, she picked up a piece of firewood and went at him.[40]

Herndon interprets this fireplace incident, which he picked up from a servant in the Lincoln home, as evidence of his hero's "domestic hell." Actually, it suggests Mary's frustration with Lincoln's emotional distance, and it shows her inability to contain her anger. To some extent, her anger was justified. She probably felt hurt by the implicit snub in Lincoln's lack of response to her requests, though his absorption in his book by no means indicated a lack of love for her. She could be horribly frustrated with his refusal to become a total part of her.

Desperately in need of Lincoln, Mary often summoned him home from the office to help handle household emergencies, especially those relating to the children.[41] For much of her life, however, she had to cope without him, as he rode the circuit or went off campaigning for months at a time. Her response to his absences was decidedly ambivalent. She wanted the income that the lucrative practice on the circuit brought, and she longed for the fame of political success, yet his absences could devastate her. In 1859 she sent a note to ask Ozias M. Hatch, who was planning to leave for Chicago, to contact Lincoln there and tell him *"dear little Taddie"* was ill. "The Dr. thinks it may prove a *slight* attack of *lung* fever. I am feeling troubled & it would be a comfort to have him, *at home*. He passed a bad night. I do not like his symptoms, and will be glad, if he hurries home."[42] But Lincoln stayed

in Chicago to make a speech and did not start home for several
days.[43]

The Lincoln's Springfield neighbor James Gourley once stated:
"I don't think that Mrs. Lincoln was as bad a woman as she is represented; she was a good friend of mine. She always said that if
her husband had stayed home as he ought to that she could love
him better; she is no prostitute, a good woman. She dared me
once or twice to kiss her, as I thought, refused, wouldn't now."
Gourley also reported that once in terror Mary had wakened him
and pleaded hysterically with him to come spend the night in her
house. Lincoln was away and apparently the maid was letting
men slip in the back door to visit her. Mary frantically appealed
to Gourley: "Come—do come & stay with me all night—you can
sleep in the bed with Bob & I. I don't want boys: they go to sleep
too soon & won't & can't watch. Come do—Sleep with Robt &
myself."[44]

The relative abundance of information obscures rather than
clarifies the Lincolns' complicated relationship. Herndon does little to help. For him, Lincoln's "domestic hell" was a central fact
of the hero's life. Herndon listed Lincoln's agonies at home as one
of three reasons for his melancholia (the other two were his supposed illegitimacy and his genetic endowment).[45] "Poor Lincoln," Herndon thought, "was woman-whipped."[46] Mary berated
her husband for answering the doorbell himself rather than sending a servant; for using his own knife in the butter; and for lying
on the floor to read a newspaper or a book. It might seem odd that
Herndon could view Mary so favorably as a young woman and
yet see her as such a shrew after marriage, when "she became
soured, got gross, became material, avaricious, insolent."[47] He explained the change by reference to Ann Rutledge. "Mrs. Lincoln's knowledge that Lincoln did not love her and did love another caused much trouble between them. I say, Lincoln told her
he did not love her. The world does not know her, Mrs. Lincoln's
sufferings, her trials, and the cause of things."[48] In Herndon's
view, what had been admirable pride and genteel breeding in

This photograph of William Herndon was taken about five years after Lincoln's death. Herndon had been Lincoln's trusted and quite competent law partner from 1844 to 1865. After Lincoln died, Herndon worked for many years gathering materials for (and then writing) his famous and controversial biography. *Ostendorf Collection*

Mary became aristocratic, haughty, and imperious manners. "She was cold as a chunk of ice," he believed.[49]

Relations between Mary and Herndon were bad from the start. As a young man, he once asked her to dance at a ball. Intending to compliment her, he told her she danced like a serpent. This she took as a distinctly ungracious comment,[50] and soon a kind of silent war developed between them. She never relented. When, in 1863, Herndon traveled to Washington to try to get a job for a friend, he ran out of money and had to borrow twenty-five dollars from Lincoln. Mary snubbed him. Privately, he complained of her wickedness and felt sorry for her poor husband.[51]

In the triangular relationship of Lincoln, Mary, and Herndon, a curious set of exclusive intimacies developed. From her point of view, her love and needs excluded anyone else from a closeness to Lincoln. He had to envelop her, comfort her, love her as a hus-

band *and* as a father. The lover expects fidelity but the child demands absorbing attention; in Mary the lover and the child
merged. Herndon also sought an impossible closeness with Lincoln. All he wrote about Lincoln implies wonderment and awe.
Lincoln seems to have recognized the idealizing needs of his junior partner and skillfully played on them. Though Herndon was
only nine years younger, Lincoln liked to lecture him as a father
would a boy. When Herndon was arrested for drunkenness he
turned to Lincoln to bail him out and help him save face. And
after Lincoln died, Herndon lived only to produce what he hoped
would be the definitive biography of the great man.

Lincoln thus aroused the love of one man and one woman who,
like children in a situation of intense sibling rivalry, detested each
other. When open warfare broke out between Herndon and Mary
in 1865, it only brought to the surface the suppressed tensions
that dated from the early 1840s. There was a sexual basis for this
rivalry. It is most explicit in Herndon's insistent and even obsessional interest in Lincoln's sex life, which he believed had been
richly varied before Lincoln's marriage. He leaves to the imagination the question of whether Lincoln consummated his relationship with Ann Rutledge, but he leaves no doubt that Lincoln enjoyed the pleasures of farmers' daughters, prostitutes, and
others.[52] Lincoln's closeness to Speed upset Herndon; he could
not understand it but wished for something like it for himself.
Then Lincoln married and, in Herndon's eyes, became oddly
devoted to his nasty little wife. "Lincoln had terribly strong
passions for women," Herndon once declared, "could scarcely
keep his hands off them, and yet he had honor and strong will,
and these enabled him to put out the fires of his terrible passion."[53] The fires of terrible passion probably were Herndon's
own, and so were the frustrations, the ungratified longings.
Raw, elemental jealousy prompted the virulent hatred between
Herndon and Mary as each sought possession of the elusive
Lincoln.

On the issue between Herndon and Mary, most authors have
taken one side or the other. Edmund Wilson, agreeing with
Herndon, has referred to the "tantrums and aspirations of his
[Lincoln's] rather vulgar wife."[54] On the other hand, Ruth

Painter Randall and Irving Stone (*Love is Eternal*) have come to Mary's defense. Mary is a complex figure that elicits mixed responses. She was a blend of willful, stubborn, outspoken manners and a quiet passive femininity. She defined her life in Lincoln's shadow and then refused to stay there. She could be warm and genuine one moment and manipulative, petty, and imperious the next. At times she was in a rage, at other times collapsing with a migraine headache. "And you are entirely free from head-ache?" Lincoln wrote her on April 16, 1848. "that is good—good—considering it is the first spring you have been free from it since we were acquainted."[55] In addition to her short-term vacillations, Mary underwent a long-term change. The bubbly, vivacious, engaging young woman almost seems a different person from the dour, self-pitying widow.

Herndon's material tends to support the view of Mary's contrariness. For example, Herndon relates an incident with a Mr. Tiger, which he picked up third hand. Tiger's niece, Sarah, had worked for Mary as a maid sometime in 1850. All went well until Mary got into one of her "insane mad spells" and insulted and slapped the girl, who ran home to her uncle. Tiger went to see Mary. He found her standing in the yard, which was strewn with Sarah's trunk and clothes. He attempted to learn Mary's side of the story, but rational discussion seemed impossible. "Mrs. Lincoln got madder and madder," Herndon comments, "boiled over with her insane rages, and at last struck Tiger with a broom two or three times." Tiger, now angry himself, sought out Lincoln for an apology and reportedly found him telling jokes at the Edwards store. He called him outside and demanded that he punish Mary and apologize to him. Lincoln sadly appealed to him: "Friend Tiger, can't you endure this one wrong done you by a madwoman without much complaint for old friendship's sake while I have had to bear it without complaint and without a murmur for, lo, these last fifteen years?"[56]

It matters little whether Lincoln was in the Edwards store, or when the episode occurred (Lincoln had not known Mary for fifteen years by 1850), or whether he said exactly what he is quoted as having said. It does matter whether something like this incident occurred at some time during the Lincolns' Springfield

years. And that seems likely. Furthermore, the point of the anecdote—Mary's erupting, irrational anger—finds adequate docu-
mentation in a variety of sources. Neighbor Gourley noted that
Lincoln and Mary got along fine "unless Mrs. Lincoln got the
devil in her." Lincoln would then pick up one of his children and
walk off, paying no heed to her "wild furious condition."[57] Mrs.
George C. Beal reported that she and her mother once went to
call on the Lincolns. As they approached the house the back door
flew open and Lincoln came rushing out. Mary was fast on his
heels throwing potatoes at him.[58] Another of Herndon's infor-
mants told of Mary chasing Lincoln with a butcher knife. Lincoln, apparently realizing that people were watching, stopped
short and wheeled around, caught Mary by the back of her neck
and seat of her pants, and carried her inside the door, saying,
"There, now, stay in the house and don't be a damned fool before
the people."[59] Herndon also recalled from his personal experience
Lincoln's frequent gloom at the office when chased from home.[60]
And so it goes. Visitors, friends, neighbors, relatives, journalists
after 1860, the devoted and the spiteful, all commented on Mary's
ferocious and unpredictable temper. The little girl who stomped
her feet—because she could not secure a disoriented world and
capture the attention of her busy and remote father—gave way to
a housewife who startled those around her with periodic out-
bursts of furious, irrational rage.

The Lincolns generally stayed at home in the evenings. An Irish
servant, Mrs. Mary Gaughan, recalled that they were "very domestic in their tastes. . . . although they were great entertainers
and had numerous guests. They very seldom went out visiting,
preferring the pleasures of their own home." Mary would work
around the house or sew; Lincoln would read.[61] Their home was a
private sphere that both of them protected. A young friend of
Robert's from Phillips Exeter Academy, Frank Fuller, who visited the Lincolns in July 1860, noted how warmly Mary had received him and how interestingly she had talked of poetry with
him. Lincoln impressed him even more favorably.[62] To some, the
Lincoln privacy seemed unnaturally exclusive. Ward Hill Lamon

thought the home "forbade the entering guest,"[63] and Herndon believed that Lincoln dared not invite his friends home.[64] This view implies that Lincoln needed to protect himself against Mary, but, in fact, the Lincolns' private style reflected her character and needs, not his.

Mary's life centered on giving birth, on making the household "work," on adjusting to Lincoln's irregular presence. Robert was born in 1843, Eddie in 1846, Willie in 1850, and Tad in 1853. Eddie died at the age of four, but as late as 1856 Mary still had three lively boys, aged thirteen, six, and three. They absorbed her attention. As she commented later, if she erred in her child rearing, it was because she was too indulgent.[65] She took pride in the boys' appearance and fussed over their clothing. In 1853 she asked a friend, Elizabeth Dale Beck, who was traveling to St. Louis, to buy a white fur hat for the baby Tad. "I should like white trimmings & white feather," she wrote, "if you find any to your taste, of the prettiest quality."[66] Some years later Mary, giving a party for Willie on his ninth birthday, sent hand-lettered invitations to over fifty of his young friends.[67]

Mary was always deeply involved in the children. For "any big man or woman" who visited the Lincoln home, Herndon said, Mary would dress up the boys, trot them out, "and get them to monkey around, talk, dance, speak, quote poetry, etc., etc." The boys' performance would inspire her to excessive praise, which would annoy the visitor and embarrass Lincoln. "After Mrs. Lincoln had exhausted the English language and broken herself down in her rhapsodies on her children, Lincoln would smooth things over by saying: 'These children may be something sometime, if they are not merely rare-ripes, rotten types, hothouse plants. I have always noticed that a rare-ripe child quickly matures, but rots as quickly.' "[68]

This account suggests Mary's conflicted identification with the boys' natural exhibitionism. She seemed unable to set limits for herself or them. Lincoln would put her down, gently but firmly, and thus show her, his "child-wife," when to stop. Similarly, on June 12, 1848, he responded to her wish to come visit him in Washington (she was in Lexington): "Will you be a *good girl* in all things, if I consent? Then come along and that as *soon* as possible."[69] Earlier that year he had told her to stop putting the "honorable" on her letters to him. "I like the letters very much, but I would rather they should not have that upon them. It is not necessary, as I suppose you have thought, to have them come free."[70]

Mary, who needed Lincoln's fatherly help and support, found that problems with the children proved to be an effective basis for manipulating him into a more central place in the household. Some problems, of course, were real. Children can hurt themselves, run away and get lost, eat poison left for rats, fall into rivers. Mary, however, seemed full of fears even when all was well. When she sensed a hint of danger she panicked, and when disaster actually struck she collapsed. In the middle of a letter to Speed in 1846 Lincoln noted that a messenger had come to his office to tell him that Bob, then three, was lost. Lincoln rushed home, only to discover that the boy had already been found and whipped. By the time he returned to his letter, Lincoln jokingly guessed that Robert had run away again.[71] But Lincoln was not always there to help Mary; indeed, he was seldom there when she most needed him. A neighbor, Elizabeth A. Capps, recalled how hysterical Mary became if a child was lost and how, when Robert ate some lime, she started screaming in helpless terror, "Bobbie will die, Bobbie will die" (Capps's father came to the rescue and washed the boy's mouth out).[72] The child in her spilled over anxiously to the children she tended.

Mary's psychological vulnerabilities made her unusually susceptible to the devastating effect of death. Everyone, of course, must face the loss of loved ones, but few experience the relentless procession of deaths that Mary did. On July 16, 1849, her father died; in January, 1850, her grandmother; and on February 1, 1850, her little Eddie, who had never even had his picture taken.[73] At the loss of her son, Mary went into deep mourning, cried bitterly, even stopped eating. Lincoln once bent over her and pleaded with her, "Eat, Mary, for we must live."[74] "God gives us our loved ones," she wrote much later, "we make them our idols, they are removed from us, & we have patiently to await the time, when, He reunites us to them. And the *waiting* is so long!"[75] The Lincolns responded to the wrenching loss of Eddie by deciding to have another child; within a month Mary was pregnant. The hope of renewed life, Lincoln's devoted support, and the new meaning of religion in her life gradually brought Mary out of her despair. By spring she was well enough to travel with Lincoln and Robert to Lexington to visit her family.

Mary had always had trouble with separations, and after 1850 she developed a morbid fear of loss, especially when Robert left for Exeter in 1859 (and then for Harvard in 1860). On August 28, 1859, she wrote her friend Hannah Shearer that she felt "quite lonely" now that Bob was gone. It seemed "as if light & mirth, had departed with him."[76] She wrote long letters to him, and she traveled a good deal, but the inner emptiness remained. She confided to Hannah Shearer, on October 2, 1859: "Since I last wrote you, I have been wandering. Mr. L & myself visited Columbus & some beautiful portions of Ohio, & made a charming visit to Cincinnati. I am again at home and Mr. L- is in Wisconsin. I miss Bob, so much that I do not feel settled down, as much as I used to & find myself going on trips quite frequently."[77] The following summer Mary reported to Adeline Judd that her boy Robert had been gone a year and she felt *"wild to see him."*[78]

Mary's capacity for denial was quite profound. As a sad widow after 1875 (when she was briefly institutionalized on Robert's initiative), she came to feel quite differently about the separation from her son in 1859. By 1877 Robert seemed to her a "bad son" and a "wretched young man, but old in sin" with a "mean nature," a person who must yet render account to his Maker: "And God, does not allow, sin, to go unpunished." Mary continued: "In our household, he was always trying to obtain the mastery, on all occasions—never daring of course to be insolent, to my amiable devoted children or myself, when my beloved husband, was near, it was a great relief to us all, when he was sent to school, *then* we had a most loving peace." One thing Mary was certain of: *"Distance* or time does not weaken *remembrance."*[79] In this letter to Edward Louis Baker she failed to note the unconscious substitution of her devoted young friend Baker for Robert. She doted on Baker, who was the grandson of her sister, Elizabeth Edwards. All of her intense hatred for Robert she poured out in this letter to Baker, a letter that served to eliminate Robert and put Baker in his place. It helped her to mourn the "loss" of her hated son.

In her marriage Mary had devised a variety of strategies for handling her extreme sensitivities. She manipulated Lincoln, bringing him home to handle minor crises with the children; she fleetingly identified with her boys in an effort to find escape; and she tried to center attention on herself and her problems with periodic rages. She also sought—in clothes, money, furniture, and other objects—substitutes for the confused and uncontrollable world of people. She always accumulated her possessions aggressively, taking particular pride in her clothes. When she was a child, her homemade hoop became a symbol of her call for recognition and love from her father and for distance from her stepmother. Later, she pushed hard to escape from the Globe Tavern and then furnished and enlarged her own house, despite some tension with Lincoln over the costs.[80] She saw that both she and her children always kept up with the fashions. Henry Villard noted her "splendid toilette" at the February, 1861, farewell party for Springfield friends.[81]

But clothes and things proved inadequate substitutes, and she manipulated them with the same ambivalence as she did people. The first hint came as early as 1848 when Lincoln wrote her from Washington: "Last Wednesday, P. H. Hood & Co., dunned me for a little bill of $5.38 cents, and Walter Harper & Co., another for $8.50 cents, for goods which they say you bought. I hesitated to pay them because my recollection is that you told me when you went away, there was nothing left unpaid. Mention in your letter whether they are right."[82] Herndon, in thinking Mary became materialistic and avaricious after her marriage, accurately but ungenerously captured her desperate need to acquire.

The losses Mary experienced from 1848 to 1850 marked the end of one phase of her life: her relatively gay, open, vivacious youth that had merged into her early years of marriage. After 1850 she was very definitely a mature woman, a matron really, with the lines beginning to harden around her mouth, her body growing plump and soft, and her hands hardening with toil. After the birth of Tad in 1853 she developed serious gynecological problems. "My disease is of a womanly nature, which you will understand has been greatly accelerated by the last three years of mental suffering." So she wrote her friend Rhoda White on May 2, 1868. "Since the birth of my youngest son, for about twelve years I have been more or less a sufferer."[83] Mary's disease may have played a major role in shaping her life after 1853. It probably ended sexual intercourse between the Lincolns, who had previously spaced the birth of their children quite regularly,[84] but who had no more children after that year. And if abstinence proved necessary because of Mary's condition, it was further reinforced by the separate bedrooms that were built into the remodeled and enlarged house in 1856. Mary was only thirty-five in 1853, probably still far from menopause and the end of pregnancy fears. There were then no effective contraceptives, and abortion would have been out of the question for the Lincolns. Four children were perhaps enough anyway. But the end of a sexual relationship seemingly contributed to the charting of a new course in the marriage. Mary turned increasingly outward and away from her complete absorption in home, husband, and children, though without direction or unifying purpose. After 1853 her domestic style clearly began to alter. Social obligations, frequent parties, politics, and her husband's career assumed more and more attention. Mary never abandoned her original commitment to her home and her children, and so she hovered uncertainly between her self-conception as a passively devoted wife and her emerging identity as a semi-public figure.

On November 23, 1856, and again on February 16, 1857, Mary wrote a long letter to her sister, Emilie Todd Helm, and reflected this recently consolidated position between the private and semi-public spheres. The letters deal with politics, parties, family, friends, church, and marriages, and they are among the best examples of Mary's discursive style. Lydia Matteson is about to marry. The Bakers are still with the Edwardses. Louisa Iles has recently married. Robert Scott is courting Julia Ridgely, whose brother Charley is to marry Jennie Barrett this winter. O. B. Ficklin came to tea; he is as "rough & uncultivated as ever altho some years since married an accomplished Georgia belle," who apparently should have changed things. Dr. Smith, their minister, plans to resign because he cannot live on the limited salary he is given.[85] The winter has been quiet, partly because of the scarlet fever among children. Still, there has been a round of parties. "Within the last 3 weeks, there has been a party, almost every night & some two or three grand fetes, are coming off this week." Mary herself is still recovering from a party she has just given for 300 people. Three days ago Governor Bissell gave a large party. Miss Dunlop is spending the winter in town and looking very pretty, but "the beaux do not appear so numerous as the winter you passed here." Dr. and Mrs. Brown are on hand; he has charge of the First Presbyterian Church now.[86]

And so it went. Mary reported to her friend Hannah Shearer that there had been "a continued round of *strawberry* parties" and that during the past week she had spent five evenings out. She also reported giving a "strawberry company for 70 people."[87] Isaac Arnold described her as "busy, animated, and gay" at these gatherings. According to this former Springfield friend, she was the chief attraction of fancy parties with her "genial manners" and "wit and humor, anecdote and unrivalled conversation."[88] The journalist Henry Villard filed a story on the party the Lincolns gave as a farewell to their Springfield friends just before their departure for Washington. He noted that hundreds attended. "Mrs. Lincoln's splendid toilette gave satisfactory evidence of extensive purchases during her late visit to New York."[89]

Mary's lifelong fascination with politics found ready expression after 1854 as Lincoln's renewed interest in public issues converged with her tentatively expanding concerns. The young woman, who had acted so "unladylike" in 1840 on behalf of Harrison, continued to follow political events after 1842, and in the mid-1850s her interest became a passion. She strongly supported Lincoln's ambition, even though his speeches, the meetings, and the relentless campaigning took him away from home. She liked to attend the functions where he spoke, and she thrilled to his oratory. When, in 1858 he mused on his political career up to that point, he recalled that his greatest ambition as a young man in New Salem had been to be a member of the state legislature.

[89]

Eventually he convinced himself he was capable of becoming a Senator. "Mary insists, however, that I am going to be Senator and President of the United States, too."[90]

Mary was more than the little woman at home; she supported Lincoln's drive upward and provided a stable center of gravity for his reach out into the chaos of politics in the 1850s. She seemed totally identified with his successes and failures. Gustave Koerner recalled seeing him in a hotel lobby in Alton before his debate there with Douglas in 1858. Lincoln, an old friend and political ally of Koerner, asked him to come upstairs and see Mary, then told him: "Now, tell Mary what you think of our chances! She is rather dispirited."[91] Two years later Mary wrote her friend Hannah Shearer: "I scarcely know, how I would bear up, under defeat. I trust that we will not have the trial."[92] Lincoln recognized the extent of Mary's investment in his career and could respond sensitively to her fears. On election night in 1860 he waited quietly in the telegraph office as the returns came in. When he had won New York (and the election) he turned to Lyman Trumbull and said: "I guess I'll go down and tell Mary about it."[93]

Mary's involvement in Lincoln's career and her strong support for his ambition has led to the mistaken idea that she played a major role in shaping his political ideas.[94] Her influence never extended that far. On November 23, 1856, she tried to explain his position on slavery to her sister Emilie Todd Helm. She said he had supported Frémont for the Presidency, but was not an abolitionist. "All he desires is, that slavery, shall not be extended, let it remain where it is." She herself had preferred Millard Fillmore in the same election. "My weak woman's heart was too Southern in feeling, to sympathize with any but Fillmore." What really appealed to her about him was his nativism. "If some of you Kentuckians, had, to deal with the wild Irish, as we housekeepers are sometimes called upon to do, the southerners would certainly elect Mr. Fillmore next time."[95] Lincoln had only disdain for the base prejudice that fueled the nativist movement. On August 24, 1855, in a long letter to his old friend Joshua Speed, he attempted to define where he stood in the muddled political world. "I am not a Know-Nothing. That is certain. How could I be? How can any one who abhors the oppression of negroes, be in favor of degrading classes of white people?" It is bad enough, he continued, to exclude Negroes from a position of equality guaranteed in the Declaration of Independence. The Know-Nothings would exclude alike Negroes and foreigners and Catholics. "When it comes to this I should prefer emigrating to some country where they make no pretence of loving liberty—to Russia, for instance, where despotism can be taken pure, and without the base alloy of hypocrasy."[96] Mary had come a long way politically from her slave-owning past to endorse Lincoln's opposition to the spread of slavery, but she remained stubbornly unsympathetic with his egalitarian beliefs.

Mary Lincoln was hardly a popular first lady. "The Hell-cat," Lincoln's secretary John Hay observed on April 9, 1862, "is getting more Hell-cattical day by day."[97] Again he wrote: "The devil is abroad, having great wrath. His daughter, the Hell-cat, sent Stackpole in to blackguard me about the feed of her horses. She thinks there is cheating round the board and with that candor so charming in the young does not hesitate to say so."[98] Hay had long since learned to manipulate Mary and he always seemed to dislike her. He even lacked empathy for her difficult period of grief in April, 1862.[99] In Randall's view he failed to understand that "mental illness was involved,"[100] though in fact he seemed quite convinced she was crazy. The press relentlessly criticized her. Newspapers then were generally intensely partisan, and partisan feeling ran high during the war. Noah Brooks, who was to replace John Hay, only obliquely praised Mary in a dispatch for his California paper: "It is not a gracious task to refute these things [the criticisms of Mary], but the tales that are told of Mrs. Lincoln's vanity, pride, vulgarity and meanness ought to put any decent man or woman to the blush. . . . Mrs. Lincoln, I am glad to be able to say from personal knowledge, is a true American woman."[101]

All the complexities of Mary's character from earlier years carried over into the White House. Her new position underlined her real or apparent faults but obscured her virtues. Her contemporaries never knew how often she visited hospitals and prisons in Washington, for she did not gather reporters around her during the visits.[102] She never seemed to lose completely her empathic touch, but her compassion was evident only in quiet and private ways. Her friend Hannah Shearer lost a son late in 1864. Mary wrote her: "Since we were so heavily visited by affliction, almost three years since, the loss of our darling idolized Willie, with the sensitiveness of a heavy sorrow, I have shrank, from all communication, with those, who would most forcibly recall my sorrow to my mind. Now, in this, the hours of *your* deep grief, with all my *own wounds* bleeding afresh, I find myself, writing to you, to express, my deepest sympathy, *well knowing* how unavailing, words, are, when we are broken hearted."[103]

Mrs. President Lincoln was not a simple midwestern housewife thrust suddenly onto center stage where she found the attention—and criticism—impossible to handle. For much of her life she had dreamed of and even prepared for the position she occupied as first lady. In some ways she proved ready for the demands of her position. She turned out to be a competent and gracious hostess, with her "levee" on Friday evening, reception on Saturday afternoon, and balls and dinners on special occasions. The French nobleman de Chambrun seemed quite impressed with the social style of her White House.[104] At first many of the leading ladies in Washington snubbed her as a parvenue.[105] She responded bitterly and used her position when she could to undermine her tormenters.[106] She faced an inherently difficult situation. Her position required that she regularly entertain political friends and opponents, travelers from near and far, and diplomats. Yet the war occupied the entire period of her stewardship over the White House. Many critics were bound to see any entertaining as, at best, frivolous and, at worst, a criminal waste of public money when soldiers without blankets were dying in defense of the country.

Mary's southern background contributed to the harshness of the criticism. After all, she had come from a slave-owning family that remained decidedly southern in its loyalties after 1861. Seven of her immediate male relatives fought for the Confederacy, including three half-brothers, one brother, and three broth-

Mary Lincoln in her inaugural gown in 1861. *Ostendorf Collection*

ers-in-law.[107] She seemed to feel no attachment to these members of the Todd clan. She told Reverend N. W. Miner, a Springfield neighbor who visited the White House during the horrendous battle of Shiloh in April, 1862, that she had two brothers then fighting for the South in that very battle. "I hope they are either dead or taken prisoner," she commented vigorously. Miner was taken aback, but Mary explained: "They would kill my husband if they could, and destroy our Government—the dearest of all things to us; and I repeat it—I hope they are either dead or taken prisoner."[108] Mary expressed the same sentiment to her seam-stress Elizabeth Keckley on the death of her brother Captain Alexander Todd. "He made his choice long ago. He decided against my husband, and through him against me. He has been fighting against us; and since he chose to be our deadly enemy, I see no special reason why I should bitterly mourn his death."[109] In her public role, however, Mary never seemed able to convince everyone that she was loyal. In the minds of many, she bore the stigma of a traitor.

Refusing to leave politics entirely to Lincoln, Mary meddled in small matters of influence and large matters of policy. Even be-fore the inauguration she had let the excitement of her new posi-tion go to her head. In a confidential letter of January 17, 1861, she urged David Davis to use his influence on Lincoln to keep the offensive Norman Judd out of the cabinet. She knew that a word from Davis would "have much effect."[110] When she traveled east to buy clothes, she dispensed gratuitous political advice all along the way.[111] Writing to Lincoln from New York, November 2, 1862, she hinted that "all the distinguished in the land" were concerned that he replace McClellan,[112] and she asked that Alexander T. Stewart receive an army promotion—Stewart owned a prestigious New York store to which she was apparently in debt.[113] By then, she had accumulated a host of shady figures and sycophants who attended dutifully to her vanity and their own greed. Among them were Henry Wikoff, a great talker, flat-terer, cheat, and liar; his friend Dan Sickles, flamboyant and dis-reputable; and Oliver S. Halsted, a munitions lobbyist in search of big deals.[114] All three received the devoted attention of a needy

Mrs. Lincoln, who prided herself on the intuition that told her what people were really like.[115]

Elizabeth Keckley, a mulatto seamstress and a former slave who had worked for the wife of Jefferson Davis, began service with Mary soon after she moved into the White House. In time Elizabeth became a close friend, one to whom Mary confided secrets that apparently she told no one else. This relationship has contributed to the questionable notion that Mary played an important role in shaping Lincoln's attitudes toward blacks and his policies on emancipation.[116] Mary herself encouraged this idea, as when she wrote Elizabeth (October 9, 1867) that she had never failed to urge her husband to be an extreme Republican.[117] Actually, she had exerted little influence on Lincoln in regard to this or any other political subject. As early as January, 1861, she had been forced to turn to David Davis to influence Lincoln; she had lost a voice in the new government before it even began. In late November, 1864, she dashed off notes in which she asked Oliver S. Halsted and Charles Sumner to prevent the appointment of Nathaniel Banks to the cabinet. It never seemed to occur to her simply to talk with her husband about the matter.[118]

The Presidency and the war created a vast chasm between the Lincolns. Mary tried reaching out but without much success. On November 3, 1862, she wrote from New York: "I have waited in vain to hear from you, yet as you are not *given* to letter writing, will be charitable enough to impute your silence, to the right cause." She begged: "One line, to say, that we are occasionally remembered will be gratefully received by your very truly, M. L."[119] A year later Mary, again in New York, wired Lincoln: "Reached here last evening. Very tired and severe headache. Hope to hear you are doing well. Expect a telegraph to-day."[120] He responded: "All going well. A. Lincoln."[121] Mary's inability to bridge the gulf between herself and Lincoln intensified her well-established physical and emotional problems. Anson G. Henry, who visited the White House in February, 1864, found that she was in bed, "not being very well."[122]

The mounting tension climaxed in March, 1865. Lincoln had ridden out separately to City Point to review some troops. Mary came along behind in a carriage with Colonel Horace Porter. She either began the day with a migraine headache or acquired one in the carriage when it hit a bump and she severely knocked her head. She arrived somewhat late and the review had already begun. Lincoln ended the review with a beautiful young woman, Mrs. Ord, riding beside him in front of the troops. Mary went berserk with jealousy. The officers in her carriage had to restrain her physically from jumping out. When Mrs. Grant tried to calm her, Mary angrily accused her of complicity in the affair. And when Lincoln and Mrs. Ord came up, Mary lashed out at Mrs. Ord and reduced her to tears. Then she turned in furious anger on Lincoln as the generals, their aides, their wives, and the Army of the Potomac watched. Lincoln put his arm around her and turned her aside, calling her "Mother" and speaking softly. Gradually he quieted her.[123]

Had it not been for the demands of war, Lincoln might have been more reassuring to Mary all along. In his heart he seemed to remain devoted to her. At one White House reception he turned to a woman at his side and called her attention to the beautifully dressed Mary. "My wife is as handsome as when she was a girl, and I, a poor nobody then, fell in love with her; and what is more, I have never fallen out."[124] When he was killed in Ford's Theater he was holding her hand.[125] But most of the time his preoccupations were too great for him to be close and involved in Mary's world in anything except a peripheral way. Besides, he tired of her impetuosity and her unforgiving hatreds. On April 9, 1865, returning from Richmond on a boat, Mary spied Washington from a distance and commented with a shudder that the city was full of enemies. Lincoln responded with an impatient gesture. "Enemies," he said, "never again must we repeat that word."[126]

The wartime Lincolns were apart physically and emotionally. Mary, lacking the resiliency of her youth, had a heavy public task to perform as manager of the White House. Lincoln, of course, was under almost inhuman pressure from his election to his death. There were few fleeting moments when Mary could share an intimate word with her husband. Guests or relatives usually accompanied the two on carriage rides.[127] Lincoln ate little if any breakfast and began work early and stayed late. He and Mary tried to keep together as a family for the midday and the evening meals, but the demands of the war and the office frequently interfered. As they long since had decided to sleep apart, no loving embrace ended the long and difficult day.

In the early part of the Presidency Mary tried to define for herself a politically important position in a kind of kitchen cabinet—without success. She also aggressively embraced her role as hostess, but ran into relentless criticism. By the end of the first year in Washington, things had soured for her. She was ridiculed in the press and in Washington society both as a hostess and as a person. Many doubted her loyalty to the Union. Lincoln was caught up in the war, and the war was going badly. For her, the only source of comfort was the children, who were always there, dependent and needing, from whom she could get a measure of strength and renewal.

Willie's death early in 1862 removed what was perhaps the last prop to Mary's tenuous hold on reality. She adhered to the ritualized Victorian forms of mourning but in her devastating grief carried everything to excess. She went to bed for months and cried uncontrollably. She discontinued entertaining for the rest of the year, and, as she had done after Eddie's death, she even stopped eating for a time. She wrote Julia Ann Sprigg on May 29, 1862, "We have met with so overwhelming an affliction in death of our beloved Willie a being too precious for earth, that I am so completely unnerved, that I can scarcely command myself to write." Mary begged Julia to visit her and ease her "crushing bereavement."[128]

Mary's anger at the loss expressed itself even against God. "How often I feel rebellious," she wrote on July 26, 1862, "and almost believe that our Heavenly Father, has forsaken us, in removing, so lovely a child from us!"[129] Later she repressed this anger toward God and turned it on herself. In 1864 she wrote her old friend Hannah Shearer that with Willie's death she had passed through a "fiery furnace of affliction" (which was a metaphor she borrowed from Lincoln). She went on to say that Willie's death had been a kind of divine punishment for getting too wrapped up in "our own political advancement."[130] Mary's partly conscious reasoning apparently was that God willed her to care for her children but she had abandoned them in the search for political advancement. So He took Willie away.

A fascinating series of letters from Elizabeth Edwards, who came from Springfield to stay with her sister through the worst period of mourning, to her daughter, Julia, provide a unique opportunity to follow the course of Mary's reaction to Willie's death—and the strains it put on those close to her. At first Elizabeth felt only sympathy for Mary. She wrote Julia on March 1 (Willie had died on February 20): "Your Aunt Mary still confines herself to her room, feeling very sad and at times, gives way to violent grief. She is so constituted, and the surrounding circumstances will prevent, a long indulgence of such gloom."[131] The next day Elizabeth told Julia how glad she was to be with Mary and comfort her. For Mary has been "utterly unable to control her feelings. . . . Mary has confined herself to her room, and bed, until this morning, when I persuaded her to put on the *black dress*."[132] Later that month, on March 12, Elizabeth reiterated her sympathy for Mary and expressed a touch of self-satisfaction at her efforts. "I feel very much for her, and am satisfied that my presence is more soothing than anything else at present."[133]

Already beginning to tire of Mary's relentless suffering, Elizabeth noted how depressing it was to be absorbed in Mary's sorrow. She also expressed the hope that her niece Mary Wallace would substitute for her in a month or two. By April 1 she had come to feel that Mary was indulging her grief. Elizabeth's request to be replaced became insistent. "Your Aunt Mary wonders if Mary Wallace will not feel like coming on, when I am ready to leave—Mention it to her—and I would advise it by all means."[134] Elizabeth was quite aware of Mary's antagonism toward most members of the Springfield Todd clan and seemed to fear those old hatreds would keep Mary Wallace from replacing her. Elizabeth therefore went to some length to convey to Julia that Mary's desperate state would override such feelings. "Without a doubt," Elizabeth wrote Julia on April 9, "she [Mary Wallace] will be treated with the greatest kindness, for a companion is absolutely necessary for her Aunt, who is at times very gloomy."[135] Elizabeth began to feel trapped in Mary's clawing needs. On April 19 she wrote Julia that, "The daily routine here is especially irksome to me."[136] By April 26 Elizabeth was past sympathy for Mary and concerned only with her own escape. She told Julia that Mary was so "nervous and dependent upon the companionship of some one" that she would definitely be friendly to any visitor, even one from the family. And she noted, "The truth is I am not very happy."[137] Elizabeth left soon on the pretext of an urgent summons from home. Mary Wallace never came.

Elizabeth Keckley later described another aspect of Mary's unhinged state after Willie's death. For months Mary was unable to mention Willie's name or look at his picture. She never again entered the guest room where he had died or the Green Room where he was embalmed. "There was something supernatural in her dread of these things," Mrs. Keckley reported, "and something that she could not explain."[138] Mrs. Keckley also reported the scene when Lincoln threatened to institutionalize Mary if she failed to recover.[139] In her despair Mary turned to spiritualism to recapture contact with Willie. There was a séance held at the Soldier's Home in the summer of 1862 and some indication that the séances continued long after that. Lincoln, suspecting fraud, successfully had at least one of Mary's spiritualists exposed.[140] Mary eventually repudiated the more extreme claims of the spiritualists—for example, that during a séance one actually converses with the dead—and retreated to a more religiously legitimated, though still rather mystical, idea that she described in a letter of November 20, 1869: "I am not EITHER a spiritualist—but I sincerely believe—our loved ones, who have only, *'gone before'* are permitted to watch over those who are dearer to them than life."[141]

A large part of Mary's sanity died with Willie. Her dreams and fantasies seemed absorbed with his death. In time Eddie and others long dead joined the ghosts. Emilie Todd Helm, who visited late in 1863, noted in her diary how Mary came to her one night in a "deep pit of gloom and despair" and reported that Willie came to her every night and stood at the foot of her bed "with the same, sweet, adorable smile he has always had." Sometimes he came with Eddie and twice with her brother, Alec.[142] Emilie was frightened at her sister's unnatural behavior, but she went on to make the psychologically astute observation that Mary's hold on the dead in part reflected her fears about Robert's going into the army.[143] This was an important issue with the Lincolns. Robert was an able-bodied, adult male throughout the war. Lincoln felt it was unfair for him to send hundreds of thousands of young men to their deaths in the war while Robert remained safely ensconced at Harvard.[144] But the desperation of Mary's opposition convinced him to wait until Robert's graduation in 1864. Even then he delayed until the first part of the following year, when he sent Robert as a personal aide to Grant, and thus safely removed him from battle.[145]

There had always been a sense in which Mary's response to the unloving and uncontrollable world of people was to seek substitute gratification in money, clothes, furniture, and various possessions. Things at least stood still, could be admired and fondled, and never died. Yet her ambivalence toward people spilled over to their inanimate surrogates. As she lost her own center of gravity during the war Mary turned with alarming vigor to her clothes and household furnishings for fulfillment. One of the first letters she wrote after Willie's death was to Ruth Harris to order some mourning clothes. The bonnet she requested was to be elegantly plain and genteel. She ordered the crape to be made of the finest jet black English variety and the trimming to be small and delicate. In everything, Mary commanded, Harris was to use only the very best material.[146] Any gift that arrived at the White House she felt was hers personally. These gifts ranged from grapes from Ohio and cider from New York to an elaborate tablecloth from Constantinople, yards of lace and China silk, fabrics embroidered in France, books, jewelry, anything at all.[147] She also bought vast quantities of everything. At the start of her stewardship of the White House, Congress authorized $20,000 for her to fix up what all agreed had become a rather dilapidated old house. Mary briefly had a marvelous, if manic, spree purchasing only the best furnishings for the White House. There was quickly an uproar over her extravagant purchases. But, even worse, she had forgotten to keep track of her expenses and overran her appropriation substantially. When Lincoln found out he was furious and determined to pay himself for Mary's purchases of "*flub dubs*" as Lincoln reportedly called them. In the end, however, Congress paid.[148]

Mary spent her own money with equal indiscretion. In 1866, when she was desperately trying to sell some of her White House possessions, Mary listed her *unused* jewelry, hoping for close to a full refund from the New York store where it was purchased. The items included earrings, a gold card case, a diamond ring, a pearl bracelet, a set of onyx breast pin and earrings, a pair of enameled sleeve buttons, and on and on.[149] Mary could be intermittently tight with money. When she interviewed Elizabeth Keckley in 1861 she stressed her poverty and hoped Keckley's terms would be reasonable.[150] But Mary's caution hardly prevailed. By the summer of 1864 her debts were enormous and she lived in constant anxiety that Lincoln would discover the truth (though it is difficult to believe Lincoln was not aware of the situation). She had to telegram creditors, telling them their payment was coming soon. Once she made a revealing slip. She wired George A. Hearn of New York, "Will you send your check today?"[151] As the pressure mounted Mary feared most of all that Lincoln would not be reelected and her secret debts would be revealed. She poured out her heart to Mrs. Keckley and became obsessed with her fears of Lincoln's political fate. By September she saw her problems as partly the result of her husband's honesty. "Poor Mr. Lincoln," she wrote on September 23, 1864, "who is almost a monomaniac on the subject of honesty."[152] When at last the victory came Mary drew a deep sigh of relief.[153] But her happiness proved short-lived.

Mary's final chapter is an unrelieved tale of sadness. She had collapsed after the earlier deaths, but the loss of Lincoln on April 14, 1865, affected her traumatically. She went to bed, numb, lost, confused, utterly helpless. For five weeks she lay there unable to supervise packing or make preparations for the future. She later repressed all memory of the first few days following the assassination. She was unable to attend the funeral service in Washington on April 20. De Chambrun stopped by that afternoon to leave his card and noted Mary was still "completely insane."[154] Her only extended human contact in this desolate period (except for Tad) was with the kindly doctor, Anson G. Henry, who had long ago attended Lincoln in his worst depression, that of January, 1841. Henry wrote his wife in May, 1865, that Mary refused to be comforted. Still he spent several hours a day with her, talking largely about religious matters and the hovering spirits of the dead, and these discussions seemed to relieve Mary somewhat.[155] Henry also helped Mary in her struggles with the city of Springfield to bury Lincoln where she intended (Oak Ridge Cemetery, just north of town). Several enterprising Springfield citizens, wishing to honor Lincoln and perhaps also with an eye on the commercial merit of the idea, proposed a downtown burial site with an appropriate monument. The body was halfway across the country, wending its slow way home, when Mary discovered what was afoot. She asked Henry to write the letter. "I have been requested by Mrs. Lincoln to say," wrote Henry on May 1, 1865, "that if her wishes and directions in regard to her husband's remains are not complied with she will remove them to Chicago next June."[156]

Mary had always been ambivalent about Springfield. The fight over Lincoln's remains hardly endeared her to the citizens or made a return there desirable for her. She also could not face living so close to the grave. After a brief visit to Oak Ridge Cemetery in December, 1865, Mary wrote a friend that, "The further removed I am, the better, it will be, for *my reason*, from *that* spot."[157] Mary felt this keenly, for her constrained financial situation made it increasingly difficult to survive anywhere except Springfield, where, of course, she owned a home. Lincoln left an estate of liquid assets valued at $83,000. David Davis was the administrator of the estate until it was settled in 1868. He performed well, for during these three years he paid the interest regularly to Mary and the boys (about $1,500 each) and increased the capital to $110,000, which was divided three ways in 1868. In December, 1865, Congress voted Mary a one-time sum of $25,-000.[158] Mary always felt unfairly treated because Congress at first refused and then only reluctantly voted her a pension in 1869. But she always had assets and an adequate income, except for her debts from her personal spending sprees in the White House. These debts drove her to abstraction.

Mary chose to live in Chicago. There she stayed in some dreary rooms in a Hyde Park hotel, secluded, alone, bitter, broken with grief, racked by migraines, pouring out her heart in letters to almost every correspondent. On May 9, 1865: "I go hence, broken hearted, with every hope almost in life—crushed." On May 14: "In my crushing sorrow, I have found myself almost doubting the goodness of the Almighty." May 29: "To rejoin my Husband, who loved me so devotedly & whom I idolized, would be bliss indeed. I am scarcely able to sit up & fear it will be some time, ere I can summon strength of mind or body either, to receive friends." July 11: "I have almost become blind with weeping." And a different letter on the same day: "I am realizing, day by day, hour by hour, how insupportable life is, without the presence of the *One*, who loved me & my sons so dearly & in return, was idolized. Tell me, how *can*, I live, without my Husband, any longer?" July 17: "If it was not for dear little Taddie, I would pray to die, I am so miserable." July 26: "The world looks darker to me than ever & my heart aches, for my bereaved sons." August 17: "My heart is indeed broken, and without my beloved husband, I do not wish to live. Life, is indeed a heavy burden, & I do not care how soon, I am called hence." November 29: "I have been so wild in my despair over the loss, of my idolized husband." December 8: "Only those, who suffered & lost . . . can fully understand the return of anniversaries." December 11: "My overwhelming sorrow, removes me, from the world." And finally, December 24: "I pour my sad tale, into your sympathizing ear."[159]

Over the years Mary returned often to the theme of her grief. The sampling of her 1865 letters suggests the extent of her pervasive sense of gloom. She never really resolved these feelings of loss, anger, and helplessness, which in turn accentuated the more unlovely characteristics of her personality. She was intensely envious when Ulysses S. Grant received several houses and a large pension after the war while the family of the martyred President had to struggle.[160] "Alas, alas my burden of sorrow is too heavy for me to bear," she moaned once in self-pity to Elizabeth Blair Lee on August 25, 1865.[161] A few months later her tone was almost a parody of self-pity. "Yet I cannot express to you, how painful to me, it is, to have *no* quiet home, where I can freely indulge my sorrows—*this is* yet another of the crosses, appointed unto me."[162] Her brooding envy of Grant consumed much of her energy. "Life is certainly, *couleur de rose* to *him*—," she wrote Sally Orne on December 30, 1865, "if it is, all *darkness & gloom* to the unhappy family, of the fallen chief."[163]

Mary's self-absorption had always made her relatively insensitive to the feelings of others; after 1865 her despair blinded her to the ways she manipulated people. In August, 1865, for example, Mary wrote Sally Orne a long, self-pitying letter that began with an attempt to evoke pity in Mrs. Orne: "Bowed down & heart broken, in my terrible bereavement. . . ."[164] Mary dwelt on her afflictions at the loss of her devoted and loving husband and declared she would welcome death, which would give her a chance to rejoin Lincoln. Mary's real purpose, however, was to get Sally Orne to sell the dress Mary had worn at the Second Inaugural Ball. Mary bleakly painted her financial picture. She said her pension was $1,500 per year, which was a little misleading. She and Tad together received $3,000, which would have been adequate except for her wartime debts. She then described the dress and asked Mrs. Orne to sell it in New York. Apparently, the idea of selling something excited Mary, for she went on to mention to Mrs. Orne some magnificent material she would like to sell.[165] Nothing came of these feelers to Sally Orne, so Mary turned hopefully to Elizabeth Keckley; that in turn led to the great clothes scandal in 1867. Mary's idea had been to sell all her old dresses in New York. Mrs. Keckley agreed to help. The two met furtively and tried to peddle the clothes through a pair of disreputable brokers. With Mary's support, the brokers first tried bribing politicians, then gathering the support of well-known figures, and, finally, taking all her dresses on tour. From the beginning Mary manipulated Mrs. Keckley in a variety of conscious and unconscious ways. Mrs. Keckley genuinely wanted to help and endured a great deal herself as events unfolded. But it seems Mrs. Keckley also resented the way she had been handled through it all—in 1868 she published her book (an "as told to" volume), *Behind The Scenes*, which revealed all the unhappy details of the clothes scandal as well as the impulsive purchases Mary made while in the White House that had originally created her indebtedness. The book even included twenty-four of Mary's most personal letters.

Mary's real and imagined financial problems, her grief and her loneliness were all endlessly complicated by her physical problems. Whatever was wrong gynecologically seemed to worsen after the assassination. And the headaches were a continuous torment. The five weeks following the assassination and the train trip to Chicago had been one great headache. After that her life revolved around her headaches. In December, 1865, Mary told Mary Jane Welles that she was incapacitated for three days of every week with severe headaches.[166] The following May, Mary again mentioned that for three days a week her headaches were so severe she could barely sit up.[167] Sometimes she overcame her worst agonies to write letters to friends, but that was only when urgent financial pressures forced her out of bed.[168] At the Chicago insanity hearing in May, 1875, a doctor testified she had told him that during one of her headaches "an Indian was removing the bones of her face and pulling wires out of her eyes."[169] This was used as evidence that she was hallucinating, which seems partly true. Randall, however, points out that Mary's vivid picture may simply have been a graphic attempt to describe her pain.[170]

Mary was sad and suffered greatly, but she kept her spunk. She may have humiliated herself in badly planned attempts to raise money, but she never repudiated her debts. She lived alone and went hungry rather than move in with relatives (at least until after her institutionalization in 1875). She never accepted defeat. She dragged herself from bed to write spiteful, angry letters and then returned to lie awake hating. And she never lost her interest in politics. She regularly absorbed the contents of seven papers: the Chicago *Tribune*, *Times*, and *Evening Journal*; the Illinois *State Journal*, for news of friends and enemies in Springfield; the New York *Times* and the *Tribune*; and the Washington *World*.[171] She hated the way journalists dealt with her and the world, calling them vampires,[172] but she could not stop reading.

The fight in Mary, however, should not obscure the desperation of her state. She was physically and emotionally a wreck. She was helpless, in debt, and constantly making bad decisions about her life. Her personality was increasingly brittle. Her warmth, intense loyalty, and empathy could no longer stem the tide of envy, greed, suspiciousness, and sensitivity to slight that spurred feelings of revenge, stubbornness, and self-absorption. Not surprisingly (in psychological terms), what emerged finally as the trait that was to bring about her institutionalization was her paranoia. She wrote Dr. Henry on July 17, 1865, of her overwhelming sorrow at all the enemies she had to contend with.[173] She came to feel betrayed by her political friends—David Davis, James Harlan, Edward Stanton, and James Speed—on the pension issue. "All, they desire is to be inquisitive and they are *not* friends & will *never* assist us—Therefore, let this, be an end, to *them.*"[174] In time these fears and pervasive feelings of danger gave way to actual paranoia. The turning point seemed to be the death of Tad in 1871. Smoke from a neighboring chimney suggested the city was about to burn. When she entered a public dining room, she whispered, "I am afraid; I am afraid." In March, 1875, she and her son, Robert, stayed in separate rooms in a Chicago hotel. She was terribly restless and once left her room improperly dressed. Robert tried to calm her by putting his arm around her and leading her back. Mary turned away violently, screaming, "You are going to murder me."[175]

There was a real basis to some of her fears. Robert was having her followed by a Pinkerton detective in early 1875. And the actual trial was a carefully staged setup. The day before it was to begin Robert called together several physicians and an old friend of his father, Leonard Swett. Robert got the doctors to agree that he had a case for the committal of Mary. He then asked Swett to be the one to pick her up at the hotel at 1:00 P.M. and take her to the 2:00 P.M. trial. Mary knew nothing of these arrangements. She was of course astounded when Swett arrived the next day but went along without physical resistance. She refused to take Swett's arm, however, and suggested to him that he should attend to his own crazy wife when he finished with her. At the trial Robert and Swett at first had some trouble with their prearranged de-

fense counsel, Isaac Arnold. It seems he expressed some misgivings about carrying out his task since he was personally convinced of Mary's insanity. Swett persevered, however, and
pointed out that Arnold had to defend Mary or she would get
some "mischievous lawyer" who would "make us trouble."[176]

The trial itself brought forward depressing evidence of Mary's
state. Various witnesses testified to her paranoia. John Fitzhenry,
a hotel waiter, said he was called to her room where he found her
"carelessly dressed" and complaining of vague fears. Charles
Dodge, another hotel employee, reported she complained to him
of a stranger in her room who was about to molest her. Other
witnesses reported her hallucinations. A certain Maggie Gavin
testified Mary heard voices through the wall. Robert himself
made that more specific: she had met a wandering Jew in Florida
who had taken her pocketbook and now talked to her through the
walls. There was also plenty of evidence presented of her super-
fluous buying and the risks of her walking around with $57,000 in
securities sewn into her petticoats. It was an embarrassing trial
for all concerned. People like Swett felt guilty and Robert himself
never really got over it.[177]

Mary sat through it all quietly, but on the evening of its completion she tried to commit suicide. She slipped past the guards at
her hotel room and went to buy some laudanum from a local
druggist. However, he recognized her.[178] After that, Mary spent
three months in Bellevue well cared for by Dr. R. L. Patterson.[179]
In the fall Mary's sister, Elizabeth Edwards, took her home to
Springfield. Mary's behavior continued to worry Robert. He
wrote Elizabeth Edwards on January 17, 1876: "I am very much
afraid that things are going on from bad to worse as they did last
spring—and that if they get worse it will be necessary to place
my mother again under Dr. Patterson's care."[180] Robert backed
off, however, and Mary stayed in Springfield.

Her life ended sadly. On June 15, 1876, a second trial judged
her sane and restored her rights. After that she traveled frequently but kept the Edwardses as her base. She wrote volumi-
nously, mulling over the past with friends and fretting over her
finances with her Springfield banker, Jacob Bunn. In her last
years she seemed numb with hurt. Her old friend and neighbor,

N. W. Miner, who had since moved to New Jersey, saw her once in New York in 1881. Mary had traveled there for medical treatment. Miner was aghast when he met her: her hair was prematurely gray, her eyes half-closed with excessive weeping, and she was staying alone in an old and dingy hotel.[181] She died in her sister's home in Springfield on July 15, 1882, at the age of sixty-three. She spent the last few months sleeping on one side of the bed. The other space she kept for Lincoln.

The first known photograph, from sometime in 1846. Lincoln was thirty-seven years old, hopeful, reflective, uncertain. *Library of Congress*

Chapter 5

A Little World
Made Cunningly

In this troublesome world we are never quite satisfied.
ABRAHAM to Mary Lincoln
April 16, 1848

 Y the 1840s Lincoln had "made it" in the cherished American sense. He was far beyond his rural roots and rapidly emerging as a sought-after lawyer and political leader among Illinois Whigs. He owned a nice home, had married well, and children were entering his life in regular intervals of three to four years. The first photograph of Lincoln, taken in 1846, nicely captures the contentment of a successful man with a promising future. He would often joke of his "poor, lean, lank, face,"[1] but in this picture at least there is a hint of bourgeois self-satisfaction in the slight tilt of the head and jaunty thrust of the chin. He seems to be a young man who expected to be taken seriously.

And yet there is a tension in the eyes that has an almost haunting quality. They are surprisingly round and deep, set off in the photograph by shadows, which only enhances their mysteriousness. Nor can the mystery of Lincoln's eyes be dismissed as an artifact of early photographic technique (the subject had to sit motionless for several minutes while the plate was exposed). "My old, withered, dry eyes," Lincoln said on hearing a moving speech by Alexander H. Stephens in 1848, "are full of tears yet."[2] He was thirty-eight years old. A decade later, in a fragment on the struggle against slavery, Lincoln referred to his "own poor eyes" that might not last to see the final victory. The eyes, it seems, captured Lincoln's early sense of life's mournful tasks, which in turn aged him prematurely. Before his fortieth birthday Lincoln contrasted himself with the young men of Illinois politics.[3] In his private life he was "father" to Mary's "mother."[4] He joked at times of his need for spectacles and his poor eyesight,[5] but there is something curiously sad and moving when a healthy, vigorous middle-aged man refers to himself as old.[6] The eyes suggest a kind of premature insight that carried its burdens and took its toll. Profundity was a part of Lincoln's earliest style.

Two points are quite well documented in Lincoln's relationship with Mary. The first is that from the outset Lincoln developed a powerful attachment for his vivacious young wife. A week after the wedding (November 4, 1842) he ended a business letter with the cryptic note, "Nothing new here, except my marrying, which to me, is a matter of profound wonder."[7] Later the following spring James C. Conckling met Lincoln in Bloomington and reported that he had "found Lincoln desperately homesick and turning his head frequently towards the south."[8] After the stress of their tumultuous courtship, Lincoln seemed to embrace Mary fervently, to find deep needs for love and devotion satisfied in her. Separation came as a painful experience.

It is equally clear that by the 1860s Lincoln believed Mary bordered on insanity and required a patient, humane tolerance. He watched her collapse after Willie's death in 1862. When her sister's help proved futile, he exerted a measure of control and told her she must restrain herself or he would have her committed.[9] He carefully and discreetly exposed the fraudulent psychic medium to whom Mary turned in the spring and summer of 1862.[10] Somewhat later he reportedly talked openly about Mary's problems when confronted with evidence of a schemer who had used his friendship with Mary to further some illegal business.

"The caprices of Mrs. Lincoln, I am satisfied, are the result of partial insanity," he said once to a visiting reporter, and asked whether her malady was "beyond medical remedy to check before it becomes fully developed?"[11]

These two ends of the spectrum frame the essential issues in Lincoln's complicated relationship with Mary. From the beginning she met some important needs in Lincoln, but her own problems gradually diminished her central emotional position in his life. These problems were sufficiently severe to cause Lincoln himself to see her as nearly insane. The psychological movement along this emotional spectrum occurred erratically and is difficult to place in chronological sequence. Nevertheless, there is a marked change in all facets of Lincoln's life with Mary around 1854. The coincidence of this dating with larger political events is hardly accidental. It suggests that a multitude of private and public concerns prompted an emotional reordering of Lincoln's self-organization at this time.

Life at Eighth and Jackson subtly combined themes of intimacy and distance. In this tight house, which until 1856 consisted only of the first floor, the Lincolns defined their family style. Four rooms and a kitchen separated the functions of daily life. On either side of the entrance two parlors—one formal, the other informal—clearly expressed the family's genteel aspirations. The bedroom for both the Lincolns and their children was at the back of the formal parlor, behind a partition that has since been removed. (In the warmer months, two children could sleep in the crawl space on the second floor.) These close sleeping quarters joined intimate relations with child rearing. It is striking how the arrangement of the house spatially allocated the back corner and smallest room to the most intimate family activities. The most conspicuous space is reserved for the parlors. The home itself, in other words, de-emphasized intimacy in favor of more formalized encounters sitting around the fire, talking, playing with the children. Next to the bedroom was the dining room laid out with respectable dignity: a table with four chairs, a serving table, and a sideboard. On top of the sideboard was a sillabub set (for serving custard), a favorite item in the homes of eighteenth-century

English aristocrats. Behind the dining room and quite separate from the four central living rooms was the kitchen. It was ample and well equipped but apart, no longer the central motif so characteristic of room arrangements in earlier periods.

The architecture of the house confirmed and reinforced the domestic aspirations of the Lincolns. It looked inward, away from the world, turning closely around a central axis. The world was deliberately excluded, a private enjoyment of family domesticity deliberately pursued. In this, of course, the Lincolns typified a style of family life that was increasingly important and prevalent after 1820, especially among white, urban, middle-class families. The Lincolns, however, perhaps even more vigorously than most, sealed off the family unit from outside contagion. Few friends "dropped by" and the neighbors kept an amicable but respectable distance: few of the reminiscences of neighbors describe scenes occurring within the house. Herndon groused about the way Mary excluded him, David Davis, and other friends from the Lincoln home.[12] Lincoln was willing to tolerate Mary's idiosyncratic exclusion of people like Herndon from the home because it reflected his own protective conception of the hearth. In a sense, a tightly cohesive nineteenth-century family like the Lincolns' survived only so long as it could effectively maintain the sharp line between itself and the community.

The Lincolns also kept apart from their troublesome relatives. Lincoln frequently visited his country kin near Charleston, but they never visited his home in Springfield.[13] The one exception was a daughter of Dennis Hanks who showed up as a domestic in the Lincoln home in 1844. The relationship between her and Mary, however, was a disaster and the poor girl was driven away.[14] The relationship with the Todds was somewhat more complex. The Lincolns married without the Todd family's approval, but Mary's father, when he met Lincoln, was quickly won over. He even gave Mary money. It is speculation, but it is difficult to believe a man as proud as Lincoln relished such gifts that tied his wife to her father. But it is not speculation that the relationship between Lincoln and the other Todds was highly strained. Matters even reached the point of a lawsuit in 1853, when Mary's tempestuous brother, Levi, accused Lincoln of embezzling funds collected for Robert Todd on an earlier suit in Illinois. Lincoln was enraged. He wrote his lawyer in Louisville that he found it difficult to suppress his indignation at the charge.[15] When the lawyer delayed in settling the case, Lincoln's frustration mounted and he let him know that the matter upset him a great deal.[16] The case left a bad taste in Lincoln's mouth. Perhaps it helped him deal with the Todd's southern loyalties during the war.

The Lincoln family's need for exclusivity serves also to provide perspective on Mary's difficulty in keeping servants. Anyone from the outside was an intruder. Mary wanted her maids to be "submissive."[17] She wrote in 1859 to her friend, Hannah Shearer: "My seamstresses bear such different testimony to my honesty & justice, that it is a matter of unimportance & therefore, we will forever drop the subject."[18] Lincoln, it seems, tried to handle the situation by paying some servants extra to endure his wife.[19] But in a larger sense both Mary's refusal to deal with the issue and Lincoln's slipping money to servants to buy peace reflect a vital, unspoken agreement in the family to keep the world at bay, to solidify or attempt to solidify a cohesive domestic unit.

The sources do not allow a complete reconstruction of the rhythm of daily life for the Lincolns. One can only gain glimpses of this little world cunningly turned in on itself. The formality of the dining room and the parlors suggest a rigorous scheduling of domestic behaviors. Dinner was probably normally served at the same time each night, and an evening pattern of talking, reading, and then sleeping kept to. There is a sense in which Lincoln deviated somewhat from the script. To Mary's dismay he lounged on the floor at times, answered the door with his tie loose, and allowed himself to slip into distant worlds of thought and perhaps periodic depression. Money was his concern. Lincoln, who from the mid-1840s on earned a very respectable $1,200 to $1,800 a year, bought his own rather expensive suits and ties and handled such matters as the purchase of a new carriage,[20] but he left the responsibility for food, children, and household in Mary's hands. He certainly paid the bills and probably gave Mary adequate pocket money to run the house. He also allowed her to use various charge accounts in town. In the 1840s these expenditures seemed within reasonable bounds. There is no reason to suspect tension over money, though Mary's delight in material possessions may have helped her endure Lincoln's active and lucrative work on the circuit.

Lincoln's absences from his home are a crucial and highly controversial issue in grasping the rhythm of his life with Mary. No discussion of Lincoln and Mary, their home and children, or indeed the deeper meanings of Lincoln's thought can ignore his mature pattern of distancing and separation. The facts are fairly clear; their meaning ambiguous. Two interests, law and politics, pulled him away. The pull of politics was erratic and obviously regulated by outside factors. Lincoln was a loyal Whig throughout the years before 1854 and, during election years, regularly met requests to talk on the issues and in support of local candidates. In 1844 he worked vigorously and unsuccessfully to garner support for his candidacy to the United States House of Representatives. Then, in 1846 he defeated Peter Cartwright after a busy two months of campaigning. From the fall of 1847 Lincoln was in Washington and, except for the few months of the stay when Mary and the children were there, he was apart from them. The pace of Lincoln's political work slacked off some between 1849 and 1854 but remained an important ingredient in his life. After 1854, however, politics increasingly consumed Lincoln. His success as a lawyer—and notable fees like the $5,000 charged to the Illinois Central Railroad in 1857—supported long periods of politicking.

The more constant pull on Lincoln was the circuit. Unlike most other lawyers, Lincoln was unique in his practice of attending every court on the circuit and remaining until the end.[21] Herndon embellished here a good deal: he had Lincoln growing sad as the other lawyers started home for the weekend to see their wives and babies; they learned not to encourage Lincoln to come with them.[22] Herndon's account appeared in a letter he wrote to his coauthor, Jesse Weik in 1887. The final presentation of this matter in the 1889 biography called in the authority of David Davis, who was quoted as saying how odd it was to everyone that Lincoln never went home on Sunday from the circuit. "At first we wondered at it," Davis said, "but soon learned to account for his strange disinclination to go home. Lincoln himself never had much to say about home, and we never felt free to comment on it. Most of us had pleasant, inviting homes, and as we struck out for them I'm sure each one of us down in our hearts had a mingled feeling of pity and sympathy for him."[23] The editor of the 1930 edition of Herndon's book, Paul Angle, could not contain himself on this point and added a gratuitous footnote that Lincoln worked hard on the circuit and must have been too tired to travel home on Sunday. But Judge David Davis also worked prodigiously on the circuit. He seldom missed traveling home on his day off, no matter how tired he might have been. He even found time while listening to dull cases to write passionate letters to his young wife.[24] It was undoubtedly a bother to travel on horseback along muddy roads for a brief stay from, for example, Taylorville to Springfield. But it was not an impossible trip; the other lawyers regularly traveled that twenty-five miles and other routes on weekends.

To get a sense of the pattern of Lincoln's absences from home, one need only cull the remarkably complete three-volume study, *Lincoln Day by Day,* which traces Lincoln's activities on a daily basis for his entire life. In 1843, for example, Lincoln took two one-day excursions in the spring before leaving on the court circuit on April 12. He remained away until May 4. On his return he managed to remain pretty much at home through the summer, except for one-day trips on May 22, June 5, and July 15. Then on September 6 he left for the fall circuit and stayed away until September 25, when he returned for a weekend, and left again to return October 9. He was then home until October 16 when he left for another week of circuit work. He took a final two-day trip that year in early November. In the course of the year Lincoln had been gone a total of some ten weeks, broken down into an extended absence in the spring and an even longer one in September and early October. Few trips occurred between mid-October and early April. Throughout the summer Lincoln traveled erratically. One interesting point to note is that Lincoln broke up the five-week fall term with a weekend visit home. At least sometimes he came home.

The pattern for 1843 holds for most of the following decade

(except when Lincoln was in Washington). Lincoln seldom went away from home until the spring term of the circuit began in April and then he usually broke up his trip into two or at most three week units. In 1844, for example, Lincoln was away from April 3 to April 16, May 6 to May 20, May 27 to June 6, July 15 to July 21, September 5 to September 16, September 21 to October 7, and October 21 to November 11. He also took several one-day trips. That year he was gone some fourteen weeks. In the next couple of years Lincoln followed a similar pattern, though in 1846 he took his first really extended trip when he was gone eight weeks between June 1 and July 25 campaigning for the House seat. After Lincoln returned from Washington in March, 1849, he tried to minimize his travel. He was gone only one week in June and was out on the fall circuit from September 20 to September 25 and October 1 to October 13. In 1850, however, legal work took a heavy toll. He was gone for two weeks between April 3 and April 18, four weeks between May 1 and June 1, four weeks for a summer trial in Chicago, which ran from June 30 to July 26, a couple of one-day excursions in August, then six weeks on the circuit from September 18 to October 31. The last trip of that year was from November 14 to November 21.

A subtle shift had occurred in the pattern of Lincoln's absences between 1843 and 1850—they had lengthened. In the early days of his marriage he seldom stayed away more than two weeks and determinedly broke up longer trips into two- and three-week units. By 1850, however, he took five long trips that lasted one, four, four, six, and one weeks, in that order. The six-week trip on the fall circuit (September 18 to October 31), apparently without a visit home, is the most striking. The same pattern holds true for the next few years. In 1852, for example, Lincoln was gone for six extended trips: three weeks in April, four in May, one in June, five in September and October, two in November, and, un-usually, two more in the first part of December. In 1854 Lincoln seemed so caught up in circuit life that he stayed out during the spring term for six and one-half weeks from April 5 to June 30.

After the mid-1850s Lincoln again altered the rhythm of his travels, quite dramatically increasing both the frequency and du-ration of his trips. Several factors contributed to the change. He was more noted and therefore in greater demand as a lawyer. He was also more centrally engaged in political activities, which meant more short visits throughout the state to speak. It all crowded in. In these years the travel was made easier by the railroads, which by the mid-1850s had a fairly extensive set of routes throughout Illinois. The existence of the railroads, however, did not seem to bring Lincoln home more often; it just took him away more frequently. During 1856, for example, Lincoln was away from home a total of nearly twenty weeks. He remained out on the spring circuit for eight weeks (April 2 to May 29) and then took thirteen more trips that year. Six of these trips were one- to three-day excursions, but of the remaining seven, four were at least a week, two were two weeks and one—when he was out on the fall circuit—three and one-half weeks (October 3 to October 27).

This "objective" evidence of the pattern of Lincoln's absences from Mary and home can also be approached more subjectively. Herndon noted in a letter written August 4, 1857, that he had to start some court work because Lincoln was absent.[25] There is nothing really remarkable about the reference in Herndon's letter except that it is made gratuitously. It suggests that Herndon felt Lincoln was usually absent. Lincoln himself often mentioned facts of his travels in letters, because so much of his mail reached him on the run.[26] He also used his absences to ward off students who wished to apprentice themselves with him. For example, he told Isham Reavis in 1855 that he was "from home too much" for it to be advantageous for a young man to read law with him.[27] Three years later he used essentially the same excuse with James T. Thornton: "I am absent altogether too much to be a suitable instructor for a law-student."[28]

All this evidence of Lincoln's absences from home suggests a number of important conclusions. Lincoln established the general pattern of persistent separation from home at the very beginning of his marriage. Obviously, complex motives and, most of all, real need for an income prompted frequent trips on the circuit. He was good at that kind of work, he found it afforded pleasure, and it yielded a good income. The general pattern of separations was

that few lasted over two weeks, and the most likely time of separation was in the spring and fall. Lincoln was always home between December and April and usually absent only for short
trips in the summer. The most important exception in the first
decade or so of the marriage was between spring, 1848, and
spring, 1849, when Lincoln was in Washington (Mary was with
him briefly in Washington but soon left to stay with her family in
Kentucky). After the early 1850s the pattern of that first decade
accelerated markedly. The total number of weeks Lincoln was
away increased from an average of twelve weeks a year to approximately twenty weeks a year *and* the rhythm changed. In the first
decade of marriage, Lincoln seldom left his home for more than
two weeks; in the 1850s the same kinds of activities (riding the
circuit, for example) took him away for as long as eight straight
weeks.

It seems that during the first decade or so of his marriage, Lincoln wrestled with his conflicted intimacy with Mary and home.
He needed to leave often but took emotional sustenance from the
episodic refueling he received at home. To push this idea somewhat further, it seems probable that Lincoln embraced the peri-
odicity of his relationship with Mary, the closeness–separation–closeness that defined its contours. In the early years at least
he thought of her while absent (as the Conckling letter shows)
but thought of being absent while with her (for example, the vi-
gnette about the Lincolns in front of the fireplace discussed in
chapter 4). This kind of complex tie to Mary carried with it a
deep devotion and fidelity; the stories of Lincoln's sexual capers
are ludicrously apocryphal. But conflict created a need for regulated distance from Mary. The background for such a pattern was
perhaps Lincoln's childhood experience of the death of his
mother and of the resulting need to repeat that loss and his desire
for recovery in minute doses as an adult. To "lose" Mary when he
departed for the circuit evoked significant feelings of dread and,
probably more often, depression in Lincoln. He needed the circuit life, however, both to support his material aspirations and to
free him temporarily from a transference figure of such potent
significance. Once separated, however, Lincoln seemed desirous

of returning and reestablishing ties with Mary. He came back often in these years and was apparently away no more than absolutely necessary.

The memories of Whitney, Herndon, and Davis are thus quite wrong and misleading if one collapses the entire eighteen years between 1842 and 1860. These old friends are, however, right on target for the period after the early 1850s. Lincoln was quite willing, even eager, to travel a great deal. He rode the circuit without returning home for as long as eight weeks. He never seemed reluctant to be away; on the contrary, his cohorts on the circuit remember him as a boon companion. He seldom wrote home.[29] And he kept adding new legal and political responsibilities to an already tight schedule. The creative tension that defined Lincoln's relationship with Mary in the 1840s and early 1850s loosened considerably after 1854.

For Mary, of course, Lincoln was an intensely idealized figure on whom she came increasingly to lean for life itself. Lincoln in turn welcomed and perhaps needed such idealization and adoration. What emerges in the few leters Lincoln wrote Mary during their separation in 1848 is a wistful loneliness and an immersion in family life, colored by a fatherly remoteness that created distance as it united. The background of these letters was Mary's departure from Mrs. Sprigg's boardinghouse in Washington after a stay of several months. She was quite unhappy with the accommodations and probably disappointed that no one paid any attention to her as the wife of a junior Congressman. This separation lasted a year, though the letters date from the early period of Mary's absence. Whether other letters were written and lost is uncertain. For some reason a special dread descended on Lincoln in that spring of 1848. "In this troublesome world," he wrote on April 16, 1848, "we are never quite satisfied. When you were here, I thought you hindered me some in attending to business; but now, having nothing but business—no variety—it has grown exceedingly tasteless to me. I hate to sit down and direct documents, and I hate to stay in this old room by myself."[30]

Lincoln then proceeded to comment on mundane but clearly meaningful details of family life mentioned by Mary in her earlier letters. He commented on the robbery in Mary's grandmother's

house and thought it was unwise for her to stay alone. He asked
Mary to send his greetings to John Parker. Lincoln then told her
he had tried to find the "little plaid stockings" for Eddie but was
unsuccessful: McKnight was out of business now and Allen had
none of that description. Lincoln then commented that an old
friend of hers from St. Louis would be leaving Washington soon
and offered to drop a package off in Lexington. If such topics
tended to preoccupy Lincoln, one can also see clearly his fatherly,
controlling tone in the way he handled certain items of business.
For example, Lincoln expressed pleasure Mary was enjoying herself but cautioned against hurting her father by getting too close
to the family of one of Robert Todd's staunch personal and political enemies. It is remarkable Mary should need such advice. Lincoln followed up this passage immediately by alluding obliquely
to Mary's disruptive presence in Washington. "All the house—or
rather, all with whom you were on decided good terms—send
their love to you. The others say nothing." The comment appears
to be a backhanded way of underlining his caution not to offend
her father needlessly by her wanton friendships.

Scolding in turn gave way to a gentle reprimand. As we have
seen, Lincoln asked Mary to please leave the "Hon." off her letters to him. He granted that her motivation was probably to insure free posting, but he assured her it was unnecessary. Lincoln
was uncomfortable with the pretentiousness of the modest title.
He would rather be an honorable "Mr." than an unnoticed and
ignoble "Hon." The gap between the false dignity of his real position in Washington and his soaring ambitions could not be covered by recourse to title. Mary, who so fiercely identified with
Lincoln's ambitions, in this sense prodded him with the title.
Lincoln withdrew from embracing such empty symbols and in
the process established an important point with Mary.

The reprimand over the title put Mary in her place and
permitted Lincoln in his secured position of authority to be
tender and fatherly. He referred condescendingly to her frequent headaches, noting that this was the first time since they
had met that she did not suffer from them. He even allowed himself a hint of sexual play, though in a vein that underlined her
hefty and aging body. "I am afraid you will get so well, and

fat, and young, as to be wanting to marry again. Tell Louisa I want her to watch you a little for me. Get weighed, and write me how much you weigh." Lincoln was lonely and yearned for contact with Mary. And yet his expressions of love, modest but real, deliberately dwelt on Mary's excruciating migraines and her fat body. Lincoln took away something vital as he provided crucial sustenance, distanced as he expressed love, and in every way forcefully clarified his position of authority. It is no wonder Mary idealized him; that was the only emotional position he allowed her to assume.

The next letter sharply defined Mary's subordinate position to Lincoln as it playfully acceded to her wish to come visit him in Washington. He opened with excuses for not answering right away (essentially that he was tired and busy). Lincoln then addressed directly the matter of her visit and the unspoken problem it posed. "Will you be a *good girl* in all things, if I consent?"[31] The allusion here is clearly to problems Mary caused before at Mrs. Sprigg's, her tantrums and general discontent with Washington. Lincoln perhaps occupied a humble niche in Congress, but he was sufficiently self-conscious of his position to try to avoid any obvious embarrassments. If Lincoln put Mary down, however, he quickly recovered himself. For he added after this proviso: "Then come along, and that *as soon* as possible." In fact, as he thought about the visit (if free from turmoil) he became quite openly eager to see her: "Having got the idea [of a visit] in my head, I shall be impatient till I see you." And Lincoln concluded the letter after discussing some money matters: "Come as soon as you can. I want to see you, and our dear—*dear* boys very much. Every body here wants to see our dear Bobby."

Mary then delayed some before she left Lexington, causing Lincoln anxiety. Having gotten the idea in his head, he wanted a family reunion. He even ended his third letter (July 2, 1848) with a note of impatience: "Father expected to see you all sooner; but let it pass; stay as long as you please, and come when you please. Kiss and love the dear rascals."[32] This last and final letter in the series was otherwise unusually full of family concerns. Lincoln told Mary to be sure to arrange matters with the mail. He also mentioned friends and relatives. "Give my kindest regards to your uncle John," Lincoln noted, "and all the family. Thinking of them reminds me that I saw your acquaintance, Newton, of Arkansas, at the Philadelphia Convention." These letters suggest in concrete ways the assorted needs for which Lincoln turned to Mary for gratification. Somehow it all gradually unraveled. Their sense of private space radically shifted. After 1856 they moved from a tight four-room house that looked in on itself to a genteel home that allocated space generously. This expanded new house gave the family members much greater privacy as it turned outward to the world: Lincoln's separate bedroom doubled as an office where he met many important political figures in the later 1850s.

Lincoln's shifting field of vision after 1854 had enormous consequences for the country; it also tended to leave Mary alone, abandoned to meet her mounting needs without emotional resources. Deep childhood wounds reopened in Mary as the distance between husband and wife increased. His perception of her insanity, which was undoubtedly partly true, also perhaps carried a measure of desire on his part. His essential human kindness kept him near her, and she could never have survived without it. But in another sense her insanity filled the emptiness Lincoln created as he expanded his vision. The change around 1854 represented a complex shift from a conflicted private world of meanings that never worked themselves out to a public arena of political rhetoric that Lincoln domesticated. The personal issues for Lincoln proved remarkably continuous as he translated his private experience into an idiom that made sense of much larger concerns. After 1854 Lincoln turned outward and attempted, as Erik Erikson might say, to solve for all what he could not solve for himself alone.

Lincoln's relationship with Mary carried the essential weight of his conflicted ties to home and family. But the children also represented another crucial aspect of his domesticity. "My Friends," Lincoln said to those gathered at the depot on his departure for Washington on February 11, 1861, "No one, not in my situation, can appreciate my feeling of sadness at this parting. To this place, and the kindness of these people, I owe everything. Here I have lived a quarter of a century, and have passed from a young to an old man. Here my children have been born, and one is buried." The future was ominous. "I now leave, not knowing when, or whether ever, I may return."[33]

Such direct public reference to his children was rare for Lincoln. On the question of the children, myth and the projected fantasies of various authors cloud our vision even more than usual in the Lincoln story. The most abundant source is Herndon, and, of course, he had an ax to grind whenever he mentioned Lincoln's domestic affairs. Mary hopelessly idealized Lincoln's relationship with the children, and Lincoln himself, as usual in personal matters, left few verifiable written clues concerning his relationship with the children. Furthermore, there is little information from the children themselves. Only Robert lived to maturity, and he was generally reticent about revealing concrete details of his childhood. Robert was caught up in his painful relationship with his mother and, subsequently, saw his role as protector of his father's story from meddlers like Herndon. We are left, therefore, with only bits and pieces of often questionable evidence from which to draw conclusions. One must tread cautiously.

At the most superficial level Lincoln clearly seemed to love and enjoy his children, as well as children generally. According to Ward Hill Lamon, an old friend, Lincoln was extremely fond of his children and was patient, indulgent, and generous with them. He often walked in the country with them on Sunday afternoon, "giving himself up entirely to them," rambling in green fields and cool woods, "amusing and instructing them for a whole day at a time."[34] The Lincolns' neighbor, Noyes W. Miner, later illustrated Lincoln's love for children with an evocative anecdote. Troops of children from the block would watch for Lincoln's return from his law office for meals. They would then "gambol by his side, and as many as could get hold of him, would swing from his hands. He had a kind word & a smile for all."[35] Mrs. George C. Beal, the daughter of a Lincoln acquaintance, recalled much later her experiences visiting the home. Lincoln would give her "hossy" rides. He would hold her hands and put her on his leg, chanting, "This is the way the lady rides—Nim—Nim—Nim!" Then he would speed up some. "This is the way the gentleman rides—Prim—Prim—Prim!" Then at full gallop: "This is the way the countryman rides—Giddy-up—Giddy-up—Giddy-up!"—which led to shrieks of delight. It seems Lincoln would play these games with the little girl while Mary and Mrs. Beal's mother were in the adjoining room "gossiping."[36]

This kind of post-assassination anecdotal material may well reflect simply the need to see Lincoln as a Christ-like figure, suffering the little children to come unto him. Another group of anecdotes, which have a hint of vitality, are perhaps more authentic. One time a neighbor, Mrs. Bradford, saw Lincoln pushing a baby carriage down the street (a decidedly unmasculine thing to do in this period). She upbraided him for doing Mary's work rather than being down in his law office. Lincoln looked at her (probably suppressing a comment about busybodies) and said, "I promised" and went on about his business.[37] Another time Lincoln was carrying Tad, who always received special attention, to his office, even though the boy was already half-grown. Frances Wallace, Mary's sister, told Lincoln that the boy could easily walk and thus implicitly chided him for overindulgence. Lincoln replied: "Oh, don't you think his little feet will get too tired?"[38]

This theme of Lincoln's gentleness with children and indulgence of them to a fault occurs repeatedly in the literature. From Mary's perspective it was admirable. "Mr. Lincoln," she told Herndon in 1866, "was the kindest man and most loving husband and father in the world." Furthermore, he gave everyone in the family "unbounded liberty" and was "exceedingly indulgent" with the children. What indulgence meant specifically for Mary is unclear, but it involved a loving recognition of the boys' achievements and an absence of restraint. Mary quoted Lincoln to Herndon: "It is my pleasure that my children are free, happy and unrestrained by parental tyranny. Love is the chain whereby to bind a child to its parents."[39] For Herndon such indulgence of the children was despicable. Herndon, it seems, came to hate the little Lincoln brats. Lincoln often brought them to the law office on Sunday and let them play while he worked. They would pull the books from the shelf, bend the points of the pens, overturn ink-stands, scatter law papers, and throw pencils into the spittoon. As Herndon put it in a letter (though Weik censored it for the book), they even "pissed on the floor." Lincoln would work calmly through it all. Nothing disturbed his serene good nature.[40]

In order to put Herndon's account into perspective, it is worth noting that this picture of Lincoln's brats in the office was tied directly to Herndon's unflattering characterization of Mary. The reason Lincoln brought the children to the office at all was so Mary could go to Church *"to show her new bonnet."*[41] Further-more, Herndon saw the boys' behavior as somehow Mary's fault. Herndon himself was unable to handle the anger he felt toward the boys who, as extensions of Mary, drove a wedge between himself and Lincoln. He frankly confessed wanting to wring the boys' necks and pitch them out the window when Lincoln brought them to the office. He held back, however, out of respect for Lincoln, "and left for parts unknown."[42]

Lincoln's "indulgence" of his children thus carried contradic-tory meanings for different observers. For our purposes, however, it is worth stressing the points of agreement. Lincoln seemed eager to let the children grow without much parental restraint, to find their own way in a complex world. In modern terms, he was permissive. He was quite willing to flout social codes of behavior that defined his role as in the office and Mary's as with the chil-dren. The officious intrusions of friends and relatives along those lines had no effect on him. His large, doting spirit also seemed to spill over to other children, and he became the delight of the block. His tolerant, humane kindness, which so appealed to Mary and made him able to bear her odd behavior through many trials, blinded him to obvious faults of his children. He seemed to encourage their freedom and to let discipline go by the wayside.

Nevertheless, Lincoln's ties to his children were complex. The pattern of Lincoln's separations from Mary also meant he was away from the boys. Lincoln in large part was an absent father. Mary basically raised the children. It was her interaction with them that set the contours of their personality. The boys' wild-ness perhaps reflected Lincoln's tolerance, but surely it also grew out of Mary's trouble in dealing with the people in her life. One reason Lincoln could tolerate so much from the children may have been that he saw them so infrequently.

Lincoln wrote Mary on July 2, 1848, that "Father" expected to see her and the boys soon.[43] One can read this to show what a "good" father Lincoln was, but it is striking that Lincoln wrote the note because it had been so long since he had seen his family. He also used the third person to refer to himself. This grammatical distancing tended to elevate Lincoln within the family, to split him off so to speak as a godlike figure apart from the rest. It also separated himself from his own experience. Only rarely—as in his autobiography, when matters also touched close—did Lincoln fall back on the third person to talk about himself. It was a sign of ambivalence. And in this letter to Mary the ambivalence seemed to center on fatherhood.

The birth of Lincoln's first son on August 1, 1843, was a joyous event. It seemed to relieve him of a confused sense of potency and togetherness that had undermined much of his earlier relationship with Mary. It is interesting in this regard that the baby before birth was directly tied to Joshua Speed to whom Lincoln wrote when Mary was five months pregnant, "About the prospect of your having a namesake at our house cant say, exactly yet."[44] Lincoln followed this letter with several more to Speed that urged him to visit Springfield. On May 18 he assured him that a room could be prepared at the Globe Tavern.[45] And on July 26 he urged Speed again to visit with Fanny, for "We are but two as yet."[46] It is unclear when the name "Robert" for the baby replaced "Joshua," but the source is clear: Robert was the name of Mary's father.

The best and only extended account of Lincoln's feelings about any of his children came in a letter he wrote to Speed on October 10, 1846. The lead topic of the letter was to report the birth of another boy, Eddie, on March 10, 1846. Lincoln, however, proceeded quickly to a discussion of Robert. The boy was "short and low," Lincoln reported, and probably always would be. He was talking all right and seemed "quite smart enough." But Lincoln was oddly uncomfortable with Robert's talents. "I some times fear he [Robert] is one of the little rare-ripe sort, that are smarter at about five than ever after." Robert was then just three. Lincoln, it seems, felt an ambivalent fondness for his firstborn, a recognition of Robert's potential that carried with it an inability to tolerate the competitive thrust of Robert's intelligence.

Robert was also something of a troublemaker for Lincoln, full of "that sort of mischief, that is the offspring of much animal spirits." As Lincoln was writing his letter of October 10 to Speed from the office, a messenger came to fetch him home to find the lost Robert. By the time Lincoln returned home the child had been found and whipped, so he went back to his office to finish describing the scene to Speed. Lincoln concluded his letter ironically that Robert by then had probably run away again.[47] Lincoln thus unburdened himself about his son—in a way never again to be repeated—to his old friend, Speed, whom Lincoln once again placed in the role of emotional intermediary. As Speed once helped Lincoln reach out to Mary, Lincoln now wanted him to help deal with his son. The situations, however, were entirely different. Speed could, of course, do little, and besides Lincoln was well past the period of his greatest psychological openness to systematic outside influence.

But Lincoln's disappointment with Robert and his antagonism toward him continued. Two years after the letter to Speed, Lincoln dreamed of something bad happening to Robert. It seemed to foreshadow the future. He wrote Mary: "I did not get rid of the impression of that foolish dream about dear Bobby till I got your letter written the same day."[48] There are several second-hand reports of prophetic dreams Lincoln had during the war, but they were only recorded later and their meaning is clouded by the passage of time. The reference in this letter, however, is quite specific. Lincoln had had some dream of young Robert that boded evil. He apparently felt it was sufficiently real to be prophetic and had to write Mary immediately to assure himself of Robert's safety. Having heard that all was well, Lincoln dismissed the dream as "foolish." Before that, however, it was clearly a serious matter. It is speculation no doubt, but Lincoln's dream of evil befalling his oedipal son (Robert was five at the time) probably reflected his own ambivalence toward his firstborn. Robert obstructed in some way Lincoln's largely unconscious grandiosity, holding back by his presence the father's tendency to fill the male space within the family.

In other ways, too, Robert carried a heavy burden of expectation for Lincoln. All of the father's educational deficiencies and social aspirations united in Robert. Thus the eldest boy was to have the kind of schooling that Lincoln never had. He was even to go to Harvard. There is some indication it was Lincoln's idea that Robert attend Harvard.[49] Robert, however, remembered it as his own idea in his brief autobiographical statement for the *Harvard Class Book* of 1864. In that statement, Robert described the inadequacy of his educational experience in the 1850s at Illinois State University (which was then in Springfield): "The government was very easy, and we did just what pleased us [,] study consuming only a very small portion of our time." Robert eventually came to question the value of such laxity: "I became aware," he continued, "that I could never get an education in that way and resolved to enter Harvard College." He imagined it would be easy to get into Harvard, but soon had the "honor to receive a fabulous number of failures." He resolved, however, "not to retire beaten" and took President Walker's advice to take a preparatory year at Exeter. The year at Exeter worked out well, though Robert had to give up his hope of entering Harvard as a sophomore in 1860. He was "obliged" to enter as a freshman in 1860.[50]

Robert seemed proud he had stuck by his goal of getting into Harvard. "After the commencement in 1860," he said, "I was able to inform my father that I had succeeded in entering College without a Condition—quite a change from the previous year." At Harvard, Robert managed with gentlemanly C's; he studied enough, he said, to satisfy himself without being overly earnest about it. He was active in a variety of enterprises in college and was proud to report his election as vice-president of the Hasty Pudding Club.[51]

Robert thus fulfilled Lincoln's contradictory feelings about education. Lincoln recognized the inadequacies of his spotty and erratic schooling. At the same time, as a self-made man, he took pride in the learning he acquired on his own. Some of the advice he gave young lawyers suggested, in fact, that they forget formal schooling altogether. Just read, he said, and keep on reading.[52]

Robert Todd Lincoln in 1860, the year he entered Harvard College. *Ostendorf Collection*

Robert had all the best and yet never quite made the mark. If he excelled, it meant confronting his awesome father directly. If he failed totally, he equally risked losing a large measure of love. So he ambled along.

There was, however, a certain closeness between Lincoln and Robert. Lincoln visited him at Exeter during that first winter away from home; in fact, a reason for accepting the invitation to speak at Cooper Union in New York in 1860 was to combine it with a trip to see Robert.[53] Robert eagerly welcomed his father, who made quite an impression on his schoolmates. They spent some time together alone, though most of their few days together were crowded with speeches Lincoln had to make.[54] A more striking encounter between Robert and his father came during the war. Lincoln often walked to the telegraph office in the War Department alone at night to check the progress of a battle. Robert recalled later that during the winter of 1865 he told his father he wished that he would not do that at night without letting him know, so that he could accompany him. Lincoln as a result woke Robert up on a "number of occasions" and the two walked together to the telegraph office.[55]

In many respects Robert was much like his father. For example, he was reported to have a good sense of humor. An English observer once commented that Robert "when once he had shaken himself free from his jokes, was vigorous enough."[56] In his autobiographical statement there is a measure of cute humor in his reference to his "fabulous failures" in the Harvard exams and how some "filthy lucre" got him out of a scrape at Exeter.[57] He seemed to play on words as his father did, though less gently; sarcasm often infected Robert's jokes:

Not very long ago in trying a suit, Mr. Lincoln addressed the defendant, Mr. Windet,—a man who was hopelessly insolvent, but given to great schemes about which he did a great deal of talking. Mr. Lincoln pronounced the defendant's name with the accent on the first syllable. The gentleman corrected him saying, "Mr. Windet, if you please, sir, Mr. Windet" accenting the last syllable. Mr. Lincoln replied very quietly: "I beg your pardon, sir; but I think that I am to be excused for not knowing whether to associate more of wind or debt with you."[58]

The letters he wrote seldom show any humor at all. At best he mustered a sense of irony. "Please accept my thanks for your kindness in sending me the bag of 'Lincoln' Coffee," he wrote John Hanna in 1884. "It is rather singular that this brand should be used in Costa Rica, and it gives me great pleasure to receive it on account of this peculiar circumstance."[59]

Robert was also ambitious, shrewd, capable. He was a successful lawyer in Chicago through the 1870s. Between 1879 and 1884 he then served competently as Secretary of War. After that he returned briefly to various legal and business interests in Chicago before accepting (somewhat reluctantly) appointment as Minister to Great Britain. He returned to Chicago in 1893 to begin a long and prestigious association with Pullman Railroad Company. He became president of the company in 1901 and in the course of the next decade steered it through its greatest period of financial growth.[60] After 1911 he went into semiretirement as chairman of the board. He spent as much time as possible in his beloved Vermont home, which he named Hildene. There he played golf, wrote letters, and dabbled in astronomy. He died in 1926, just short of his eighty-third birthday.

In a sense Robert lived out with a vengeance his father's upwardly mobile aspirations. Robert became a millionaire and the confidant of the powerful. He served on important boards and ran one of the nation's leading companies. He lived sumptuously and socialized only with the best people. He went to England in part because of the "social benefits" that came with the job.[61] Robert also seemed to identify with Lincoln's alienation from Thomas, which in Robert became a generalized feeling of shame about his father's rural roots. He disdained the bad spelling of the frontier.[62] Thomas Lincoln, Robert said, "was poor and unable to give him [Lincoln] an education."[63] He also suggested that Lincoln's parents, who lacked opportunity, were lazy: "It is well known that my father's parents were poor and unlearned, and without opportunity," he wrote in 1884, "if they had the inclination, of doing more than keep slight traditions of their relations, and I know little of what those were."[64]

Robert treasured his father's memory and saw himself as the caretaker of the Lincoln tradition. His ownership of the Lincoln papers gave meaning to his role as protector. He let no one see the papers, except Nicolay and Hay for their approved biography. As a stubborn final gesture, Robert also imposed a twenty-one–year cloture on the papers after his death in 1926 to frustrate Albert Beveridge, whose work on Lincoln Robert disliked.[65] During his lifetime Robert received hundreds of letters requesting relics, mementos, autographs, or information from the Lincoln papers. For many respondents Robert developed a form letter that his secretary, Charles S. Sweet, could send out. But Robert himself responded directly to a surprising number of these requests. He was particularly likely to write back when asked about photographs or paintings of Lincoln. In 1887, for example, he told Ewing Hill that "I do not know of any portrait of him [Lincoln] standing erect which is at all satisfactory. There is such a large painting in the President's house, but if I owned it I would burn it."[66] He said he liked the Volk life mask because it showed Lin-

Robert Todd Lincoln in 1889 as Minister to Great Britain. He was rich, respected as an astute lawyer, and powerful politically. *Ostendorf Collection*

coln without a beard. He preferred that to the ones with a beard, which for Robert were less "familiar."[67] Robert replied without irony or resentment to one extraordinary request for an original copy of the Gettysburg Address.[68]

Robert had strong views about what was acceptable and what should be discarded in the books on his father that came pouring out after 1865. He was "indignant" about Ward Hill Lamon[69] and felt Herndon was entirely untrustworthy.[70] In 1884 he tried to discourage a publisher from putting out a book by Jane Swisshelm. Her material, Robert felt, was a "miserable mess of misstatements," "trash," and "invention," and it would be a "wretched thing" to publish it.[71] He did, however, approve of Nicolay and Hay's work and felt Isaac Arnold's one-volume study the best short biography available. Robert wanted everything to be right (that is, factually correct) about Lincoln, but he refused access to the material that would have made for accuracy.

[133]

He provided information to selected respondents over half a century and seemed baffled why everyone kept getting the Lincoln story all wrong. He hoped silence would stifle the inquisitive but instead it only spurred them on.

Scholars for nearly a century have been angry at Robert because he kept them away from the Lincoln papers. But what has not been appreciated is the vital meaning of the papers for Robert. The secrecy accomplished several psychological objectives. It kept Lincoln alive and close to Robert in a special way. Any human relic carries this meaning, but Robert built his self-conception around his unique connection to his father. In his letters, for example, Robert wrote somewhat tiresomely of which were the best and worst photographs or paintings of Lincoln, whose biography was awful, whose good, and he diligently recorded his own memories of selected events. This circumscribed focus on the past preserved Lincoln for his son. It also controlled Lincoln and kept him near, as Robert never could as a child. In the Lincoln legacy Robert retained a hold on his father that gratified enduring childhood longings.

Robert found painful any situation that publicly honored his father with him present. As a rule he religiously avoided such events, although he often felt obliged to provide lengthy, somewhat gratuitous explanations for his actions. For example, in January, 1900, he turned down a request to speak at a birthday ceremony honoring Lincoln. "I do not know whether my reasons for this are sufficient," he wrote, "but they seem very good to me. While I am most sincerely gratified for the admiration of his character, which is the burden of so many speeches at meetings of this kind, I am more comfortable in reading them than I would be in a company listening to them; and if I were present, it would very commonly happen that I would be much embarrassed in trying to avoid speaking myself. This I am most unwilling to do."[72] Such scenes seemed to overwhelm him. He refused to attend the reburial of his father's remains in 1902 and stayed away from the dedication in 1909 of the cabin in which Lincoln may have been born. He avoided any public encounter that risked comparing him to Lincoln; he never once gave a speech about his father.

As he aged, however, Robert came to accept the inevitable

constraints on his control of his father's memory. His acceptance of these constraints came slowly and painfully. He was enraged at Herndon's 1866 lecture on Ann Rutledge and furious at Lamon's 1872 *Life*.[73] By the turn of the century, however, Robert brushed aside much of the foolishness about his father. For example, he wrote to a friend in 1900 that a respectable businessman had reported proudly to him that his brother had served in Lincoln's bodyguard of 100 men over six feet tall. "I did not think it necessary to say to him," Robert concluded, "that there never was such a bodyguard."[74]

Robert's adult encounters with the memory of his father were complicated by the troubles with his mother. In his autobiographical statement (1864), Robert forgot to mention his mother's date of birth and his hand jiggled and forced him to write over the "my" of "my mother" when he mentioned her.[75] As a young man just out of college, Robert tried living with Mary in Chicago as he began his law practice, but the strains were incredible. Mary described, for example, Robert's overwhelming sense of shame when the "old clothes scandal" broke in 1867.[76] Later, as Mary's condition deteriorated, her paranoid fantasies about Robert confirmed his feeling that the "dreadful circumstances" surrounding his father's death had "deranged" his mother mentally. Her actions, he said, distressed him "beyond any power of description." The old clothes scandal and her hundreds of letters to all and sundry begging for money were only a part of what he had to "grieve and be mortified about." There was also "any quantity of newspaper publicity about her actions and writings. . . . It all nearly wore my life out."[77]

Robert remained confused about his mother throughout his life. He hardly ever talked about her in private and drew a public screen over the events surrounding the committal. He even tried to cover up the episode by searching out and destroying Mary's letters from the period. He gave up, however, because there were simply too many letters.[78] Robert took on his responsibility (as he saw it) to commit her with a grim, almost fatalistic determination. "I can only do my duty," he wrote on June 1, 1875, "as it is given me to see it."[79] The fatalism Robert expressed reflected perhaps his fantasy of acting out his father's wishes. The committal curiously linked him with his father's convictions about Mary's insanity and his (Lincoln's) threat to commit her after Willie's death in 1862. Robert probably sensed what his father had told Mary. But even if he somehow missed the family secret he could not avoid Elizabeth Keckley's 1868 book, which reported Lincoln's threats. The unspoken support for Robert's committal of his mother was thus his awareness, however dimly acknowledged, that he was acting as Lincoln's surrogate.

Robert lacked spontaneity and zest. His thousands of letters are characterized by a flatness of tone, a decided lack of affect. He seemed to block any mourning response to his mother's death; at least he failed to discuss her death in his correspondence.[80] Occasionally, he got mad (at Herndon, for example) and he deeply grieved over the death of his son Jack (Abraham Lincoln II) in 1890.[81] But these were the exceptions. Herndon, as we might suspect, rather overstated his case against Robert: "He has the insane rage of his mother without the sense of his father. Robert Lincoln

The impish Tad, born April 4, 1853, was a slow learner but a warmhearted child. He was the delight of both his parents and a mainstay for his mother after 1865. His death on July 15, 1871, devastated Mary Lincoln. *Mellon Collection*

is a wretch of a man." He was also a "little wee bit of a man," "silly, cold and selfish, a Todd not a Lincoln," "little, proud, aristocratic and haughty," and "his mother's 'baby' all through."[82] If we remove the venom from Herndon, it offers a measure of insight into the cold and haughty demeanor of Robert Lincoln.

The other children were different, though none lived long enough to make possible anything but the most cursory comments about their personalities. Eddie, who lived only four years and died in 1850, never even had a picture taken of him. Tad, born in 1853, was the oddity in the family, an appealing yet helpless and possibly somewhat retarded child. He was twelve or so before he could read.[83] He lisped slightly. He was delightfully impish. Lincoln went to great lengths to entertain Tad. He played blind man's bluff with him, for example, and would trip over furniture to insure Tad would escape.[84] During the war, Tad ran wild in the White House. He dressed up in uniforms and interrupted cabinet meetings. He drove Nicolay and Hay to distraction. But he never upset Lincoln, who responded easily to

Willie, who was born on December 20, 1850, was his father's favorite child. His death on February 20, 1862, cast a long shadow over the lives of both his parents. *Chicago Historical Society*

Tad's helplessness. He was like a puppy whose uncomplicated presence helped drain off some of the family tensions and conflicts.

Finally, there was Willie, born in 1850, who was the favorite. He was lively, poetic, and smart. Willie, according to Mary's niece, Elizabeth Todd Grimsley, was a "noble, beautiful boy." He had "great mental activity," an unusual intelligence, a wonderful memory, and was frank and loving.[85] The impression one gets is that Lincoln so obviously favored Willie it never had to be remarked upon. Willie's death in 1862 etched massive new lines of sorrow in Lincoln. "I never saw a man so bowed down with grief," wrote Elizabeth Keckley on Lincoln's reaction to the boy's death, "murmuring 'My poor boy, he was too good for this earth. God has called him home. I know that he is much better off in heaven, but then we loved him so. It is hard, hard to have him die!' Great sobs choked his utterance. . . . I did not dream that his rugged nature could be so moved."[86]

It is interesting in this regard to compare Robert, born in 1843, with Willie, who was born in 1850. Robert was born into the family when Lincoln was most a part of it. He carried the full burden of Lincoln's conflicts over fatherhood and his contradictory expectations for his son. With seven years and one child spanning the distance between the birth of these two sons, and Lincoln's greater emotional distance from the family itself, he could relate warmly and easily to Willie. The conflicted intensity of the early years of marriage heavily burdened Robert. The freer, more atomistic sense of Lincoln family life in the 1850s allowed the talented Willie breathing space. He took advantage of it.[87]

Chapter 6

Law and Order

He studied with nobody.

A. LINCOLN on himself
June, 1860

O assessment of the mature Lincoln can proceed without some understanding of his activities as a lawyer. In practical terms it was his legal work that supported his life style and defined his place within the larger community. Lincoln seemed to find or consolidate in the law a sense of order that perhaps served as an antidote to his domestic turbulence. One might even argue that Lincoln's search for order was the defining characteristic of his adult life, public and private, and that his failure to find effective order domestically prompted an analogous engagement with larger issues in the community. In this sense, law and Lincoln's self-conception as a lawyer helped bridge the gap from private to public.

It all began somewhat inauspiciously. Speed noted that Lincoln at first lacked confidence as a lawyer and embraced his new career with diffidence. He seemed intimidated by the high-powered lawyers with whom he came into contact.[1] Lincoln, of course, lacked formal training in the law. He picked up Blackstone's *Commentaries* on John T. Stuart's urging and read intently and alone whenever he could. "If you are resolutely determined to make a lawyer of yourself," Lincoln later counseled an aspiring lawyer, "the thing is more than half done already." There is no need for formal schooling, he went on, just a determined crack at the books. "Get the books, and read and study them till, you understand them in their principal features; that is the main thing. . . . Always bear in mind that your own resolution to succeed, is more important than any other one thing."[2] "Get the books," he told someone else once, "and read and study them until you understand them in their principal features, and that is the main thing. The books and your capacity for understanding are just the same in all places. Begin with Blackstone's *Commentaries* first and after reading it through, say twice, take up Chitty's *Pleadings*, Greenleaf's *Evidence*, and Story's *Equity* in succession. Work, work, work is the main thing."[3] Lincoln even seemed to feel it was better not to have formal training in the law,[4] partly, it appears, because solitary study gets the job done faster.[5] All this was later to be romanticized greatly in the literature, but it is worth recalling that Lincoln had no other choice and was himself unusually talented. The limits of his legal knowledge were also quite apparent to his partner.[6] It has been noted that Lincoln appears never to have read a law text after he passed his exam; his knowledge came from attending carefully to each case.[7] "Mr. Lincoln," David Davis said in 1866, "was not a general reader in any field of knowledge; he was purely a practical man, and when he wished to know a fact, he trailed it up and dug it up, root and branch . . . [and] used his information for practical ends."[8]

Lincoln was what lawyers call a litigation man. More than half his cases involved real property and mortgages, simple contracts, or issues of procedure. The next largest category of cases fell in the field of personal property. There were numerous divorce cases but few wills. As he matured and his skill became better known, Lincoln included substantial work in federal trial court in his practice. Herndon noted that Lincoln was incredibly shrewd as a trial lawyer, able to sway juries by his honesty, humor, and lucidity.[9] These same traits made him a favorite of his peers. Henry C. Whitney remembered fondly Lincoln's reply to his question of whether in an attachment suit a service of the attachment writ on the defendant had the force of a summons. Lincoln pondered the matter, cast his eyes up to the ceiling for a long minute and finally replied roguishly: "Damnfino."[10]

The number of cases he handled was really astounding. He took the cases as they came: a farmer suing his neighbor for stealing his pig, a wife seeking divorce, a black suing for freedom, a property dispute, anything and everything. Lincoln believed in the ethics of his profession strongly and seemed to feel even the devil deserved an advocate. Thus, in 1847 he represented Robert Matson who was suing to recover his runaway slaves.[11] From later statements it is clear Lincoln detested the fugitive slave law, but here as elsewhere he buried his personal feelings in the interest of serving his client.

Herndon noted that Lincoln often began a day in the office sad and gloomy but that the melancholy lifted as the day progressed.[12] The work and the human contact it involved brought Lincoln out of himself as he listened to endless tales of anger, misdeeds, and woe. He searched people out, probing and questioning, trying to put them and himself at ease. Herndon recognized the subtlety of Lincoln's style but remained somewhat ambivalent about it. By the time Herndon wrote his book in the 1880s, most of his ambivalence had fallen away. A letter he wrote in 1857, however, captures better than any source what the office was like when Lincoln was there, as well as some of Herndon's deeper feelings about his partner: "I am now in my office writing this letter," Herndon told Wendell Philips, "with a good hickory fire in the stove and several good jolly fellows keeping it warm. Lincoln—the joker—the funny man—is cracking his jokes:—he beats Hale to death *in that line.* By the by—do you know Lincoln? as we say west he is a 'hoss' I am the runt of the firm and no 'hoss', yet I suppose will pass among the crowd as a Liberty lover—a fool and a Reformer."[13]

Lincoln dealt with all these clients with a casualness that is difficult to imagine today. A student clerking in the office later reported that seeds once actually sprouted in a dusty corner.[14] Lincoln had no bookkeeping system to speak of, except his hat. "I am ashamed of not sooner answering your letter," he wrote Richard

S. Thomas on June 27, 1850. "My only apologies are, first, that I have been very busy in the U.S. Court; and second, that when I received the letter I put it in my old hat, and buying a new one the next day, the old one was set aside, and so, the letter lost sight of for a time."[15] At times Lincoln simply forgot things, large and small. For example, he wrote Milton K. Alexander on June 13, 1854: "It pains me to say that I forgot to attend to your business when I was in Clinton, at court in May last. Your best way would be to address me a letter at Clinton, about the time I go there to court in the fall (Oct. 16th I think) and then it will be fresh, & I will not forget or neglect it."[16]

One careful student of Lincoln the lawyer has noted that such sloppiness was hardly out of place for the times.[17] It is certainly true that Lincoln himself saw nothing to be ashamed of in the method of his practice. He apologized for any obvious error or inconvenience he caused a client, but in general was quite satisfied with his work. At least he saw no irony in advising young law students to leave nothing until tomorrow that can be done today.[18] He advised students that the first rule of law is diligence; that correspondence should always be promptly attended to; that research and preparation must be adequately carried out ahead of time. Be thorough, he said. And most of all be honest: "if in your own judgment you cannot be an honest lawyer, resolve to be honest without being a lawyer."[19]

One reason much of Lincoln's law practice appears erratic is that it was often, if not usually, carried out on the circuit and under pressure, constantly moving, without time for adequate preparation. The circuit was a wonderfully premodern creature devised to accommodate a changing but thinly populated state. When Lincoln first became a lawyer, there were seven state circuits. The legislature elected the judges for each circuit. This system dated from the state constitution in 1818. The grouping of counties in each circuit, however, was constantly changing throughout the 1830s and 1840s, because new counties were being formed as the state's population increased and shifted north. For example, the legislature recognized twenty-one new counties between 1837 and 1839. The eighth circuit itself was formed in 1839. It was huge and originally included seven counties (Sangamon, McLean, Livingston, Macon, Dane, which later became Christian, Logan, and Menard). Over the next six years nine more counties were added (Dewitt, Shelby, Champaign, Mason, Pitt, Woodford, Moultire, Edgar, and Vermillion). At its largest the eighth circuit covered 11,000 square miles, two-thirds of the width and one-third the length of the state.

The entire court—judge, lawyers, and clerks—moved between county seats throughout the circuit. The court would be in session in each county seat for a few days to a week, depending on the volume of business, and then move on. The whole circuit was covered once in the spring and once in the fall. The court settings were usually quite humble, a log cabin adapted for the purpose or an unpretentious state building. The system itself had an impromptu quality to it that some observers at the time regarded as incompetence.[20] It was impossible to carry books along, so most cases were argued on the issue of right or wrong rather than on precedent.

There was often little time for a lawyer to prepare or even to learn the facts of a case. He might of course have made previous contact with a client and, through letters, worked out an argument based on precedent from research in Springfield. In such cases Lincoln and others worked with local "partners" or loose affiliations with lawyers in the county seats. Lincoln had some seventy-five such casual, ad hoc arrangements over the years.[21] More often, however, a lawyer was approached to handle a case as he arrived in town. An afternoon in the town square, talking and joking with the local residents the day before court opened, was the principal way to bring in business.

Conditions for the lawyers on the circuit were primitive. Much of their time was spent in arduous travel between county seats. In the years when Judge Treat presided over the eighth circuit (1843–1848), the caravan usually moved by horseback. Between 1848 and 1860, when David Davis was the judge, they moved at first by buggy over the improved roads and, by the mid-1850s, by train.[22] In the court, which met every day except Sunday, the lawyers had to argue cases without much preparation before juries that refused to recognize legal pretensions. Food and lodging varied but were never elegant. If the night had to be spent along the route between county seats, everyone might have to crowd into a log cabin, perhaps on the floor. In the towns themselves, there was seldom enough space in the local hotel for everyone in the caravan, so lawyers usually slept two (or sometimes more) in a bed. The food was abundant but usually terrible.[23] Most lawyers tried to return home on weekends but still faced long and frequent separations from wives and children. Circuit life could be frustrating, disruptive, hard, and lonely.

But Lincoln loved it. He was as happy on the circuit as he ever was in his life. He never complained of the physical hardships and seemed to thrive on the quiet loneliness of the circuit. He read Euclid in the peaceful time after others were asleep and would bounce along on his horse for hours absorbed in his book.[24] He was known to slip away quietly by himself, once to spend an entire evening at a little magic lantern show intended for children.[25] The rough male camaradarie of aspiring professionals in primitive conditions appealed to Lincoln. It provided, especially, an ideal audience for his spontaneous, warm humor.[26] David Davis used to hold mock court in the evening and laugh for hours at Lincoln's sense of the outrageous.[27] Besides Davis (who became Lincoln's 1860 campaign manager, was later appointed to the Supreme Court, and after the war handled the Lincoln estate), Lincoln made perhaps his only adult friends (after Speed) on the circuit: Elihu B. Washburne, Leonard S. Swett, Ward Hill Lamon, Henry C. Whitney, and many others.

Lincoln also thrived professionally on the circuit. He was at his best before a humble fury of decidedly ordinary citizens. He never talked down to them, and his careful dosing of technicalities with earthy humor made him enormously effective. It should also not be forgotten that professional advantage was served in two ways by circuit work: his law practice, strictly speaking, and his political career. Lincoln's acute sense of the mood, potentialities, and prejudices of ordinary citizens in Central Illinois came from long immersion in their ways. He came to grasp what they wanted—and needed—which helped him consolidate his political career. A lot of votes were at stake. Circuit work in some ways gave Lincoln the chance to campaign half of every year for most of his adult life. New York Republicans were shortsighted when

they saw him as only a dark horse in 1860. His renown throughout Illinois, based on twenty-five years of spade work among the
people, was what his wise managers hoped to build on when they
suggested Chicago as a "neutral" convention site in 1860.

One way to understand Lincoln's work as a lawyer is through
his fees. He always earned a good income from the law, but
usually his fees were quite small. A five dollar payment was not
uncommon. It was the volume of his work that made it lucrative.
He even accepted payment in kind, whether firewood or sub-
scription to a local newspaper.[28] Lincoln never took advantage of
his role as lawyer to acquire cheap land and other properties. In
this he differed from many of his colleagues (such as David
Davis, Stephen T. Logan, and C. H. Moore) who amassed personal fortunes.[29] Lincoln could be extraordinarily generous, as
when he returned ten dollars of George Floyd's twenty-five dollar
payment for services rendered: "You must think I am a high-
priced man," he told Floyd. "You are too liberal with your
money. . . . Fifteen dollars is enough for the job."[30] Still, Lincoln
expected to be paid something and could be quite insistent with
his clients.[31] He felt in general that some if not all the fee should
be paid in advance. He noticed that he was not likely to hear from
clients after their cases were settled.[32] But in dealing with anyone
over any fee, large or small, Lincoln never lost his sense of humor.
"I have news from Ottawa," he wrote a circuit partner once, "that
we *win* our Galatin & Saline county cases. As the dutch Justice
said, when he married folk, 'Now, vere ish my hundred tol-
lars.' "[33] Similarly, he once asked another circuit partner to help
him finish up a case for which he had already taken a fee. He disliked keeping the money without doing the work, he said, but he
also hated to "disgorge."[34]

One fee Lincoln received has become quite famous. As lawyer
for the Illinois Central Railroad after it was chartered in 1851,
Lincoln handled some forty cases for the company. His most important by far was the McClean County Tax case. In it Lincoln
successfully argued that railroads should be exempt from county
taxes as "public works" because they already paid state taxes.
The decision was to have an enormous impact on railroad construction generally. Lincoln recognized the value of the case, but

at first seemed uncertain what constituted a reasonable fee. He considered $2,000 but friends urged him to increase that amount considerably. In the end he charged $5,000, at which the company balked. So he sued the railroad company for the full amount, which he was awarded on June 23, 1857. The company, however, saw the payment, at least in part, as a kind of political payoff. In May, 1857 (that is, just prior to the uncontested court settlement) the Illinois Central's Chicago Director wrote privately that Lincoln "proves to be not only the most prominent of his party, but the acknowledged special advisor of the Bissell Administration [William H. Bissell was then Governor of Illinois]."[35] Most people agree Lincoln deserved the fee. It was a landmark case. In suing the Illinois Central, he was probably not consciously capitalizing on his political clout for his own material advantage. Still, no one as shrewd as Lincoln could be unaware of the connection. It seems he was more than a little conflicted about the fee. At the conclusion of the trial, the jury awarded him $5,000, but Lincoln's attorney, John M. Douglas, had to request immediately that the verdict be set aside and another jury called. This was done and a new judgment awarded for $4,800. It seems Lincoln "forgot" he had much earlier taken a $200 retainer fee.[36]

Several legal scholars have exhaustively examined Lincoln's activities as a lawyer. Much remains controversial, for example, how "great" he was as a lawyer and what kinds of precedents he set. One of these studies—John P. Frank's *Lincoln the Lawyer*— has also stressed the development of Lincoln as a lawyer. "Perhaps the largest single difference," Frank wrote, "between the Lincoln of 1840 and the Lincoln of 1860 is in his self-confidence, his sense of personal assurance. . . . The tone changes. Diffidence is replaced by authority."[37] Certain of Lincoln's human traits made him a good lawyer from the beginning: a personality that attracted clients; an aptitude for organizing materials to highlight the essential; a gift of selectivity; a restrained and effective verbal expression; an unusually retentive mind; and a capacity for hard work. Nevertheless, Frank felt he could clearly identify a young lawyer Lincoln and a mature lawyer Lincoln. In the early years, for example, he tended to brand the fellow on the other side a liar. The mature Lincoln saw all people as seekers after truth. In his early practice Lincoln represented some flatboatmen suing a dam, which he showed obstructed a navigable river. He won eighty-five dollars for the defendants. Later, he shifted to the other side—the famous Rock Island Bridge case. Here he represented the bridge (and behind it the railroads that crossed the Mississippi on the bridge) against the boat that hit the bridge. If boats can go up and down the river, he argued essentially, why should trains not be allowed to go across it?[38]

Young Lawyer Lincoln, Frank argues, approached the law as a tricky game of variances, pleadings, niceties, and petty details.[39] This observation is worth dwelling on for a moment. The law for Lincoln before the early 1850s was a tool for use, something outside of the self to foster prestige, bring in money, defeat opponents. Lincoln tended to focus on the details of his cases, to try to trip up witnesses, and to react indignantly to the lies of the witnesses. He was not a bad lawyer at all, but he was an ordinary one; every important case with which his name is associated came after 1854 (except for the Duff Armstrong murder trial of 1841, which was more frosting than cake). He found his way slowly in his chosen profession. It took time and, I would argue, both experience *and* change in other areas, before he could work at his best, or, in Frank's terms, before law could become "an approach to life, a merger of engineering, surveying, economics, social wisdom, as well as precedent tightly analyzed."[40]

Chapter 7

The Domestication
of
Political Rhetoric

It will become *all* one thing, or *all* the other.
A. LINCOLN
June 16, 1858

HANGE came in many shapes for the mature Lincoln. It is clearest in his political development. Thus, he took positions on three major issues as a representative in the Thirtieth Congress (1847–49). He came out strongly against the Mexican War; he tried to introduce a bill in Congress to abolish the slave trade in Washington, D.C.; and he worked against Henry Clay and for General Zachary Taylor in the 1848 Presidential struggle. Lincoln was, in other words, antiwar, antislavery, and anti-Clay. In each case he either failed completely to accomplish his objectives or met with only partial success. The country was joyfully militaristic, especially the South, and welcomed the huge acquisitions of the 1848 Treaty of Guadalupe Hidalgo with Mexico. In terms of slavery, Lincoln only succeeded in identifying himself with extremists without altering the slave trade at all. He badly misjudged both his support and the strength of the opposition. And in working against Clay Lincoln managed to acquire the smell of a traitor without any offsetting advantage; Zachary Taylor, who beat Clay for the nomination and won the election, proved singularly unresponsive to Lincoln's requests for a position in the new administration. In each case, it seems Lincoln chose the wrong issue at the wrong time in the wrong place. It took years to undo the damage. It was a mark of Lincoln's greatness that he acknowledged to himself the extent of his failure as a Congressman and pulled back gracefully to reflect, grow, change for some five years. When his next opportunity came, in 1854, he was not unready for the challenge. Neither he nor the country was ever again quite the same.[1]

Lincoln's "Spot Resolutions" were introduced in the House of Representatives on December 22, 1847. In legalistic language Lincoln tried to force President Polk to admit that the actual spot where fighting began was in Mexico, not the United States; if true, that made the United States the aggressor. The first two of Lincoln's eight "interrogatories" directed President Polk respectfully to inform the House of Representatives, first, "Whether the spot of soil on which the blood of our *citizens* was shed, as in his messages declared, was, or was not, within the territories of Spain, at least from the treaty of 1819 until the Mexican revolution" and, second, "Whether that spot is, or is not, within the territory which was wrested from Spain, by the Mexican revolution."[2] Lincoln over-lawyered himself in these interrogatories, which treated Polk as though he were a humble witness on the stand. The technique of asking detailed, probing questions to which only affirmative or negative answers can be given and then from those answers reconstructing a logically ordered chain of events is really only appropriate for the courtroom. In the complex world of parties and politics and the formalized tensions between Congress and the executive, the device Lincoln was using to unmask Polk was inappropriate. Lincoln felt we were the aggressors in the Mexican War and that the whole venture was unjust and imperialistic. He should have said so in ways he uniquely could.[3]

It would be easy to chalk all this up to inexperience. Lincoln was new to Congress and uncertain how best to mount an effective Whig response to Polk's war. He had little sense of his own support and even less appreciation of the resources of the executive. He was also not fully seasoned as a lawyer; he lacked a full grasp of when to use and when not to use legalistic devices. Nor had he fully developed his own political speaking style. His major speeches before 1848—the Young Men's Lyceum speech in 1838 and the Temperance Address in 1842—are windy pronouncements with little nuance, subtlety, or eloquence. Lincoln seems young in 1848 in every respect. He was a freshman Congressman, a young lawyer, and a developing statesman.

Lincoln's opposition to the war was principled and determined. Such were the concerns of Congressman Lincoln. As he said in another context (but only two weeks after the resolutions were introduced and one week before a major anti-Polk speech he gave on January 12, 1848), "if we once yield to a wrong principle, that concession will be the prolific source of endless mischief."[4] The interrogatories themselves were an attempt to discredit President Polk and to prove to the world the aggressive intents of the United States against Mexico from the beginning. Lincoln reacted angrily to his law partner's disagreement with his position. "I regret this," Lincoln commented on Herndon's vote for the Ashmun Amendment censuring Polk, "not because of any fear we shall remain disagreed, after you shall have read this letter, but because, if *you* misunderstand, I fear other friends will also."[5] Lincoln proclaimed to Herndon he would "stake his life" on the claim that if Herndon had been in his place he would have voted the same way. The vote on the floor had directly questioned the justice of the war. As a Congressman he could hardly run from his responsibility to cast his vote. And surely he had to vote his conscience, "to tell the *truth* or tell a *lie*. I can not doubt which you would do."[6]

Lincoln's next letter to Herndon was a detailed response to Herndon's letter (since lost) opposing Lincoln's position on the war in general political and constitutional terms. From the context of Lincoln's response, it seems Herndon argued that the constitutional provision empowering the President to repel invasion justified Polk's unilateral action. Lincoln went to the heart of the matter and pointed out that such a position went beyond even what the President or his supporters argued. "Their only positions," Lincoln continued, "are first, that the soil was *ours* where hostilities commenced, and second, that whether it was rightfully *ours* or not, *Congress had annexed it*, and the President, for that reason was bound to defend it...." Both these positions, Lincoln felt, were manifestly wrong and yet tenaciously clung to. The danger lay in the principle and the precedent: "Allow the President to invade a neighboring nation, whenever *he* shall deem it necessary to repel an invasion and you allow him to do so, *whenever he may choose to say* he deems it necessary for such purpose—and you allow him to make war at pleasure." And that was exactly what the framers of the Constitution sought to avoid. Kings had always made wars and impoverished their people. Our Constitution was deliberately designed to preclude such action. Your view, Lincoln concluded in his letter to Herndon, would place our Presidents where kings have always stood.[7]

Lincoln's response to his law partner is a masterpiece of argument. It is subtle, clear, closely reasoned. Lincoln returned intelligently as was his wont to the words and intent of the founders to clarify an important political issue in the present. But why did he bother to go through it all with Herndon? Perhaps Lincoln thirsted for reelection and this letter was an attempt both to enlist Herndon's considerable energies toward that goal and to stave off local opposition to his antiwar position. If this were true, the letter was clearly meant for public consumption. There are, however, several problems with this view. Lincoln never dealt with Herndon on anything indirectly; if he had *really* been writing the Whig establishment in the letter to Herndon and hoped his partner would know to circulate it, he would have said so. It is also not clear that Herndon himself was that much of a political asset. He had a certain recognition, even clout, among young Whigs in the district, but he was hardly in a position of leadership to bring around someone like Stephen T. Logan to see the validity of Lincoln's position on the war. It is not even clear, for that matter, that local Whigs other than Herndon objected to Lincoln's antiwar position.[8] Furthermore, Lincoln was extremely sensitive to a complicated agreement he had affirmed before his election that rotated the Whig nomination among several contenders. Thus, unless the situation changed, he was committed to withdraw after one term. He was frankly ambivalent about the arrangement and told Herndon essentially that he would respond positively to a draft. ("I could not refuse the people the right of sending me again," he put it delicately.) But he was in no position to politick for renomination. His "word and honor" forbade such maneuvering.[9]

The only reasonable explanation for Lincoln's eloquent plea to Herndon is that Herndon was the only person listening. Lincoln's ambitions, indeed, his grandiosity, lay thinly disguised below the surface. His purpose in the interrogatories was to gloriously unmask Polk and force an acknowledgment of wrongdoing (whether Lincoln believed the damage by then could have been undone is another question). "Let him [Polk] answer [the interrogatories]," Lincoln thundered from the House floor, "fully, fairly, candidly. Let him answer with *facts*, and not with arguments. Let him remember he sits where Washington sat, and so remembering, let him answer, as Washington would answer. As a nation *should not*, and the Almighty *will* not, be evaded, so let him attempt no evasion—no equivocation."[10] The same evil genius, the dictator of the Lyceum speech a decade earlier, blended with the figure of Polk, only now the danger was real and present rather than potential. Polk had acted like a king, capriciously and independently, and dragged the country deliberately into war. The dictator so dreaded at the Lyceum seemed to have sprung up unawares. To disarm him was thus to slay him, to play a David to Polk's Goliath.

But the worst indignity of all occurred—no one really seemed to hear or care. The interrogatories themselves suffered the fate of inattention. Polk blandly ignored them and left it to prowar Democrats in the House to reply condescendingly to Lincoln's charges. Not one Whig rose to his support.[11] Lincoln was isolated and alone with his righteous pretensions. Lincoln suffered this indignation in silence, though there are hints of a depression in his April 16, 1848, letter to Mary, which began "In this troublesome world, we are never quite satisfied" and went on to lament how much he hated to stay in his old room by himself directing documents.[12] Lincoln had unleashed his wish for power, recognition, dominance, and fame. The forum had been the political arena, a public setting, where he had made an inauspicious showing. The resulting inattention Lincoln experienced as a blow of the first order. He responded in pained depression, quietly withdrawing from the fray.[13] He only expressed his feelings to Mary, though to her the idiom was personal and private rather than public and political. The public and private were as yet apart, unintegrated. Lincoln had reached beyond his grasp.

The second major initiative Lincoln took as Congressman was to attempt an abolition of slavery in Washington itself. All sensitive observers, including some southerners, agreed that it was unseemly to allow slaves to be publicly traded in the nation's capitol. There is no indication Lincoln reacted in horror to the sight; indeed, there is no indication at all of his feelings on the matter. The bill he tried to introduce on January 10, 1849, therefore, came as something of a surprise.

Lincoln's attitudes toward slavery and race before 1848 are quite murky and certainly lack the clarity given them by most later observers. It plays unjustly with the sources, for example, to quote from Lincoln's 1855 letter to Joshua Speed as evidence of Lincoln's early views on slavery and race. In that 1855 letter Lincoln described strong feelings about slavery from as early as 1841. "You may remember," he told Speed, "as I well do, that from Louisville to the mouth of the Ohio there were, on board, ten or a dozen slaves, shackled together with irons. That sight was a continual torment to me. . . ."[14] Lincoln's contemporary description of the same scene (interestingly enough, in a letter of August, 1841, to Speed's sister, Mary) struck quite a different note. Lincoln introduced his description with a general, almost philosophical comment on what he had seen: "By the way," he wrote parenthetically in a paragraph that began with chatter about the "vexatious delays" in his trip, "a fine example was presented on board the boat for contemplating the effect of *condition* upon human happiness." A Kentucky gentleman had bought twelve slaves and was taking them by boat to his farm further south. Lincoln described in some detail the manner of their captivity: "They were chained six and six together. A small iron clevis was around the left wrist of each, and this fastened to the main chain by a shorter one at a convenient distance from, the others; so that the negroes were strung together precisely like so many fish upon a trot-line." This animal imagery (which occurred throughout Lincoln's thinking about blacks later) seemed to suppress the agonizing human experience of the slaves he saw. To compare the slaves with fish on a trotline was to see them as objects.[15]

But even as he distanced himself, Lincoln's empathy provided an insight: "In this condition they were being separated forever from the scenes of their childhood, their friends, their fathers and mothers, and brothers and sisters, and many of them, from their wives and children, and going into perpetual slavery where the lash of the master is proverbially more ruthless and unrelenting than any other where." It should be remembered that Lincoln was writing to the daughter of a slaveholding family. He may have expressed his real feeling of sorrow for these slaves being taken from their families more gently than he might have in another context. He also built in an implied contrast—which was undoubtedly understood by Mary Speed—between the family togetherness of slaves in Kentucky, the scenes of their childhood, their fathers and mothers, brothers and sisters, and the cruelty of what they would encounter on the "farm in the south" where things are proverbially worse. Lincoln thus remained sensitive to Mary's feelings in describing a scene he found distressing, balancing her feelings against his for the slaves in tow. Yet the conclusion of his description, which was really the point of the story, was that, despite the unhappy circumstances the slaves faced, "they were the most cheerful and apparently happy creatures on board. One, whose offense for which he had been sold was an over-fondness for his wife, played the fiddle almost continually; and the others danced, sung, cracked jokes, and played various games with cards from day to day. How true it is that 'God tempers the wind to the shorn lamb,' or in other words, that He renders the worst of human conditions tolerable, while He permits the best, to be nothing better than tolerable."[16]

A large measure of self-reference seemed to shape Lincoln's re-action to this scene. September, 1841, fell in the period of his most severe and extended depression. In fact, his visit to the Speeds' home in Kentucky was an artifact of that depression, an effort to restore his spirits and renew his close friendship with Joshua. Mary Speed knew well of Lincoln's "blues," which he discussed toward the end of this very letter. In some way, his de-scription of the boat scene is a parable for himself. As the blacks display only happiness in great misery, so Lincoln, living in rela-tively happy conditions, feels only the agony of depression. This personal meaning of the passage in the letter seemed entirely ac-cessible to Lincoln, though one cannot be certain, for he failed to make the connection explicit. But whether or not it was con-scious, Lincoln seemed unable to go beyond his own misery in reacting to the boat scene; he failed to distinguish his sense of de-jection over his conflicted relationship with a woman who still loved him (Mary Todd) and the depths of sadness those slaves on the chain had reached. All human misery was only a mirror of his own unhappiness, feigned gaiety (or suppressed misery) a be-havior lesson for him to learn. That a part of himself knew better is apparent from his subsequent reconstruction of the scene in the 1855 letter to Joshua. By then there was no facile lesson to be learned, no Scripture quoted, just the real feeling that sprang from empathy with people in a different and terrible situation: "That sight was a continual torment to me." Thus it seems Lin-coln's memory of the scene changed over the years. If he felt tor-ment for the slaves in 1841, it was a very personalized, largely unempathic, kind of misery. It is far more likely that he simply remembered the scene differently as his personal feelings and po-litical convictions changed.

The only other direct source[17] we have on Lincoln's views on slavery before 1848 provides a fascinating link with his aborted action on the slavery question in Washington as a United States Congressman. In 1837 the Illinois House, responding to memori-als on slavery from several southern states, strongly condemned abolitionism, reaffirmed the constitutionally protected right of slave states to own slaves, and asserted that slavery could not be abolished in Washington without consent (and presumably compensation). Lincoln and Daniel Stone, another Whig from Springfield, objected to several particulars of the resolution and on March 3 entered their own protest in the House. Lincoln and Stone affirmed the resolutions in substance and objected only to a wording that made no moral judgment on slavery itself. The original resolution of the Illinois House read: "That we highly disapprove of the formation of abolition societies, and of the doctrines promulgated by them." The Lincoln/Stone protest read: "They [that is, Lincoln and Stone] believe that the institution of slavery is founded on both injustice and bad policy; but that the promulgation of abolition doctrines tends rather to increase rather than to abate its evils."[18] This position was typically Lincolnesque: clear, even courageous, in statement of essential moral purpose but moderate in dealing with political realities. The Illinois winds obviously blew kindly over the slave states. Lincoln dissented, but gently. He went on record against both slavery and abolition, branding one morally evil and the other politically immoderate, which for Lincoln was another form of evil.

The reformist leverage in the Illinois House resolution and in the Lincoln/Stone protest was the statement on slavery in Washington. Both the resolution and the protest affirmed the constitutional right of southerners to own slaves, but both also indicated slavery might legitimately be abolished in Washington with the consent of its citizens. This 1837 position thus defined an agenda for Lincoln: leave slavery alone where it existed; oppose abolitionism; demonstrate moral fiber by working politically to end slavery in Washington. This agenda gave Lincoln the kind of delicate middle position he so enjoyed occupying. After 1837 he appeared to drop the issue. He took no political action on it again in the Illinois House (where he served two more terms as Whig leader before retiring). He dealt, of course, with some legal matters that touched slavery, but it seems that before 1848 he seldom reflected on the issue of slavery itself (other than his letter to Mary Speed). There are two exceptions worth noting. First, in his address to the Springfield Washington Temperance Society on February 22, 1842, Lincoln referred in passing to that happy day when the drunken bondage will be broken and "a viler slavery, manumitted." When that victory is complete, "when there shall be neither a slave nor a drunkard on the earth" how proud the land will be.[19] Second, in a letter to Williamson Durley on October 3, 1845, Lincoln went to some length to spell out his political principles generally. These included a recognition of how divisive slavery was for party unity; how abolitionists had been "wonderful" (Lincoln says sarcastically) in their opposition to Clay in 1845, which helped bring about the annexation of Texas; and how basically evil slavery was and yet how important it was to protect it in the South. He concluded with the hope that slavery would die out.[20]

The issue of slavery became a central concern of the Thirtieth Congress. The land acquired from Mexico in 1848 opened up the constitutionally thorny issue of whether slavery could be extended into new areas. Opponents (including Lincoln) tried numerous times to pass the Wilmot Proviso, an amendment first offered in 1846 that would have prevented the expansion of slavery into any areas acquired from Mexico. Proponents of extension used increasingly intemperate language to defend the right to extend their peculiar institution. Furthermore, the spectacle of the slave trade in the heart of Washington probably did offend Lincoln. And whatever inclinations he felt toward abolition were undoubtedly encouraged by Joshua Giddings, another junior Congressman who stayed at the same boarding house (Mrs. Sprigg's) where Lincoln lived while in Washington.[21] It is important, however, not to put too much emphasis on the impact of abolitionists on Lincoln. He had always condemned them as extremists and felt decidedly uneasy when his own antiwar stand put him on their side.[22]

Lincoln's agenda in 1848 drew essentially on his formulation of slavery reform in 1837.[23] He moved slowly but seldom forgot the past. He apparently drafted his measure sometime in the fall of 1848 with the support of people like Joshua Giddings. He also referred on the House floor to fifteen leading citizens who supported his measure; when challenged for their names he chose not to produce them. The claim suggests Lincoln went to some trouble to line up support for his bill. It was also perhaps true that his support was more fragile than he realized. The explicit reason he gave later for quietly dropping the matter was that he lost the support of his former backers.[24] The measure went absolutely nowhere. Lincoln first read the bill to the House on January 10, 1849, as a "proposition" which he intended to submit. Three days later he gave further notice of his intention to introduce the bill, but he then never brought it up.

Lincoln's original title of the bill was "an act to abolish slavery in the District of Columbia by consent of the free white people of said District, and with compensation to owners."[25] Lincoln proposed that no person then living in the District of Columbia nor anyone born there after January 1, 1850, should ever be held in slavery. But there were several qualifications. Children born to former slave mothers after January 1, 1850, would be "reasonably supported and educated by the previous owners of their mothers to whom the children would owe "reasonable" service. He left open the age at which this dependence would end. Lincoln's plan also called for compensation to owners of slaves from the government, but left it to the white owners to decide whether they wanted to enter such an agreement. If not, they could keep the slaves they then possessed. It is difficult to imagine a more gradual emancipation plan. It made it optional for whites to participate and kept the slave children in essential bondage until their maturity. Lincoln clearly thought in very long terms when he spoke of "gradual emancipation." Furthermore, the bill "empowered and required" authorities in Washington to return fugitive slaves. It was that clause which probably lost Lincoln his abolitionist support. Lincoln's aborted effort even to introduce the bill reflected, of course, the devastating effects of the polarization on the issue of slavery that set in after 1848. Yet, oddly, he failed to read the political situation accurately, clinging instead to an agenda for action from his political youth in Illinois that proved irrelevant on a national level after the Mexican War.

Lincoln's political ideas took shape slowly in the late 1830s and the 1840s. He was from the beginning a principled moderate. "There are few things *wholly* evil," he said in 1848, "or *wholly* good. Almost every thing, especially of governmental policy, is an inseparable compound of the two; so that our best judgment of the preponderance between them is continually demanded."[26] Moderation meant tolerance, and nowhere was that more important in a revivalist age than in matters of religion. In the 1846 campaign for Congress, Lincoln was charged with being an open scoffer at religion (his opponent, Peter Cartwright, was a minister). In response Lincoln issued a handbill to the voters in his district to clarify his position. He noted that he himself believed in God but was not a member of any church. His sense of religious fidelity was strikingly practical and rested on the convergence of his personal feelings with those of the community. He made it clear that he himself could not support a candidate who openly scoffed at religion. "Leaving the higher matter of eternal consequences, between him and his Maker," Lincoln said, "I still do not think any man has the right thus to insult the feelings, and injure the morals, of the community in which he may live."[27]

Lincoln's early sense of community bridged the gap between neighborhood and nation. Nothing done at the federal level, he thought, could be without some advantage for local communities. The navy, for example, founded and supported essentially for defense in time of war, also protects the merchant marine. For anyone in the twentieth century this point is easy to recognize; it is even banal. But Lincoln argued just as strenuously that nothing is so *"local* as to not be of some *general* benefit." For example, the Illinois-Michigan canal considerably cheapened the price of sugar from New Orleans for citizens of New York.[28] These points went to the heart of the debate over "internal improvements" or the economic development of the nation that required federal initiative (and, usually, federal money) as well as a basic sense of national identity. It also carried a basic sense of economic optimism, a faith that economic growth and development bring with them moral improvement.[29]

In those early years a political style also emerged, one firmly grounded in attention to details. The situation among central Illinois Whigs in the 1840s was complicated by an agreement at Pekin in 1844 to pass around the party's congressional nomination. However, no two politicians seemed to have quite the same understanding of what was actually agreed to; and, besides, ambitions tended to cloud vision.[30] As Lincoln prepared for the 1846 election, he watched closely how Whigs in his district were thinking about the Pekin agreement—and about him. It would seem he read an astounding number of local papers. "The Pekin paper," he wrote a friend who was presumably in a position to affect the Beardstown paper's editorial stand, "has lately nominated or suggested Hardin's name for Governor, and the Alton paper, noticing that, indirectly nominates him for Congress. I wish you would, if you can, see that, while these things are bandied about among the papers, the Beardstown paper takes no stand that may injure my chance, unless the conductor really prefers Genl. Hardin, in which case, I suppose it would be fair."[31] Lincoln reaped great advantage from his close reading of the papers. He told Hardin himself (who was his opponent for the nomination) that it was unfair for Hardin to think harshly of Lincoln because a paper friendly to Lincoln recommended Hardin for the governorship (thus removing Lincoln as an opponent). Lincoln pointed out how little control one has in these matters, for "*what*, or *how*, ought I to think of you because of your paper at Jacksonville doing the same thing for *me* twice?"[32]

Lincoln watched everything closely. "I would rejoice to be spared the labour of a contest," he wrote a friend in 1846, "but 'being in' I shall go it thoroughly, and to the bottom." He then recorded a county by county analysis of his support that reflected a great deal of careful head-counting.[33] This letter was part of an active campaign to garner support. His letters around this time were often marked confidential and suggest many more such letters were written than have survived.[34] There is throughout all this correspondence a healthy assertiveness, a fiercely competitive spirit but one well within bounds. He defined a goal and then set to work aggressively to attain it. He felt wronged by Hardin's refusal to abide by the Pekin agreement but, rather than stew about it, he decided simply to take on the challenge and win. He succeeded.

At the national level in Congress things were rather more complicated. It was impossible for Lincoln to control events as he could in central Illinois. He was only a freshman Congressman and his party was weak, divided, leaderless. Henry Clay claimed few followers. He was old and discredited, generally regarded as something of a relic from the past. Lincoln seems never to have considered supporting Clay for the 1848 nomination. "Our only chance is with Taylor," he wrote in 1848. "I go for him, not because I think he would make a better president than Clay, but because I think he would make a better one than Polk, or Cass, or Buchanan, or any such creatures, one of whom is sure to be elected, if he is not."[35] And, again, "Mr. Clay's chance for an election, is just no chance at all."[36] Lincoln indeed was "decidedly" on Taylor's side and worked hard (and with some success) to bring Illinois around for the Mexican War hero.[37]

There were many things to consider in 1848. Once in Washington Lincoln probably realized quickly how weak Clay's base of support really was. In the aftermath of a war it was also desirable for the Whigs to have a military hero as standard-bearer. Furthermore, Taylor appeared to hold political views Lincoln could support. At least Lincoln could see enough flexibility in Taylor to allow for the implementation of Whig policies. He realized, however, that he could not be too sure. In a pro-Taylor speech Lincoln gave in Congress on July 27, 1849, he avoided defending Taylor and instead spent most of his time ridiculing the Democratic candidate, another general, Lewis Cass. Lincoln argued that Taylor at least had said he would support whatever proposal came to him from the people via their representatives in Congress. Taylor was willing to trust the people. Besides, "on the prominent questions of Currency, Tariff, internal improvements, and Wilmot Provision, Gen. Taylor's course is at least as well defined as is Gen. Cass'."[38]

Lincoln worked hard for Taylor in the campaign and spent a good deal of time stumping Massachusetts, where he made a good impression. He argued strenuously that the central issue of the campaign was the extension of slavery. On this issue Taylor himself was perhaps vague, but the Whigs were clearly opposed to it; Cass and the Democrats supported extension. Thus both candidates in some ways lacked luster, but one leaned toward evil, the other toward essential Whig positions. Furthermore, it would be disastrous for Conscience Whigs and abolitionists to support Van Buren's third-party candidacy in the Free Soil Party: that would only serve to draw off support from Taylor and insure the election of Cass.[39] In the end Taylor won the election, including Massachusetts. Illinois, however, went for Cass, though Lincoln's district stayed with Taylor.

Lincoln's stance against Clay and for Taylor reflected the sober realities of politics. Nevertheless, Lincoln's easy abandonment of Clay in 1848 involved a decided shift in his political loyalties. It seemed then—and later—that no one in antebellum America was a more devoted follower of Henry Clay's ideas than Abraham Lincoln. As George Fredrickson has noted, Lincoln "quoted Clay, paraphrased him, and at times virtually plagiarized from him, not merely for the practical political purpose of winning recalcitrant Whigs to the Republican cause but because he indeed thought of himself as taking up where Clay had left off."[40] Fredrickson was talking of Lincoln's statements during the 1850s, but Lincoln's fondness for Clay dated from the beginning of his career. He admired Clay's commitment to a national concept that transcended parochial, particularly southern, concerns. He held up as a model Clay's compromising moderation in the political process. And most of all he felt Clay's admittedly ambiguous position on slavery was the only reasonable stance to assume. It seemed that Clay epitomized all the virtues Lincoln so greatly valued: honesty, dignity, wisdom, vision, and a fierce devotion to the process of law in a fledgling republic. Clay defined the spirit and letter of compromise that Lincoln felt were essential to the preservation of the Union.

Lincoln's anti-Clay stance in 1848 seemed to make political sense. Yet his position took its psychological toll and left him with a sense of regret for precipitously abandoning his ideological idol. Clay died on June 29, 1852. One week later Lincoln delivered a moving eulogy to Clay in the Hall of Representatives of the State Capitol. It was one of only four eulogies Lincoln ever delivered[41] and certainly the only one with real emotion. The speech, which extended to some fifty-five hundred words, extolled Clay's "mighty mind," his "gallant heart," the "mighty sweep of that graceful arm," and the "magic of that eloquent tongue." In the speech Lincoln detailed the positions Clay took on crucial issues, particularly slavery. As Lincoln pointed out, Clay, as an owner of slaves, detested the institution of slavery. It was this kind of ambiguity that Lincoln believed democracy had to tolerate. "Cast into life where slavery was already widely spread and deeply seated, [Clay] did not perceive, as I think no wise man has perceived, how it [slavery] could be at *once* eradicated, without producing a greater evil, even to the cause of human liberty itself." Lincoln concluded his speech with particularly effusive praise for the central place of Clay in our history. "But Henry Clay is dead. His long and eventful life is closed. Our country is prosperous and powerful; but could it have been quite all it has been, and is, and is to be, without Henry Clay? Such a man the times have demanded, and such, in the providence of God was given us. But he is gone. Let us strive to deserve, as far as mortals may, the continued care of Divine Providence, trusting that, in future national emergencies, He will not fail to provide us the instrument of safety and security."[42]

This fascinating document operates at several psychological levels. Most obviously, the speech placed Clay among the august political figures whom Lincoln invested with the full force of his idealizing needs, making Clay one of the glorious fathers who supplanted his own inadequate father. It is thus striking how close in time the eulogy (July, 1852) was to the death of Thomas (January, 1851). Thomas was ignored, even, in a sense, abused while Lincoln heaped the greatest glory onto Clay. At the same time, Lincoln seemed to identify with Clay, perhaps in the psychoanalytic sense of regressive identification: "Mr. Clay's lack of a more perfect early education, however it may be regretted generally, teaches at least one profitable lesson; it teaches that in this country, one can scarcely be so poor, but that, if he *will*, he *can* acquire sufficient education to get through the world respectably."[43]

But the most interesting aspect of Lincoln's attitude toward Clay was that the eulogy seemed a kind of personal atonement for having opposed Clay politically for the Whig Presidential nomination. Even in 1848 there were hints that Lincoln felt guilty for his abandonment of Clay. Certainly, Democrats charged Whigs with callous hypocrisy in their refusal to nominate Clay for the Presidency. In his July 27, 1848, speech Lincoln noted that a "gentleman from Georgia" (Mr. Iverson) had charged the Whigs with a desertion of all their principles and with having turned Henry Clay out, "like an old horse to root." Lincoln seemed to take the charge personally. "This is terribly severe," he said. "It can not be answered by argument; at least I can not so answer it." Lincoln could only defensively turn the charge back on the Democrats. "I merely wish to ask the gentleman if the Whigs are the only party he can think of, who some times turn old horses out to root. Is not a certain Martin Van Buren, an old horse which your own party have turned out to root? and is he not rooting a little to your discomfort about now?"[44]

Ironically, it turned out that Lincoln's support of Taylor was not even politically shrewd. When the election was over, he hoped for some reward. But as with everything else for Congressman Lincoln, there were unforeseen problems. The job he wanted was that of Commissioner of the General Land Office, a cabinet-level post. "In these days of Cabinet making," he wrote William Schouler on February 2, 1849, "we out West are awake as well as others . . . the West is not only entitled to but is in need of, one member of the cabinet."[45] Indeed, Lincoln was awake and under tremendous pressure from politicians back home about the job he himself coveted. He told David Davis on February 12 he had received 300 letters about the Land Office Commissioner's job. Lincoln felt he could get it for himself, but if he did he would have every man in the state snarling at him about it.[46] On February 20 Lincoln used the same metaphor in a letter to Speed: ". . . there is nothing about me which would authorize me to think of a first class office; and a second class one would not compensate me for being snarled at by others who want it for themselves. I believe that, so far as the Whigs in Congress, are concerned, I could have the Genl. Land office almost by common consent; but then Sweet, and Don: Morrison, and Browning, and Cyrus Edwards all want it. And what is worse, while I think I could easily take it myself, I fear I shall have trouble to get it for any other man in Illinois."[47] At some point in late February it appears he decided to recommend Cyrus Edwards for the job.[48] The other important Illinois Whig, Edward D. Baker, who had resigned his seat in Congress in 1846 to fight in the Mexican War and had become something of a hero, recommended James L. D. Morrison for the post. The stage was set for some classic political jockeying. Lincoln and Baker both had their own candidates for the office but were themselves old friends (Lincoln's second son, Eddie, was named after Baker). It seemed likely they could get together behind either Edwards or Morrison and secure the cabinet post for Illinois.

Lincoln, however, was ambivalent about Edwards because he wanted the job himself—and felt he could have gotten it but for the clamor back home. Then, in late March, a genuine and apparently spontaneously organized group led by William B. Warren began to push Lincoln for the job. Lincoln was now treading on thin ice. He responded to the group that he could accept their nomination for the Land Office if that turned out to be the only way to keep it in Illinois. In the meanwhile he told them he was bound to his commitment to recommend Cyrus Edwards and, that failing, to support Morrison (and conversely, if the Morrison candidacy failed, he indicated that Baker had agreed to support Edwards). "In relation to these pledges," Lincoln told Warren and the others, "I must not only be chaste but above suspicion." But Lincoln then hinted at the real issue, which was that by April he deeply regretted his coyness in February. For it turned out Baker had been eager all along to recommend Lincoln for the post and had turned to Morrison as a second choice. "Baker has at all times been ready to recommend me," Lincoln said, "if I would consent."[49] Lincoln had played the reluctant bride and lost his chance. Now he was trying, ever so delicately, to get it back.

The letter to the Warren group kept his own chances alive in Illinois. Lincoln then quickly turned his attention to the Taylor administration. He wrote William B. Preston, the newly appointed Secretary of the Navy, on April 10, stressing the need for the new administration to pay closer attention to its friends. He agreed with Taylor's refusal to empty out all public officials in true Jacksonian style just because the Whigs had won the election, but he urged strongly that the administration be careful to fill any vacancy that occurred naturally with a Whig.[50] The support of his Whig friends for openings in his district was a task Lincoln was working on as he struggled for his own job. He had written numerous letters of recommendation in the early part of

April regarding various positions in Illinois and seemed to be following the situation closely.[51] As of April 25, all of Lincoln's recommendations were in trouble.[52] His influence in Washington seemed to be "broken down generally."[53] Furthermore, there was an immensely complicated struggle between the two men Lincoln had recommended for one minor office; somehow Lincoln himself was blamed for double-dealing, which made him feel stabbed in the back.[54]

The real worry, however, was further trouble in the Land Office position. For now Justin Butterfield of Chicago had suddenly become the front-runner. Lincoln was astounded. On April 25, he wrote a hurt letter to Josiah Lucas, a clerk in the Land Office in Washington. He noted that Butterfield was a personal friend and perfectly qualified for the job, "but of the quite one hundred Illinoisians, equally well qualified, I do not know one with less claims to it." Butterfield had worked strenuously for Clay and against Taylor; and Butterfield's sponsor, Lisle Smith, was also a Clay man who, despite Lincoln's "most earnest entreaties," had filled vacancies from Lincoln's district at the Whig nominating convention in Philadelphia with Clay supporters. "It will now mortify me deeply," Lincoln concluded self-righteously, "if Gen. Taylor's administration shall trample all my wishes in the dust merely to gratify these men."[55]

Lincoln had abandoned Clay for Taylor; now, oddly, those who had stayed with the Great Compromisor were triumphing over him for position in the government. Lincoln tried desperately during the next few weeks to save the situation. He complained to other cabinet members.[56] He tried to reach those who might have Taylor's ear.[57] He shot off letters to anyone, in fact, whom he thought could head off the Butterfield appointment.[58] He even, finally, wrote President Taylor himself.[59] It was all to no avail. The final irony was that his thirst for the office had become apparent to Cyrus Edwards, who now blamed Lincoln for never really advancing Edwards's own name for the office. Edwards in fact was so angry he threw his weight behind Butterfield. Lincoln, hurt and confused, claimed that Edwards was wronging him very much.[60] In the end, the Taylor administration offered Lincoln a consolation prize, the secretaryship of the Oregon Territory. He refused.[61] The offer was then expanded to be governor. He again refused.[62] He feared the isolation, it seems, and by then his pride was too wounded to take second best. Besides, Mary objected to the Oregon job.[63]

Lincoln's three initiatives as Congressman had all failed. He had never achieved adequate recognition either at home or in Washington for his antiwar position.[64] He had erred in judgment on the slavery bill. And his political work against Clay and for Taylor brought shame without compensation. Furthermore, each of these failed initiatives haunted Lincoln. Stephen Douglas thundered out in the 1858 debates: "Whilst in Congress, he [Lincoln] distinguished himself by his opposition to the Mexican war, taking the side of the common enemy against his own country ([audience:] 'that's true') and when he returned home he found that the indignation of the people followed him everywhere, and he was again submerged or obliged to retire into private life, forgotten by his former friends. ('And will be again')."[65] Lincoln's Congressional stance on slavery later blended into his position after 1854, but the beginning of the charge against him as an abolitionist dated from 1848–49. And, finally, a feeling lingered that Lincoln had stabbed Clay in the back in 1848.[66]

In fact, Lincoln had not really failed in Congress. The scholarly consensus is that he performed reasonably well for a freshman Congressman.[67] But his own sense was one of failure. He was profoundly depressed at his inability to perform up to the level of expectation of his grandiose ambitions. Unless one appreciates how much Lincoln expected of himself, his depression seems odd and misplaced. But it is in these terms—general and psychological rather than narrowly political—that Lincoln's statements to Herndon about committing political suicide in Washington make sense.[68] His expansive ambitions had soared beyond his reach. The perhaps inevitable frustration that resulted left Lincoln feeling empty and depleted. The depression and studied withdrawal from politics after 1849 was not surprising.

In those private years between 1842 and 1854, Lincoln's one important foray into politics and the public world beyond the self was his term in Congress. His sense of failure in that effort must be measured against his absorption in the private concerns of his

These photographs from the 1850s portray different aspects of Lincoln's complex face. As in all the pre-Presidential photographs, they show a beardless Lincoln.

relationship with Mary, raising a family, building his career as a lawyer. It was a decade-long period of consolidation with sights focused intently inward. It seems he tried fleetingly to find a public self too soon. The public issues at that point were only marginally his own. There was no coincidence, no merging, of public and private issues in 1848, only disjunction.

On June 16, 1858, in the sultry heat of the legislative chamber, Abraham Lincoln spoke to the assembled members of the State Republican Convention. That afternoon the convention had nominated him as its candidate for the United States Senate. Lincoln spoke to accept the nomination and to outline his sense of current issues and future agendas.

The speech began with a rhetorical flourish—constituting some 7 percent of its total—that has immortalized the speech in our political history:

> If we could first know *where* we are, and *whither* we are tending, we could then better judge *what* to do, and *how* to do it.
> We are now far into the *fifth* year, since a policy was initiated, with the *avowed* object, and *confident* promise, of putting an end to slavery agitation.
> Under the operation of that policy, that agitation has not only, *not ceased*, but has *constantly augmented*.
> In *my* opinion, it *will* not cease, until a *crisis* shall have been reached, and passed.
> "A house divided against itself cannot stand."
> I believe this government cannot endure, permanently half *slave* and half *free*.
> I do not expect the Union to be *dissolved*—I do not expect the house to *fall*—but I *do* expect it will cease to be divided.
> It will become *all* one thing, or *all* the other.
> Either the *opponents* of slavery, will arrest the further spread of it, and place it where the public mind shall rest in the belief that it is in course of ultimate extinction; or its *advocates* will push it forward, till it shall become alike lawful in *all* the States, *old* as well as *new*—*North* as well as *South*.[69]

The phraseology captured people's imagination immediately. The local Republican paper loudly voiced its approval while Stephen Douglas (Lincoln's opponent in the senatorial race), the Democrats, and their local Springfield organ bemoaned Lincoln's radical message that seemed to call for war (that at least was how they chose to interpret the speech). Because of Lincoln's increasing national prominence and the stature of his opponent in this election, the house divided speech received extensive coverage. From New York and Massachusetts to Illinois and the western territories the evocative idea of a house divided against itself as a metaphor for the divisive ills of the nation struck a responsive political and religious chord.

In William Herndon's analysis the apparently incendiary flavor of Lincoln's rhetoric in this speech later fused with the myth of the martyr. Herndon reports that Lincoln read him the speech a few days before delivery. Herndon was aghast at the tone of the opening salvo and wondered whether it would be politic to take such a radical stance. "I want to use some universally known figure [of speech]," Lincoln supposedly replied, "expressed in simple language as universally well-known, that may strike home to the minds of men in order to raise them up to the peril of the times. I do not believe I would be right in changing or omitting it, I would rather be defeated with this expression in the speech, and uphold and discuss it before the people, than be victorious without it."[70] If his exaggerated and quite un-Lincolnesque response to Herndon seems distorted—the historian Don Fehrenbacher has noted that Herndon describes Lincoln here "as a man wrapped in passion like a Hebrew prophet"[71]—there is no reason to doubt that Lincoln stuck to his bold phrasing despite his partner's qualms. Since Lincoln then went on to lose the election in 1858 to Stephen Douglas but to win the Presidency in 1860, many historians have concluded that Lincoln intended such a scenario to unfold.[72]

The question here of Lincoln's motivation is central. Anyone who studies Lincoln's political activities in 1858 will conclude that he was concentrating all of his attention on his election to the Senate. Furthermore, even if Lincoln was thinking of the Presidency in 1858, no one as shrewd as Lincoln would plan to lose in the Senate in his home state as a way of securing his party's Presidential nomination two years later. The most recent discussion of the house divided speech examines its immediate Springfield context by a careful reading of the two local papers, one Republican, one Democratic, one strongly for Lincoln, the other just as strongly for Douglas.[73] This approach to the speech clarifies Lincoln's response to the incredibly complicated political situation that confronted him in the winter of 1858. For Douglas had effectively captured the support of large numbers of Republicans by opposing President Buchanan and the spuriously generated Lecompton Constitution for Kansas. Douglas, it seemed to loyal Republicans, had opposed political chicanery, given teeth to his doctrine of popular sovereignty, and supported the free soilers who made up the backbone of the Republican ranks. Better half a loaf than none at all, argued Republicans like the influential Horace Greeley. Popular sovereignty was perhaps not an inadequate ideological foundation for Republicanism, but it seemed in the early months of 1858 that Douglas would support free soilers in the North, would be a vigorous supporter of railroads and the economic development of the country generally, and would agree to key Republican demands in return for their support in his future bid for the Presidency. At the very least, argued the eastern leaders of the Republican party, Douglas was useful in the Senate because of his strong opposition to President Buchanan. That kept the Democrats divided, which served Republican interests. Lincoln should not be encouraged.

Lincoln watched Republicans make these accommodations to the Douglas Democrats with growing alarm. For if Lincoln believed in anything by 1858, it was that Stephen Douglas was the principal spokesman for a disastrous set of policies in dealing with the issues that the country faced. The founders, in Lincoln's view, had reluctantly accepted slavery as a southern institution. They recognized its existence and even validated its perpetuation with the three-fifths compromise. Such constitutional protection justified federal laws governing the return of fugitive slaves for over half a century. It was thus illegal and unconstitutional to talk of abolition and the mobilization of a national effort to end the South's peculiar institution. Lincoln hated the realities of tracking down fugitive slaves but reluctantly accepted the practice. He told Joshua Speed in 1855: "I also acknowledge *your* rights and *my* obligations, under the Constitution, in regard to your slaves. I confess I hate to see the poor creatures hunted down, and caught, and carried back to their stripes, and unrewarded toils; but I bite my lip and keep quiet."[74]

Nevertheless, Lincoln believed that the Constitutional recognition of slavery in the South by no means meant that the founders approved of an institution that excluded a whole race from the benefits of the principles outlined in the Declaration of Independence. The only way the founders had to secure passage of the Constitution was to allow slavery to exist. But just as God defines ethical perfection, Lincoln continued, so the Constitution sets up a standard for legal action. "If we cannot give freedom to every creature," Lincoln argued in the summer of 1858, "let us do nothing that will impose slavery upon any other creature."[75] Slavery, Lincoln stated again and again in the 1850s was morally wrong, a "monstrous injustice" as he called it in 1854.[76] "I have always hated slavery," he proclaimed in 1858, "I think as much as any Abolitionist."[77] Furthermore, this powerfully negative judgment of slavery, he argued, lay behind most of the founders' thinking when they accepted the three-fifths compromise. It took one hundred years of agitation, Lincoln once noted, to abolish the slave trade in Great Britain.[78] Men like Thomas Jefferson and George Washington were tied to slavery economically but were politically and morally opposed to it. Life as they knew it in the South seemed inconceivable without slaves, but all hoped for a better day when slaves could be freed and returned to Africa, and the ideals of life, liberty, and the pursuit of happiness genuinely engaged. Lincoln of course recognized the inconsistencies in this position but accepted the muddle as all too human. His great hero was Henry Clay, who could eloquently criticize those who would blow out the moral lights around us while sipping a mint julep served by a black house slave.

Thus, the heart of Lincoln's opposition to slavery was moral and Constitutional. The people of the South, he said, have an "immediate and palpable and immensely great pecuniary interest" in their institution, but for those in the North "it is merely an abstract question of moral right, with only *slight,* and *remote* pecuniary interest added."[79] However, the "abstract" issue for

Lincoln was not as far removed from political reality as the term might suggest. "When the white man governs himself that is self-government; but when he governs himself, and also governs *another* man, that is *more* than self-government—that is despotism."[80] The moral issue was abstract only in that the Declaration of Independence defined a standard of equality that did not explicitly include the Negroes. The founding documents defined republican institutions and established the criteria for assessing the ethics of political action in modern society. The documents, however, were complex, varied, contradictory—and human. Thus Lincoln argued vehemently after 1854 in favor of the abolitionists to the extent that they opposed the extension of slavery while he also argued for the return of fugitive slaves. "Stand with anybody that stands RIGHT," he thundered. "Stand with him while he is right and PART with him when he goes wrong. Stand WITH the abolitionist in restoring the Missouri Compromise; and stand against him when he attempts to repeal the fugitive slave law."[81]

Lincoln also had strong economic views on the poisonous effect of slavery on white workers. "As I would not be a slave," he wrote, "so I would not be a master. This expresses my idea of democracy."[82] In general, Lincoln was a decided economic optimist. When he wrote about inventions or technological progress, he became almost boyish in his buoyant, hopeful, assertive enthusiasm. "All creation is a mine," he began his first lecture on discoveries and inventions, "and every man a miner." Lincoln went on to stress the uniqueness of man, who may work like animals but, unlike them, improves on his workmanship.[83] Lincoln's view of technology was clearly optimistic; it was also somewhat naive. He seemed to accept unquestionably that technological progress carried with it moral improvement. And that is the link to slavery. The slave was kept apart from the just rewards for his labor; that degraded him and his master and perverted democratic institutions. Our republican form of government as defined by the Constitution required free labor, which in turn brought opportunity, progress, hope. Slavery dashed all to the ground.[84]

Yet the evil of slavery went along, in Lincoln's thought, with a mournful sense of racial inequality between white and black.[85]

For there is no denying that at this point in his life Lincoln was convinced blacks were inferior and did not deserve social or political equality with whites. He made that point often, though most vociferously at Charleston in 1858: "... I am not, nor ever have been in favor of bringing about in any way the social and political equality of the white and black races." Lincoln would not make voters or jurors of blacks, nor qualify them to hold office, nor allow them to intermarry with whites. He believed that the physical differences of the races would always keep them from living together on equal terms and that whites would always be superior. Just because he did not want a Negro woman to be his slave did not mean he wanted her for a wife; he could just leave her alone.[86]

These are not pleasant statements. As the historian Kenneth M. Stampp has recently put it, Lincoln's speech at Charleston represents Lincoln's "fullest and most explicit declaration of belief in white supremacy."[87] Charleston, however, was not an isolated event in Lincoln's struggle with the issue of racial equality. Clearly, before that audience which leaned South in sentiment, Lincoln was rather more explicit in stating his white supremacist views. It has been frequently noted that Lincoln altered his emphasis on these matters, depending on which part of the state he found himself in; indeed, during the debates Stephen Douglas himself charged Lincoln with inconsistency on exactly this issue. But it would be naive to ignore the essential racism that informed Lincoln's thought wherever he spoke. In Peoria in 1854 he frankly acknowledged that his own feelings would not allow him to entertain the notion of political and social equality between the races. And, he added as a shrewd politician, "if mine would, we well know that those of the great mass of white people will not."[88] Even in Chicago, Lincoln stressed the numerous categories of inequality between white and black in the same breath that he claimed minimal rights of life, liberty, and the pursuit of happiness for Negroes in America.[89] The Declaration of Independence, Lincoln noted in Springfield in 1857, never intended to assert that all men are equal in all respects. Such a notion is patently absurd in any event. The Declaration simply defined basic rights and clarified a "standard maxim for free society" that, although never attained, could be admired, striven for, and perhaps in time, approximated.[90]

The fact that Lincoln held back from the notion of full equality for blacks does not necessarily cast doubt on the sincerity of his insistence that they be granted minimal rights under the Constitution. For example, when Lincoln argued that the Declaration of Independence defined a standard maxim for free society, he was nudging his fellow citizens toward giving rights to blacks that they did not then possess. In the 1850s such an assertion had abolitionist overtones, which was the label that would most harm Lincoln politically (and the one Stephen Douglas was most eager to pin on him). Lincoln made tortuous, indeed specious, distinctions after 1854, but he no longer thought of blacks as objects. They were people, albeit inferior in some odd and almost incomprehensible way. Our sensibilities tend to emphasize the prejudices that remained in the man we generally admire as a paragon of American virtue. But in the 1850s white supremacy was taken for granted; what was remarkable was that Lincoln had the courage to brand slavery wrong, oppose its extension into the territories on moral and political grounds, and risk association with abolitionism. Nevertheless, as Frederick Douglass pointed out, Lincoln was always devoted entirely to the welfare of whites. He was willing to postpone, deny, or sacrifice the rights of blacks. He came to the Presidency opposed only to the spread of slavery. His patriotic dreams embraced only whites. He supported the Fugitive Slave Law and would have eagerly suppressed any uprising. Whites were his natural children; blacks were his only by adoption.[91]

It was not easy for Lincoln to resolve his genuine and growing hatred of slavery with his white supremacist views. Furthermore, to abolish slavery was not only unconstitutional but also impractical, for what would happen to the slaves? They would become unequal members of a society in which they could never fully participate. "If all earthly power were given me," he said in 1854, "I should not know what to do, as to the existing institution. My first impulse would be to free all the slaves, and send them to Liberia—to their own native land."[92] Lincoln saw acutely that colonization of blacks would be expensive, dangerous, and time-consuming, but he also felt it might be the only viable solution. There seemed to be only two alternatives: free the slaves and keep them in America as "underlings" or make them fully equal. Both alternatives seemed to him impossible from a white perspective.[93] And so he toyed for years with colonization schemes, as absurd and offensive in retrospect as they seemed sensible and humane at the time. In 1852 he eulogized Clay's efforts since 1816 to return blacks to Africa: "May it indeed be realized! . . . If as the friends of colonization hope, the present and coming generations of our countrymen shall by any means, succeed in freeing our land from the dangerous presence of slavery; and, at the same time, in restoring a captive people to their long-lost father-land, with bright prospects for the future; and this too, so gradually that neither races nor individuals shall have suffered by the change, it will indeed be a glorious consummation."[94] Lincoln himself was an active member of Springfield's Colonization Society, to which he spoke on January 4, 1855.[95] When Lincoln talked of the "ultimate extinction" of slavery in the house divided speech, he may have had colonization in the back of his mind.[96]

The confusions, contradictions, and specious distinctions built into Lincoln's thought about the interrelated issues of slavery and racial equality in the 1850s reflected the fact that his primary concern lay elsewhere—with the preservation of the Union. For the political issue in the slavery question was not abolition but extension. And on that question Lincoln saw the country hurtling toward civil war. The Constitution was vague in what it intended to happen regarding slavery in newly acquired territories. A sensibly worked out compromise in 1820 had seemed to settle the matter forever. However, the huge acquisitions from Mexico after 1848, and renewed tensions between North and South on a variety of other fronts, fatefully reopened the whole issue of slavery's spread. After much agony and near war, a second compromise was tried in 1850. It seemed secure at first but quickly fell apart under pressure from the man most responsible for putting it together—Stephen Douglas. Douglas was an opportunist, inordinately ambitious, and very interested in the railroads. As chairman of the Senate Committee on the Territories he wanted to push through a bill in 1854 that would quickly organize Kansas and Nebraska. Effective state government would then make possible the construction of a transcontinental railroad. In one blow Douglas hoped to solve the most vexing political issue of the day and, of course, assume leadership of the country for his labors.

The key, he felt, lay in allowing the states to decide for themselves whether they would be free or slave. To justify this sidestepping of the issue of slavery, Douglas invoked the concept of popular sovereignty. For Douglas, popular sovereignty was a convenient and perfectly legitimate evasion of the moral passions that inflamed the debate over slavery. He personally did not care whether slavery was voted up or down. Let the people decide. For Lincoln, however, popular sovereignty was a grossly inappropriate concept for dealing with the question of slavery in the territories. The founders, he felt, never intended to allow slavery to extend beyond its original location in the states of the South. If left alone, it would in time whither away. But slavery must not be given a new lease on life in the territories. Thus the democratic principle of local self-government in the territories had to give way to the larger concern for legitimate government and the principles of the Declaration of Independence.

Lincoln knew immediately in 1854 that the issue of slavery's extension and its threat to the Union was his issue, one he could creatively engage and wrestle to the ground. His eloquent speech in Peoria that fall attests to his grasp of the deepest implications of the passage of the Kansas-Nebraska Act. And yet in formulating his position he struggled several years for an appropriate metaphor; until he found it, a certain groping, even indecision and confusion, characterized his thinking.

At first he tried two oddly inappropriate metaphors. In the Peoria speech Lincoln strove to explain why the founders were so circumspect in their treatment of slavery. He noted they had to strike a compromise and so included both recognition of and protection for slavery; but they did so reluctantly. The Constitution, Lincoln pointed out, never once actually used the word "slave." Instead, the slave is spoken of as a "person held to service or labor." Similarly, the African slave trade is described as "The migration or importation of such persons as any of the States NOW EXISTING, shall think proper to admit." And Lincoln continued: "Thus, the thing is hid away in the constitution, just as an afflicted man hides away a wen [tumor or cyst] or a cancer, which he dares not cut out at once, lest he bleed to death; with the promise, nevertheless, that the cutting may begin at the end of a given time."[97] Lincoln here captured the defacement of slavery in the body politic but failed to enlarge on cancer's striking capacity to spread. The metaphor thus lost its most expressive and vital element.

He also stumbled around in the Peoria speech with animal imagery that linked slaves to hogs. "Equal justice to the south, it is said, requires us to consent to the extending of slavery to new countries. That is to say, inasmuch as you do not object to my taking my hog to Nebraska, therefore I must not object to you taking your slave. Now, I admit this is perfectly logical, if there is no difference between hogs and negroes."[98] In this passage Lincoln made the connection between slaves and hogs in order to then refute it. He followed the metaphor with a curious reference to the "snaky" contact with detested slave dealers.[99] Elsewhere as well in 1854 animal metaphors pervaded his thinking. "The ant," Lincoln wrote in July, "who has toiled and dragged a crumb to his nest, will furiously defend the fruit of his labor, against whatever robber assails him. So plain, that the most dumb and stupid slave that ever toiled for a master, does constantly *know* he is wronged."[100] The economic meanings of this comparison are readily apparent. But the metaphor also suggests that the slave is a kind of lowly animal who deserves at least the few crumbs it can drag to the nest.

The rhetorical difficulty Lincoln faced was to express the meaning of the spread of slavery. That was the issue. In an editorial he wrote on September 11 for the *Journal* ("his" paper in Springfield) he again turned to animal imagery when he told a little parable:

Abraham Lincoln has a fine meadow, containing beautiful springs of water, and well fenced, which John Calhoun had agreed with Abraham (originally owning the land in common) should be his, and the agreement had been consummated in the most solemn manner, regarded by both as sacred. John Calhoun, however, in the course of time, had become owner of an extensive herd of cattle—the prairie grass had become dried up and there was no convenient water to be had. John Calhoun then looks with a longing eye on Lincoln's meadow, and goes to it and throws down the fences, and exposes it to the ravages of his starving and famishing cattle. 'You rascal', says Lincoln, 'what have you done? what do you do this for?' 'Oh,' replies Calhoun, 'everything is right. I have taken down your fence; but nothing more. It is my true intent and meaning not to drive my cattle into your meadow, nor to exclude them therefrom, but to leave them perfectly free to form their own notions of the feed, and to direct their movements in their own way!'[101]

This story ostensibly strives to brand southern whites as beastly schemers. But it conveys that message by describing slaves as dumb, ravaging cattle set loose in a green meadow. The bountiful North is invaded by rapacious blacks let loose by scheming whites.[102]

These agricultural metaphors and animal images built logically on Lincoln's earliest experience on the frontier. In many respects his idiom remained agricultural. He talked of turkeys to express his deepest childhood memories. He joked endlessly about dogs, pigs, cows, and other beasts. His letters abound in references to the wild kingdom. When he was exhausted, Herndon said, Lincoln liked to lie down on the floor and "play with a little dog or kitten to recover."[103] James Gourley, a neighbor, noted that Lincoln tended his own cow and "loved his horse well."[104] And in a sense the once shaded but then despoiled trees of the Lyceum speech in 1838 became the timbers of the house divided twenty years later. It seems he often expressed the deepest and most complex meanings in the metaphors of his rural youth. Slavery's extension, however, was not an issue he could capture in these familiar ways. It was too immediate. His profound sense of the nation's dilemma required a different metaphor.

After 1854 he sought a "right" formulation. He found it, gradually, in architectural imagery that likened the Union to a home, a house divided. The Biblical context of the house divided doctrine (Matthew 12:22–28; Mark 3:22–26; Luke 11:14–20) is curious. In Matthew, Jesus has just healed "one possessed with a devil, blind, and dumb." The people are amazed but the Pharisees suspect Satanic magic. Jesus, knowing their thoughts, says to them, "Every kingdom divided against itself is brought to desolation; and every city or house divided against itself shall not stand." If Satan casts out Satan, Jesus continues, he is then divided against himself; his kingdom cannot stand. Jesus then asks the Pharisees rhetorically, if he casts out demons by the Devil's power by whom do their sons cast them out? Jesus concludes: "But I cast out devils by the Spirit of God, then the kingdom of God is come unto you." Jesus' emphasis is on the source for healing; he wants to prove that his power to heal comes from the spirit of God. If from Satan, it is magical, disruptive, divisive. It turns the people against God's truth. If Satan casts out Satan, as Jesus puts it, he is divided against himself and therefore without power. The power of God alone must cast out demons.

The idea of a house divided, in its initial formulation, is a metaphor expressing the complex sources of motivation. Jesus' concerns went beyond simple healing. That proved nothing. What he sought to show the priests was that if God prompted his actions his kingdom was upon them. If Satan were at work, the kingdom of God would be hopelessly rent asunder. That, he says, would be disastrous, for it would pit Satan against Satan, evil against itself, man against man. No kingdom can endure such tension; no house divided can stand. The message is intensely subjective and psychologically astute. It also takes for granted that a house divided against itself cannot stand and uses that image to clarify the problem of Jesus' healing power.

Once early in his career Lincoln drew on the house divided metaphor. It was in a Whig campaign circular of 1843 that argued, among other things, for the convention system to be adopted. Whigs generally had been outpaced by the Democrats because of their reluctance to use conventions, relying instead on selection by the state legislators or by local county convention. Lincoln clearly felt his party needed to adopt the system of statewide nominating conventions to compete effectively against the Democrats, and he dwelt specifically on the last state election (1842) in his argument. Lincoln proclaimed,

Wherever in the counties the whigs had held Conventions and nominated candidates for the Legislature, the aspirants, who were not nominated, were induced to rebel against the nominations, and to become candidates, as is said, "on their own hook." And go where you would into a large whig county, you were sure to find the whigs, not contending shoulder to shoulder against the common enemy, but divided into factions, and fighting furiously with one another. The election came [and] what was the result? The Governor beaten, the whig vote being decreased many thousands since 1840, although the democratic vote had not increased any.

Thus he concluded "union is strength" and "he whose wisdom surpasses that of all philosophers, has declared that 'a house divided against itself cannot stand.' "[105]

Lincoln probably suspected that this use of Jesus' words trivialized their meaning. In any event he never again used the metaphor until 1858. During that time it had become a familiar expression through Daniel Webster's frequent use of it. It was a recognizable phrase for Lincoln to seize upon and imbue with a new meaning.[106] He once came close to using it in an 1855 letter to George Robertson, whose collection of speeches Lincoln was praising. The letter was grimly pessimistic. Lincoln noted that, like Robertson, he had long hoped for a peaceful end to slavery. But unfortunately the last thirty-six years had demonstrated that "there is no peaceful extinction of slavery in prospect for us." Henry Clay had failed miserably. The spirit of peaceful extinction apparently died along with the men of the Revolution. Colonization, he hinted, was no answer, for slave masters will never willingly give up their slaves. "Our political problem now is, 'Can we, as a nation, continue together *permanently—forever—* half slave, and half free?' The problem is too mighty for me. May God, in his mercy, superintend the solution."[107]

At last in 1858 Lincoln found his metaphor. He left behind the wens, cancers, hogs, cows, and horses and turned instead to the notion of a house divided. This was what he had sought. It blended his private self to public concerns in a uniquely creative way. It was a metaphor with personal integrity.

Chapter 8

The Group Self and the Crisis of the 1850s

We can not absolutely *know* that all these exact adaptations
are the result of preconcert.

A. LINCOLN
June 16, 1858

HERE were two distinct parts to the house divided speech. The opening flourish built psychologically on Lincoln's own experiences, feelings, and needs. His rhetorical domestication of
politics nicely expressed his own deepest concerns and could be grasped clearly by a country
dangerously close to civil war. But the heart of the speech—some
72 percent of the text—outlined a remarkable southern conspiracy to nationalize slavery.[1] Lincoln developed his theory in the
context of a brief history of recent events, which if examined dis-
passionately, he argued, showed clear "evidences of design" and
"concert of action." Lincoln felt the conspiracy was hatched
early, for the "first point gained" was the Kansas-Nebraska Bill of
1854, which had opened up the territories to slavery on the spurious grounds of popular sovereignty. Then in 1856 came the elec-

[182]

tion of President Buchanan, a weak but decidedly prosouthern Democrat. Thus was the second point gained. The third and final point came immediately following Buchanan's inauguration when the Supreme Court announced its decision on the Dred Scott case. In this decision the "machinery" of the conspiracy reached full operating condition. It declared that no black slave or his descendant could *ever* become a citizen; that neither Congress nor a territorial legislature could exclude slavery from any territory; and that it was up to the separate slave states to deal with whether a slave was made free by passing into free states. In theory, at least, this part of the decision virtually endorsed southern kidnapping of free Northern blacks.

"Several things will *now* appear less *dark* and *mysterious*," Lincoln commented, "than they did *when* they were transpiring," And he continued:

We can not absolutely *know* that all these exact adaptations are the result of preconcert. But when we see a lot of framed timbers, different portions of which we know have been gotten out at different times and places and by different workmen—Stephen [Douglas], Franklin [Pierce], Roger [Taney] and James [Buchanan] for instance—and when we see these timbers joined together, and see they exactly make the frame of a house or a mill, all the tenons and mortices exactly fitting, and all the lengths and proportions of the different pieces exactly adapted to their respective places, and not a piece too many or too few—not omitting even scaffolding—or, if a single piece be lacking, we can see the place in the frame exactly fitted and prepared to yet bring such piece in—in *such* a case, we find it impossible to not *believe* that Stephen and Franklin and Roger and James all understood one another from the beginning, and all worked upon a common *plan* or *draft* drawn up before the first lick was struck.

Lincoln's interpretation of events dramatically shifted the attention from Kansas and the other territories to Illinois and the free states of the North. We may go to sleep pleasantly in the belief that Missouri will be voted free, Lincoln argued, but "we shall *awake* to the *reality*, instead, that the *Supreme* Court has made *Illinois* a *slave* state." And as if that were not enough, Lincoln further argued that the country could also look forward to the reopening of the slave trade with Africa. If it is a sacred right of white men to own slaves, then how can it be less a sacred right to buy them where they can be bought cheapest? That clearly was Africa rather than Virginia.

The conspiracy argument of the speech clarifies significantly the force of the opening flourish. The house in Lincoln's view will not endure divided. Either slavery will be nationalized and our free institutions will crumble or the North will arrest the spread of slavery and put it on a course of ultimate extinction. Many observers immediately saw in this stark vision a call for war to end slavery. To see the inevitable so clearly appeared to hurry it along. Thus Charles Lanphier, editor of Springfield's *Register* (a Democratic paper), lambasted Lincoln for his bellicosity.[2]

Lincoln, however, neither retreated from his conspiracy theory nor relinquished it easily. He was irritated that Douglas chose largely to ignore the charge.[3] Lincoln returned to conspiracy throughout the debates with Douglas in the late summer and fall of 1858.[4] As late as September 16, 1859, Lincoln told an audience in Columbus, Ohio, that the Republican party must stand firm against the conspiracy to revive the African slave trade, pass a congressional slave code, and push through an extension of Dred Scott that would explicitly make slavery legal throughout the United States. These developments are not immediately upon us, Lincoln noted. But beware: "They are not quite ready yet. The authors of these measures know that we are too strong for them; but they will be upon us in due time, and we will be grappling with them hand to hand, if they are not now headed off."[5] And as late as June 12, 1863, he wrote: "The insurgents had been preparing for it [the war] more than thirty years, while the Government had taken no steps to resist them."[6]

It is dramatically obvious in retrospect how wrong Lincoln was in his conspiracy theory.[7] For as *he* formulated it, the conspiracy went well beyond the schemes of southern fanatics. The leaders in Lincoln's view were the pre-eminent political figures of the day: President of the United States James Buchanan, Chief of the Supreme Court Roger B. Taney, and, of course, Stephen Douglas. Since Douglas was generally acknowledged as the most important Democratic Senator, Lincoln's sense of the conspirators' base of operations included nothing short of all three branches of government: executive, judicial, and legislative. There appears to have been some collusion between Buchanan and Taney over the Dred Scott case, but beyond that it is most unlikely there was an elaborate conspiracy among Douglas, Buchanan, and Taney that was hatched in 1854, developed in 1856, and matured in 1857. For one thing, Buchanan and Douglas hated each other. Douglas expected to receive a prized position in the Buchanan administration but was instead unaccountably snubbed and isolated entirely from any position of influence. Douglas then opposed Buchanan on the Lecompton Constitution, and Buchanan retaliated by trying to remove Douglas's patronage base in Illinois. This political battle preoccupied the state in the months before Lincoln delivered his house divided speech. There is also only meager evidence of radical southerners calling for a revival of the slave trade; it is hard to imagine the leaders of the three branches of government actually planning such an act. Nor was a national slave code envisioned by serious politicians. There had been enough trouble with the Fugitive Slave Law, which was a part of the Compromise of 1850. Lincoln had not only lost perspective but also grossly misinterpreted the drift of politics.

Lincoln's misperception of events in 1858 seems paranoid. Why he responded to the rush of events with such miscalculated fervor is perplexing. It is quite possible he was simply seizing the public's mood and giving it voice. Certainly, he was a reasonable man. There is little in his early development that even hints at paranoia. He was then—and later—noted for his generosity toward his enemies, his warmth and understanding. It is clear he sensed the crisis and made it his own. He articulated its latent meanings as few others could. He gave it shape if not direction. The fact is that paranoia pervaded people's minds. Lincoln responded empathetically to their deepest fears. "He knew the American people better than they knew themselves," said Frederick Douglass.[8]

Lincoln's apparent paranoia fed on and reflected a widespread, indeed rampant, paranoia throughout the land. His opponent in the Senate race, Stephen Douglas, returned Lincoln's charges with his own, rather more deviously conceived, exaggeration of the implications of Lincoln's program for the country. During the debates Douglas exhorted his listeners to vote for Lincoln, "If you desire negro citizenship, if you desire to allow them to come into the State and settle with the white man, if you desire them to vote on an equality with yourselves, and to make them eligible to office, to serve on juries, and to adjudge your rights, then support Mr. Lincoln and the Black Republican party, who are in favor of the citizenship of the negro."[9] Lincoln repeatedly tried to answer Douglas by pointing out that he was neither an amalgamationist (in favor of bringing the races fully together) nor an abolitionist; that just because he wanted to grant a Negro woman her legitimate rights did not mean he wanted to marry her; and that his moral opposition to slavery in no way represented an abolitionist desire to forcibly free the slaves.[10] It is hard to believe Douglas was not aware of these distinctions, but then it is equally difficult to understand the meanings of Lincoln's conspiracy theory, which put Douglas at the center of a malevolent plot to nationalize slavery.

Politics in America breeds competition, suspicion, and overstatement. Individuals of roughly comparable ability and party backing struggle against each other for elected office. At stake are their own fortunes and those of their parties as well as those of the literally thousands of hangers-on who expect to benefit from victory. In America the political system as it evolved in the Jacksonian era put unusual stress on the competitive personal aspects of vying for elective office. A long tradition of virulence legitimated the most outrageous charges and counter-charges. In the fiercely contested electin of 1828, for example, Andrew Jackson was called the son of a prostitute and a Negro, a usurper, a gambler, a cockfighter, a brawler, a drunkard, an illiterate, and a person unfit for high office. His wife, furthermore, was called an adulteress. John Quincy Adams, it seems, was a panderer, who had bought the Presidency, was opposed to American institutions, and had grossly misspent public funds during his administration. Even Henry Clay was not spared. He was described as a traitor who had instigated the assassination of William Morgan to prevent the exposure of freemasonry. If 1828 is an extreme example, it is not an unrepresentative one. At all levels of government this attacking, competitive style prevailed. And the people loved it. Speeches, parades, kegs of whiskey—all helped stir partisan feeling. People endured two-hour-long speeches as the norm and then read a fiercely loyal summary and analysis of the speech in their violently partisan paper of choice the next day. It was the kind of environment that encouraged political battles and forced extreme positions on otherwise mild men. Something in American politics pushed opponents to their limits.

Until the 1850s, however, the dominant theme in this process was the coarseness of the attack, which seemed to be prompted less by paranoia than by the burning desire to win. As head of the New York Regency, for example, Martin Van Buren was a decidedly unlovely figure in the 1820s and 1830s, but he was not paranoid. Something new appeared on the scene in the 1850s. The dark shadow of paranoia that has always lurked on the fringes of American politics and culture came to block out the sun entirely. Suspiciousness reached extreme proportions. A basically conservative man such as Lincoln shuddered in terror at an imagined conspiracy to nationalize slavery. A less attractive but impressively shrewd politician such as Douglas became increasingly brittle and vulnerable. He may or may not have believed all that he attributed to Lincoln in 1858, but he certainly felt legitimately hounded by President Buchanan in their fight over control of the Democratic party after 1857.[11] Douglas also came under mounting pressure from the southern wing of the party, which wanted no compromise on anything relating to slavery. Furthermore, what Lincoln and Douglas experienced and felt was repeated in a host of leaders throughout the country. A man such as William Seward, who had resisted compromise in 1850, came to see the inevitability of open conflict to resolve the issue of slavery. Seward, interestingly enough, felt almost as strongly against nativism— the powerful movement that affirmed old ideals of the nation and vigorously opposed the recent immigration from Europe. It has been suggested that Seward lost out to Lincoln in the Republican Convention of 1860 because he (Seward) had offended nativists over the years.[12]

The case of the abolitionists is a fascinating example of the changes in politics and culture from the 1830s to the 1850s. Abolitionists had long reacted with moral outrage and a mounting

sense of frustration to the continued existence of slavery. In the
1830s, when the movement began, a strong religious fervor encouraged abolitionists to commit themselves to a variety of reform movements (especially temperance) and remain peaceful,
even pacifistic, in their means. As Lawrence Friedman has per-
suasively argued, however, the degree of genuine pacifism that
infused the abolitionists of the 1830s is open to some question.[13]
The basic issue the abolitionists failed to grapple with was
whether violence was acceptable if used defensively. All agreed
the goal was political reform through moral persuasion. The
problem, however, was that few considered how to react to violence if directed at themselves. They soon discovered that this
question of whether defensively employed violence was conso-
nant with their moral and religious beliefs was the central dilemma they faced. Thus Elijah Lovejoy, an abolitionist editor in
Alton, Illinois, saw two printing presses destroyed. On the day of
arrival of his third press he and a group of followers were huddled
inside the warehouse with guns to ward off attackers. Lovejoy
himself, though he never fired a gun, died with a bullet through
his heart in the melee that followed.

The reaction to Lovejoy's death provides an interesting litmus
test of how genuinely pacifistic the abolitionist movement was in
the 1830s. Most abolitionists never really questioned the propriety of Lovejoy's willingness to counter violence with violence.
The issue for them was the brutality of the scene, the evils of
slavery, the devastating power of the mob. Only Sarah Grimké
and a handful of other abolitionists strongly objected to Lovejoy's
decision to defend himself. Lovejoy, she felt, had seriously compromised the moral integrity of the reform movement by his willingness to defend the press with his guns.

In the 1830s this debate was remote from the political main-
stream. However, the easy accommodation to defensive use of
violence was to have fateful consequences for the abolitionists.
When they lost their firm commitment to pacifism, in a sense
they lost their moral innocence. Pacificism was clearly desirable,
but the overriding concern was the end of slavery. And that goal
became increasingly elusive for the abolitionists. They watched
with growing alarm as the political power of the white-led South,

based in slavery, seemed to grow stronger over the years. Moral reform had backfired. Southern power was spreading everywhere and its bellicosity growing more shrill every day. The abolitionists felt a mounting sense of suspiciousness, disorientation, frustration, and anger from 1848 on, which resulted in a loss of cohesion within their movement that rapidly affected the means they felt were appropriate and necessary to end slavery. Tactics were reconsidered. The old moral pacifism gave way to an accommodation to violence as the only way to end the curse of slavery. John Brown's attack on some proslavery settlers in 1856 thus helped reshape attitudes and prepare the ground for his attempted raid on Harper's Ferry in 1859. The articulate black leader, Frederick Douglass, had been informed by Brown of the raid on Harper's Ferry (though Douglass warned against the plan), and abolitionist William Lloyd Garrison applauded Brown's courage and commitment.

The interesting thing about the example of the abolitionists is that it illustrates how extreme suspiciousness can effectively undermine firmly held beliefs and even passionately valued moral codes. It is said that when the firing on Fort Sumter—and therefore the start of the war—was announced in the Senate a woman cheered lustily from the balcony; she was an abolitionist and for her only war could mean the end of slavery.[14] For the spiritual children of Lyman Beecher it was a long way from their 1830s program of moral reform through committed pacifism. Mounting frustration had fed abolitionists' fears of southern power, making them increasingly combative and eventually violent. The more the abolitionists felt out of control (especially after 1848), the more they were filled with rage.

Freud first noted how psychological symptoms often spread. Thus obsessions that begin in a relatively circumscribed form usually become a way of thinking. The Rat Man, for example, first feared that the rat punishment described by the sadistic Captain Nowak would be imposed on his father and the Rat Man's friend, Gisela. But the devastating fears he experienced in connection with rats spread to all facets of his life, and his obsessional rituals to ward off danger had to increase proportionately. In the transference, Freud arrested the spread and focused the fears, anxieties, and conflicts on himself.[15] The same spreading phenomenon is true for phobias and can be true for hysterics (for example, Anna O.).[16] The point is that the underlying conflict, once expressed in a specific form of symptomatology, will invent new variations on the same theme if for some reason the conflict itself is exacerbated. This notion of spreading symptomatology has relevance for an attempt to grasp the underlying issues of the 1850s in what might be called the group self. We must, however, make something of a translation from classical psychoanalysis to self psychology. For it is not the relationship between conflict and symptom that concerns us but the meaning of the fragmentation of experience of the group self. As individual members of small, defined groups—abolitionists, Irish immigrants in Boston, southern white aristocrats—experience intense feelings of suspiciousness, competitiveness, rage, and envy, the effects of a larger group fragmentation anxiety become evident. Nor does this issue have to be as complicated as it seems. As all of us undoubtedly know, fear and hatred feed on themselves, swallowing up dissenters in any community. A smart, empathic leader, such as Churchill, knows how to arrest the spread of such fear; an equally smart and empathic leader, but one with different motives, such as Hitler, knows how to foster spreading fear and hatred in the group self.

The suspiciousness of the 1850s in America was indeed widespread. The transformation of the abolitionist movement in the process of its accommodation to violence refracted the image of southern white bellicosity and increasing preparedness for war, for southerners also felt they were under attack. They saw abolitionists crusading against the essence of their way of life, spurring slave revolts, and poisoning minds everywhere. "The antebellum South," Kenneth M. Stampp has recently noted, "was a land troubled by a nagging dread of slave insurrections; indeed, it is impossible to understand the psychology of white Southerners, or the events of the sectional conflict, without taking this fact into account."[17] George Fitzhugh, a conservative southern ideologue, who sarcastically described the abolitionists as devoted to the "uncouth, dirty, naked little cannibals of Africa,"[18] also expressed the projective fantasies behind the paranoia: ". . . whilst they dare invoke anarchy in Europe, they dare not inaugurate New York Free Love, and Oneida Incest, and Mormon Polygamy. The moral, religious, and social heresies of the North are more monstrous than those of Europe."[19] Furthermore, the white southern sense of abolitionism was psychologically and politically expansive: it included anyone who was not actively on the side of the South. Lincoln, for example, was perceived as part of the abolitionist conspiracy to destroy the South; he would contain slavery to kill it and work determinedly to keep slaves out of the territories. Many southerners saw the election of Lincoln in 1860 as an act of aggression deliberately perpetrated against themselves. Within a month and a half after the election, South Carolina seceded; and before Lincoln left Springfield for Washington on February 11, 1861, the seven states of the deep South had seceded. After 1858 the South even turned on Stephen Douglas, who attempted to stand between North and South and find some compromise ground that would focus attention on unity, growth, and the railroads and away from slavery, secession, and war. In the debates with Lincoln it became clear that Douglas was not an unquestioning supporter of the South. The South regarded Douglas's reservations as treason to their cause and, without southern support, Douglas's 1860 Presidential hopes were doomed.

One of the many clinical signs of a disorder in the self is the patient's grandiose isolation: the cold, detached, uninvolved individual, whose brittle grandiosity serves to protect the vulnerable nuclear self against crumbling. For example, one of the patients the psychoanalyst Heinz Kohut discusses, Mr. I, began his analysis with a grandiose presentation of his exploits. He described in detail his numerous girlfriends, paintings, and poems, and his wish to be the best patient ever. The direct expression of these fantasies, especially that of being uniquely interesting, opened up the raw feelings that lay beneath: his awkwardness in social situations, his sense of inferiority to people with status and money, and his "big Jewish nose" that had once been operated on at his father's insistence. He had been a sickly child, with many colds, sore throats, and coughs, as well as bronchitis. Beneath the grandiose exterior of Mr. I lay massive self-contempt and a low sense of self-esteem. His compulsive sexual activity was not the expression of a healthy self-assertiveness, nor could it be best conceptualized in classic psychoanalytic terms as an essential sexual conflict. It reflected vulnerabilities in the self.

The clue in distinguishing normal assertiveness or neurotic conflict from grandiose isolation as a disturbance in the self is the brittle texture of the grandiosity. This idea has relevance for the group as well. For the endangered group self and the individuals who make up such a group, exaggerated notions of absolute rightness help hold together—with a Band-Aid, so to speak—the fragmenting nuclear self. The example of Nazi Germany comes to mind immediately, but the United States in the 1850s is in some ways more suggestive of an endangered group self. Most participants in the political turmoil of that decade developed a heightened—and constantly growing—sense of their own rightness. Even Lincoln grew increasingly and somewhat rigidly certain of his views. At first his position was tempered and moderate. In 1854 in a speech in Peoria, Lincoln went to some length to express his understanding of the South's position: "Before proceeding," he interjected after an assault on slavery and its extension, "let me say I think I have no prejudice against the Southern people. They are just what we would be in their situation. If slavery did not now exist amongst them they would not introduce it. If it did now exist amongst us, we should not instantly give it up."[20] By 1857 Lincoln stopped trying to empathize with the South and instead focused his attention on what the founders really intended in the Declaration of Independence as a way of supporting his own position. "They meant to set up a standard maxim for free society," he said in Springfield in response to the Dred Scott decision, "which should be familiar to all and revered by all; constantly looked to, constantly labored for, and even though never perfectly attained, constantly approximated, and thereby constantly spreading and deepening its influence, and augmenting the happiness and value of life to all people of all colors everywhere."[21] The generosity of Lincoln's outlook, however, gave way to the assertive sense of noble and moral rightness in the house divided speech (the opening flourish) that was psychologically the counterpart of the deep-seated fears of a conspiracy to nationalize slavery (the bulk of the speech). Events had pushed Lincoln to assume an increasingly shrill tone in asserting his own moral and political rectitude.

The evolution of Lincoln's articulate, pained, and sensitive thoughts on slavery from empathic opposition to a belief in conspiracy that was closely tied to his own sense of moral correctness suggests the broader significance of these issues for the group self. Indeed, it was characteristic in the 1850s to assert loudly how right you were and how wrong everyone else was. It was this holier-than-thou quality that so alienated society from the abolitionists. Their self-protective response to this alienation was to withdraw even further, which in turn heightened both their sense of superiority and of being under seige.[22] The vocal southern whites similarly grew progressively assertive and grandiose in their claims for the superiority of southern life. George Fitzhugh, for example, became a passionate defender of slavery after 1854 and an equally vigorous critic of free society and northern ideas of personal liberty.[23]

Perhaps a second, well-known clinical case will help illustrate how diffused grandiosity connects psychologically with extreme suspiciousness that borders on paranoia. One response of the endangered self is to stake out an emotional territory that far exceeds its legitimate rights. And having made such a grandiose claim on the world, one is open to, and wary of, anticipated encroachments and attacks on the self. Mr. E, another case Kohut discusses at length, used to contemplate redoing the entire architecture of the city where he lived when he rode through it on his bicycle as a child. In an eerie way these fantasies paralleled the adolescent experience of Adolph Hitler. Mr. E's report to his analyst of his architectural fantasy followed an association to the dreaded and boring childhood feeling of being stranded with his mother, who could never respond to him. "It was like always just waiting for her to die," he reported. He would feel extremely lonely in these situations and play "from morning to dark" with his toys."I thought I would go to pieces," he said. "Just thinking of it again makes my skin tingle and my spirit go blah." He recalled that when he felt that way he would rub his face on the pavement until it was sore. Then he recalled his bicycle riding and the fantasy of redesigning the city.

Frustrations and disappointments are inevitably experienced by a patient as vulnerable as Mr. E. Such patients feel perpetually exposed to attack, which must be warded off by various defensive means. Their vulnerability, in other words, makes them wary and suspicious, which not infrequently borders on (or leads to) a full-blown set of paranoid delusions. Their cold aloofness is a protective shield and masks the rage beneath. When their extraordinary demands meet with criticism or lack of response—not easily separated in the minds of such patients—they are devastated. One response to such an injury is to attack. Thus once, at the end of the last session of the week, the analyst cut Mr. E off in the middle of some difficult and painful associations, suggesting that the topic could be picked up again on Monday. Over the weekend Mr. E dreamed that he had been waiting for the analyst to be finished with another patient; it seemed like an endless amount of time. "Then he turned and shot more times than he needed to at someone who was behind him. He meant, he said, that the person was already dead, and yet he continued to shoot him."[24]

Mr. E's dream of killing the analyst came as a direct response to the injury he felt at being cut off during his painful associations. But he had himself established his vulnerabilities to this injury by his own grandiose expansion of the self that demanded, impossibly, a mirroring response of his inner state from the unseen figure behind the couch. When the analyst inevitably failed to meet these extraordinary demands and abruptly ended the hour, Mr. E experienced the resulting frustration as a violent intrusion on himself. And so he struck back.

If this sequence of feelings illustrates how, in issues of the self, grandiosity relates to suspiciousness, it also suggests how peevishness and a pervasive, wary antagonism breed on the vulnerabilities of the self. Mr. E was clearly a demanding patient who responded harshly (and often self-destructively) to "failures" from the analyst. His anger and sense of antagonism toward the world appeared everywhere. The collective analogue to this aspect of Mr. E lies in the sectional, class, and racial conflicts that increasingly devastated mid–nineteenth-century America. The American colonies were, of course, separate entities, but they were culturally homogeneous and constitutionally united in their common relataionship to England. After the Revolution each state surrendered a measure of its sovereignty to the newly formed federal government. State interests, nevertheless, as well as local or even parochial interests, remained the most significant center of initiative. For the next few decades sectional rivalry continued as an important theme. The noisy struggle over tariffs, for example, pitted the North and West against the South; banking issues tended to forge a West-South alliance against the North; and issues of internal development tended to isolate the South, which benefited relatively little from such projects. Such divisions were clearly important and kept the new country politically, socially, economically, and culturally heterogeneous.

The basis for a cohesive group self, however, was being forged. A firm idealization of the Constitution and the Declaration of Independence fed on idealizing cultural needs after the Revolution. Parson Weems's *Life of Washington* (1802), for instance, created George Washington as a mythic hero, admired for his role in shaping the war and our political institutions but revered primarily for his personal, moral virtues; it was Weems who invented the story of the cherry tree. Collectively affirmed idealizations, in turn, supported a strong sense of agreement on such things as the extension of the suffrage, the value of internal development, and the importance of the republican virtues (as they saw them) of openness, honesty, integrity, health, abundance, and strength. After the Revolution, almost all agreed, furthermore, that the Indians should be forced off their lands, blacks kept on the plantations in a condition of slavery, and the class status quo left unchanged. In the period after 1825, the imposing figure of Andrew Jackson heavily influenced the gradual erosion of state sovereignty and the emergence of a federal government that was relatively effective and increasingly powerful. In 1828, for example, the so-called tariff of abominations infuriated South

Carolina, which feared high tariffs would ruin its declining economic state. John Calhoun then formulated the first fully developed theory of the right of secession. The South Carolina Legislature responded by voting to secede if the tariff were not repealed. Jackson, himself a southerner, would not tolerate such divisive sectionalism. In 1832 he mobilized troops for a movement into South Carolina while he also pushed the Force Act through Congress. The issue was compromised and left many raw feelings, but a crucial point had been demonstrated. The new American self was not to be easily undone by internal strife.

The Jacksonians generally succeeded in sidestepping the race issue. Neither major party opposed slavery *per se*, which meant that both Democrats and Whigs agreed to preserve intact a system that kept some three million blacks in bondage. The Constitution recognized the legitimacy of slavery, and the South increasingly built its economy around the institution; the racism of northern whites and the abundance of land muted any latent discontent with existing political and social arrangements. For someone like Lincoln it was not surprising that southerners could believe slavery was wrong and yet still own slaves. Since the economic and social system of the South was built on slavery, anyone who lived there would necessarily participate in the prevailing patterns of behavior. The crucial point for Lincoln was whether you recognized the essential wrongness of slavery and hoped it would die a natural death. The correct attitude about the future of slavery need not inform present actions. There were, to be sure, northern dissenters from this easy accommodation to the existence of slavery, but the voice of opposition was generally still and went unheeded politically.

The tensions and splits in the group self were, however, fundamental. The course of events after 1848 increasingly eroded the assumptions of the Jacksonians. The major challenge came from the acquisition of vast new tracts of land after the Mexican War. No one knew what legal conditions should govern settlement of these lands. The South felt it had the right to expand slavery wherever and whenever it desired, whereas northern and western opinion grasped with a new understanding the significance of slavery spreading indiscriminately into the territories. The debate over the war itself focused the issues. The national parties that had so effectively buried sectional discord for some twenty-five years soon gave way to ideological alliances that had little to do with traditional Whig or Democratic positions. The Compromise of 1850 papered over these basic changes in the political climate, but their full meaning struck home after the passage of the Kansas-Nebraska Act in 1854. The Whig party quickly dissolved and the Democrats divided into warring factions. Disgruntled northerners—old Whigs, Democrats, nativists, free soilers—coalesced around the Republican party, which by 1856 nominated John Charles Frémont in an intensely ideological campaign.

The rapidity of these changes astounded contemporaries and continues to amaze historians. In a matter of a few years a largely stable, cohesive society disintegrated into separate and warring parts. The developments of the 1850s naturally had antecedents. Southern white culture had long since acquired distinctive characteristics that made it extremely sensitive to slights and eager to defend its rights.[25] On the other side, the abolitionists were insistent about the righteousness of their cause, and many were willing to forgo their earlier pacifism in order to achieve their goal. But it was politics and society in a new key in the 1850s. A terrible sense of urgency infected all aspects of public life. The confused party situation between 1854 and 1856, for example, created high levels of anxiety for everyone and prodded even the ordinary citizen to sort through political priorities; for the reflective, the period often became the turning point of their adult lives. Lincoln before 1854 was a comfortable Whig who opposed Jackson and Jackson-type leaders, favored strong banks and internal developments, and idealized Henry Clay. He seldom thought much about slavery, though he clearly felt it was wrong. Suddenly, after 1854, the rules changed. And Lincoln became a different person.

Sectional rivalry now disintegrated into rhetorical, and at times bloody, regional warfare. Congressman Preston Brooks of South Carolina beat Senator Charles Sumner senseless on the Senate floor on May 22, 1856, for derogatory remarks made about his relative, Senator Andrew P. Butler. John Brown's "Holy Crusade" on slavery took shape as paramilitary action that avowedly aimed at revenge and fomenting social revolution in the South. The great disappointment for Brown in the raid on Harper's Ferry was that the blacks in the area never rose up to fight in response to his call; what he failed to realize was that they never heard it in the first place. The passion of rhetoric escalated on all sides, from George Fitzhugh and Jefferson Davis to Charles Sumner, William Lloyd Garrison, and John Brown. Even traditional political rivalries acquired a shrillness that suggested underlying themes of larger significance.

As the crisis intensified in the 1850s, there were a variety of compensatory responses to the imminent collapse. There was, for one thing, a fervent spirit of revivalism that swept the land.[26] Periods of religious enthusiasm were not new in American history, but the oddly conservative character of the "New Light" movement in the 1740s gave way, after 1820, to a more expressive religiosity that featured the week-long revivals of Charles Grandison Finney. In Illinois in the 1840s Peter Cartwright was a noted preacher, able to move large crowds to hysteria and religious ecstasy, though he proved less able in his political efforts to defeat Lincoln for Congress in 1846. After 1852, at least in Illinois, something of an unconscious dread of the underlying meaning of the revivals became intertwined with the process of building the nascent field of psychiatry. Thus the records of the first mental institution in the state, Jacksonville State Hospital, list for 8 percent of admissions between 1852 and 1860 the following, closely interrelated set of causes for illness: religious enthusiasm, excessive reading of the Bible, church difficulty, spiritualism, Millerism—adherence to William Miller's Second Adventists Church—and "Spiritual Rappings."

These records suggest a confusion of cause and effect, of symptom for real illness. Nevertheless, the categories of diagnosing mental illness in the state's first institution for the insane reveal a deeply ingrained fear of intense religiosity as potentially pathological.[27]

The fragmenting self struggles desperately to heal its widening split and restore cohesion. If the spreading revivalism was one such attempt, another, of broader cultural and social significance, was the cult of domesticity that came to define the idealized style of family life in the 1850s. Changes in values leading to this cult became apparent after 1820 but greatly intensified in the 1850s. For women the cult sharply defined ideal virtues—piety, purity, passivity, and domesticity—and their loathsome opposites. The home itself became a haven or refuge from the outside male jungle of work and politics. Children were the exclusive responsibility of women in their accepted role as mothers. Sexuality *per se* was severely repressed, but a warm sentimentality suffused all the essential relationships, especially that of mother and child.

Themes in family history, even their indirect expression in popular literature, seldom appear or disappear in as short a period as a decade. However, one key source and its warm reception suggest a unique intensification of the cult of domesticity in the 1850s. Harriet Beecher Stowe's *Uncle Tom's Cabin* appeared in serial form in 1851 and was published in book form the following year. The characters in the book are etched in our consciousness by now: Eliza and George, Tom, St. Clare, Little Eva, Miss Ophelia, and Simon Legree. The dramatic appeal of the story aroused millions to the evils of slavery in the wake of the reopened debate after 1848. But it is worth noting that the central themes of *Uncle Tom's Cabin* deal with family and domestic issues. The "message" of the book is that blacks are fully human, indeed at times more upright, Christian, responsible, and worthy than their dissolute white masters, but the proof of that central point is that blacks, like whites, have families and family ties. Eliza and George, for example, are models of fidelity, integrity, and mutual respect in an age haunted by these issues. Eliza is the ideal mother. Her escape from the Shelby plantation with young Harry to avoid being sold is achieved at a great cost. The plantation is the only home she has ever known, and her escape means leaving her "loved and revered" husband. "But," Stowe notes, "stronger than all was maternal love, wrought into a paroxysm of frenzy by the near approach of a fearful danger."[28]

Finally, the complex relationship between fragmentation anxiety—the fear of disintegration—and compensatory maneuvers to heal splits in the group self is perhaps nowhere better illustrated than in the story of nativism in the 1850s. On the one hand, nativist feelings of hatred for Catholics, Irish, Germans—more simply, anyone or anything foreign—came to dominate politics in many parts of the country. Building on the tradition of antimasonry from the early 1830s, the tensions between native-born, Protestant whites and Catholic foreigners reached major proportions in the early 1850s. The nativist movement had by then already generated its own literature (for example, *The Awful Disclosures of Maria Monk*) and would soon establish its own party, the Know-Nothings. It was a party of hate, as Lincoln saw more clearly than most.[29]

The importance of nativism cannot be overemphasized. It blended curiously with free-soil, antislavery sentiment, for nativists hated the aristocratic white South as much as they did Catholic foreigners. As historian David Potter has recently put it, both nativism and antislavery "reflected psychologically a highly dramatized fear of a powerful force which sought by conspiratorial means to subvert the values of the republic: in one case this was the slavocracy, with its 'lords of the lash,' in the other, the Church of Rome with its crafty priests and subtle Jesuits."[30] In social terms as well, nativist feeling seemed to govern essential human relationships and define normative behavior. In the Jacksonville records, for example, at least 40 percent of the patients between 1852 and 1860 were foreign-born, and that figure could be much higher.[31] These patients were, on the whole, young female domestic servants, recently arrived, lonely, and different. "Homesickness" is not infrequently the "supposed cause" of illness in the admitting records.

And yet nativist sentiment built as it destroyed, affirmed essential values as it intolerantly castigated others. It was a curious kind of populism, typically American, terribly important, often profoundly misunderstood. Thus in many areas nativism carried the spirit of reform, whether it was against slavery or for temperance. Furthermore, a powerful nationalism informed all nativist programs and politics. The fact that the Know-Nothing Convention in June, 1855, disintegrated into sectional rivalry is less surprising (or interesting) than the "Union Degree" exalting nationalism that the group had instituted in its ritual. As many as 1,500,000 members of the Know-Nothing Party took the Union Degree and pledged themselves against sectional forces from either North or South.[32]

The most important and dangerous by-product of a fragmenting self is rage. Rage can express itself in almost infinitely variable ways, turning on the self one moment, a loved figure the next. Freud all but missed rage, both because of the kind of patients he saw and because of his larger theoretical interests in aggression and the death instinct. Kohut's work, however, helps us appreciate the central position of rage in human existence and its relationship to the dissolving self.[33] The loss of cohesion in the self generates rage in its wake. The rage can express itself in a kind of affect storm (for example, a child's temper tantrum) or it can become quite elaborately organized, defining an angry, hostile, and vulnerable style that attempts to ward off further fragmentation. For the group there are fascinating analogues to these characteristics of rage in the individual: the fury of war perhaps most accurately expresses the collective version of the temper tantrum, while elaborately structured systems of hate, fear, and suspicion can become built into social institutions in the same way a narcissistic patient so often organizes himself or herself around rage.

As the crisis of the 1850s matured, anger pervaded American life. War increasingly seemed inevitable. There is no easily discernible turning point in this process, which is not surprising, since it is inherently irrational. Thus the Compromise of 1850 appeared to settle the interrelated issues of slavery and the territorial expansion of the country but actually foreshadowed the dramatic realignments of the political parties four years later. A number of events in 1856 reveal the mounting rage in the group self breaking through—the caning of Charles Sumner, for example—but then all is quiet again, and there is even a degree of consolidation during the early part of Buchanan's administration.

John Brown's own rage escalated with that of the group self as the raid on Harper's Ferry in 1859 sent tremors of real war through the country. And finally the blustering and strutting of the secession crisis itself, from Lincoln's election to his inauguration, fed the deepest levels of rage as the self split into two parts. That Lincoln and his contemporaries tended to think of the spirit of the Union in terms that are understandable in the framework of self psychology suggests how deeply invested they were in the national concept. Its dissolution over a decade unraveled the fragile idealizations of the past—those collective strands of value that bound the self—and prompted an eruptive, peremptory grandiosity. The rage that this process generated in the end could only be absorbed by war itself.

One of the striking characteristics of the 1850s is the absence of effective leadership. The Presidents between 1848 and 1860 were a succession of bland nonentities—Zachary Taylor, Millard Fillmore, Franklin Pierce, and James Buchanan. The parties themselves seemed adrift at their point of greatest crisis. Only Douglas had real stature, but his fight with Buchanan after 1857 only further divided the Democratic party. Certainly the Whigs had no one of note to lead them in the early 1850s. Henry Clay was dead, Daniel Webster was dead, gone after a brief tenure was President Taylor, only the second Whig President ever elected to that office. Then as the Republican party took shape after 1854 the great dilemma was that no one spoke for it. Its growth was a spontaneous coalescence at the local level of groups that quickly realized they had a great deal in common with other groups elsewhere. There was no leader. The raucus convention in Philadelphia in 1856 nominated John Charles Frémont, whose essential weakness of character would become painfully clear to Lincoln in the early years of the Civil War. There were articulate and powerful political leaders in the land, but they either lacked power, like Stephen Douglas, or commitment to the Union, like Jefferson Davis, or were fanatics, like John Brown. The fatal lack of leadership in this critical decade greatly accentuated the unbinding of the group self. The process is ironically dialectical: the loss or absence of a

leader for the group in crisis tends to further the process of fragmentation, which in turn makes the need for an idealized figure
that much more burning. Thus, out of total collapse, civil war,
and 600,000 dead came our greatest hero who also, it happened,
was quite an effective leader.

Lincoln during the Civil War. The photograph depicts a man resolutely in charge of the country. *Mellon Collection*

Chapter 9

The Shape of a Leader

With malice toward none; with charity for all; with firmness in the right, as God gives us to see the right, let us strive on to finish the work we are in; to bind up the nation's wounds; to care for him who shall have borne the battle, and for his widow, and his orphan—to do all which may achieve and cherish a just, and a lasting peace, among ourselves, and with all nations.

A. LINCOLN
March 4, 1865

 GREAT "intensity of thought," Lincoln once counseled Joshua Speed, "will some times wear the sweetest idea thread-bare and turn it to the bitterness of death."[1] No aspect of Lincoln's character has become more tangibly real in the literature than his sad, gloomy, melancholy appearance. "No man in this agony," Harriet Beecher Stowe wrote in 1864 after a visit with Lincoln, "has suffered more and deeper, albeit with a dry, weary, patient pain, that seemed to some like insensibility."[2] One observer wrote in a letter dated February 25, 1865, that "his face denotes an immense force of resistance and extreme melancholy. It is plain that this man has suffered deeply."[3] Lincoln's friend Ward Hill Lamon called him a "man of

[205]

sorrows" who bore "a continued sense of weariness and pain" and attracted universal sympathy "because he seemed at once miserable and kind." He was, indeed, "the saddest and gloomiest man of his time."[4] Toward the end of the war the artist Francis B. Carpenter spent about six months in the White House working on a painting of the signing of the Emancipation Proclamation. After the war Carpenter wrote a detailed memoir of his impressions. The book became an important source for the public's sense of the man whose "furrowed face" was the ultimate in sadness. "There were days when I could scarcely look into it without crying." Carpenter once saw Lincoln pacing during the Battle of the Wilderness (May, 1864), "his hands behind him, great black rings under eyes." The picture seemed so full of sorrow, care, and anxiety as would have "melted the hearts of the worst of the adversaries."[5] Every time Carpenter looked up from his canvas, he seemed to see Lincoln looking haggard, weary, or with a "peculiar dreaminess of expression."[6]

Herndon described Lincoln's appearance as equally melancholy in the years before the war, and he used the same trite phrases. Lincoln's depression was "chiseled deep" in every line of his face; he was dripping with melancholy.[7] Henry C. Whitney, who rode the eighth circuit with Lincoln in the 1850s was struck by his shifting moods, particularly "when his whole nature was immersed in Cimmerian darkness."[8] Whitney described a remarkable scene one night on the circuit:

One morning [at Danville while sleeping in the same bed with Lincoln] I was awakened early—before daybreak—by my companion sitting up in bed, his figure dimly visible by the ghostly firelight, and talking the wildest and most incoherent nonsense all to himself. A stranger to Lincoln would have supposed he had suddenly gone insane. Of course I knew Lincoln and his idiosyncrasies, and felt no alarm, so I listened and laughed. After he had gone on in his way for say, five minutes, while I was awake, and I know not how long *before* I was awake, he sprang out of bed hurriedly washed, and jumped into his clothes, put some wood on the fire, and then sat in front of it, moodily, dejectedly, in a most sombre and gloomy spell, till the breakfast bell rang, when he started, as if from sleep, and went with us to breakfast. Neither Davis nor I spoke to him; we knew this trait; it was not remarkable for Lincoln.[9]

Retrospective observations on Lincoln's melancholy inevitably suggest the legend of his Christ-like martyrdom. He was shot on Good Friday and died on Saturday. The next day, the Easter Sunday sermons hammered the outlines of this myth into place. No one since has escaped its influence. The picture of Lincoln's melancholy figure fits well with a Christ-like conception of him suffering and dying for our sins. Furthermore, in the immediate postwar period the "chiseled" features of Lincoln seemed to draw unto themselves all the agonies of the war, the 600,000 dead in the long series of dramatic battles. The funeral train back to Springfield captured this sense of Lincoln's death as somehow symbolic of the war itself. Thousands poured out along the way—in New York, Buffalo, Cleveland, Chicago, and many points between—to gaze at the elaborate black hearse. Whole houses were draped and in Springfield, the end of the line, it seemed the entire town was covered with a shroud.

Lincoln complained privately throughout his life of his depression. As early as 1836 he told Mary Owens that some mysterious things "have conspired and have gotten my spirits so low, that I feel that I would rather be any place in the world than here." He asked Mary to write back "as soon as you get this, and if possible say something that will please me, for really I have not [been] pleased since I left you. This letter is so dry and [stupid] that I am ashamed to send it, but with my pres[ent feel]ings I can not do any better."[10] The following year, in Springfield, one of Lincoln's first letters was to Mary. "This thing of living in Springfield is rather a dull business after all," he wrote. "I am quite as lonesome here as [I] ever was anywhere in my life." Lincoln went on to lament that no one talked to him and that he feared going to church because he would not know how to behave himself.[11] Subsequently, of course, Lincoln experienced devastating depression in January, 1841; his letter to his wife in 1848 suggests feelings of emptiness and sadness; and contemporary reports by people such as Conkling clearly substantiate that Lincoln's melancholy was at the core of his personality.

Depression, however, comes in many shapes. In Lincoln's case it came most obviously in response to the death of those he loved.

He deeply mourned the death of his young son, Edward, in 1850, and even more so the death of his beloved Willie in 1862. His response to these deaths has been obscured somewhat by the nearly total collapse of Mary after the death of her boys. But the effects on Lincoln were powerful and enduring.[12] It is also possible that Lincoln responded sadly to the death of Ann Rutledge in 1835. The fact that he was depressed, at least, is acceptably documented in the oral history record.

The death of any close friend could also cause Lincoln pain and depression. John Hay noted in his diary on October 22, 1861: "This has been a heavy day. Last night Col. [Edward] Baker was killed at Leesburg at the head of his brigade. McClellan & the Pres[t] talked sadly over it."[13] The war itself soon absorbed these personal feelings into an expanding web of carnage. Harriet Beecher Stowe noted his "heavy eyes and worn and weary air" after Fredericksburg.[14] It is possible Lincoln came to see his own death as imminent. He always refused to take precautions against assassination and once interpreted a dream as forecasting his own death at the beginning of a second term in office.[15]

Real loss in the present becomes exquisitely painful largely because it evokes the parallel experiences of a lost and often buried childhood. In this sense the evocative meaning of a parent's death can require lifelong mourning. But death and its lingering hold can be variously symbolized in even trivial situations of separation and loss. For example, it was the separation from Mary Owens in 1836 that prompted Lincoln's feelings of sadness. The more radical break with Speed and Mary Todd in 1841 brought near disaster. Circuit life seemed to evoke melancholy in Lincoln. And enduring separations from Mary—as in 1848—aggravated his sense of loneliness and led to depression. Such response to symbolized encounters with death seemed to derive from Lincoln's association of loving and death that led him (as discussed in chapter 2) to gratuitously assure Speed, in 1842: "Why Speed, if you did not love her [his fiancée, Fanny Henning] although you might not wish her death, you would most calmly be resigned to it."[16]

Lincoln's depressions were not, however, restricted to his encounters with death or its symbolized equivalents in situations of separation and loss. He also seemed particularly vulnerable to issues of self-esteem. Political defeat could devastate Lincoln. Before the Civil War he was an experienced loser in Illinois politics. He lost his first election to the State Legislature in 1832, noting, however, in the autobiography, that those who actually knew him in the New Salem precinct voted in his favor 277 to 7.[17] Twice during the 1850s he tried for the United States Senate, losing both times: in 1855, to Lyman Trumbull and, in 1858, to Stephen Douglas. There is no indication of what Lincoln felt in 1832, but his conscious "withdrawal" from active politics in 1849 suggests a depressive response to the sense of the failure of his political ambitions after his term as United States Congressman. In 1855 Lincoln seemed resigned to his defeat by Trumbull. There is some evidence that in 1858 Lincoln was distraught at the loss to Douglas. On the evening of the defeat he said to his friend Henry C. Whitney that his life had been "an abject and lamentable failure." Whitney reported: "I never saw any man so radically and thoroughly depressed, so completely steeped in the bitter waters of hopeless despair."[18]

The depression in these cases came from Lincoln's sense of failure to realize his ambitions and ideals. The grandiose young man of the Lyceum speech (1838) gave way to a politician in the 1850s who tackled one of the nation's leading political figures (Stephen Douglas) on his own turf. Lincoln became a man unafraid to interpret the founding fathers to a country hurtling toward war. He was unabashedly majestic in the house divided speech. And when he left Springfield he saw himself as facing a challenge equal to, if not greater than, that dealt with by the founders. Yet his personal and political performances kept falling short. He seemed unable to match his own expectations. Failure at the polls dramatized the enormity of the gap between expectation and performance.

Lincoln also lived in a world of other people on whom he depended for love, support, interaction, and the maintenance of his complicated needs. In periods of vulnerability these needs were most apparent. For example, he wrote Mary Owens in 1837: "I want in all cases to do right, and most particularly so, in all cases with women. I want, at this particular time, more than any thing else, to do right with you. . . ."[19] And to Speed, Lincoln once poured out his soul on the devastating effect of losing Mary in 1841: ". . . but before I resolve to do the one thing or the other, I must retain my confidence in my own ability to keep my resolves when they are made. In that ability, you know, I once prided myself as the only, or at least the chief, gem of my character; that gem I lost—how and when, you too well know."[20] The loss of Mary in early 1841 seemed to evoke childhood memories of his mother; but perhaps even more importantly it cast Lincoln off from the one person in his life who could potentially anchor him psychologically. Speed substituted briefly and helped Lincoln find his way back to her.

The key issue for Lincoln in these intensely personal struggles was to maintain his self-esteem in his relationships with others. The "other," however, in this kind of encounter is not separate but included psychologically in the conception of the self. The political analogue of this private world of meanings for Lincoln was the stability and cohesion of the political process itself. His choice of career and early political affinities reflected an abiding commitment to order and stability in the community. In the 1850s his use of the founders' thoughts grew out of a respect for the sources of healthy continuity in the country. Yet he had to watch in horror as it all unraveled. In this sense his uncharacteristic paranoia in 1858 makes some sense: it expressed symptomatically what he felt was external but which he experienced psychologically as part of his inner life.

Lincoln's psychological uncertainty carried over into the chaos of the early months of the war. Badly prepared, the army suffered a series of military defeats. Many of the best generals defected to the South. The northern states were disunited and the border states on the verge of leaving the Union. The administration was young and halting, its relations with Congress uncertain. John Hay, one of Lincoln's two secretaries, noted in his diary on April 24, 1861: "This has been a day of gloom and doubt. Everybody seems filled with a vague distrust and recklessness."[21] And later that summer, on July 28, Orville Browning, Lincoln's old friend and now Senator from Illinois, recorded in his diary that during an extended conversation at the White House Lincoln "seemed very melancholy; admitted he was so, but said he knew of no special cause for it."[22]

Lincoln's equilibrium thus seemed to hinge on the emotional supplies served up by both intimate and formalized encounters with others. In this sense the irresistible appeal of politics was its potential for providing recognition and admiration. "Every man is said to have his peculiar ambition," Lincoln wrote in a circular for his very first campaign in 1832. "Whether it be true or not, I can say for one that I have no other so great as that of being truly esteemed of my fellow man, by rendering myself worthy of their esteem."[23] Lincoln once described himself as "too *thin-skinned*"[24] and, at times during the war, expressed a fear that he possessed no administrative ability.[25] A law lecture he once prepared began, "I am not an accomplished lawyer. I find quite as much material for a lecture in those points wherein I have failed, as in those wherein I have been moderately successful."[26]

And yet there were many rewards for Lincoln in politics, law, and work generally. His election as a captain in the Black Hawk War was an event of great emotional significance; no other success in his life (to 1860) "gave him so much satisfaction."[27] During the 1830s he played a prominent role in the Illinois Legislature and rose to the leadership of the Whig party. He loved the rough and tumble of politics and never seemed to regard speechmaking as tedious. A master politician, he could exert enormous influence behind the scenes without demeaning his own stature.[28] He worked hard as a lawyer to make a respectable income and strove vigorously for high political office. As David Donald has reminded us, a statesman is a politician who succeeds in getting elected.[29] The hard-working, shrewd, resourceful Lincoln became such a statesman. Even during his political "retirement" from 1849 to 1854, he remained active in Whig politics.[30] During the 1850s, it is true, he lost twice for the Senate, but he was also the leading figure in a complex alliance of Whigs and other smaller groups who began calling themselves Republicans. He was mentioned often for the governorship, but he was not interested.

Then at last, in 1860, he was elected President and, in 1864, re-elected.

Such success went a long way in building Lincoln's confidence and easing his transition into the Presidency. In fact, after the dark early days, Lincoln seemed newly capable of leading the North to victory. "The Tycoon is in a fine whack," wrote John Hay on August 7, 1863. "I have rarely seen him more serene and busy. He is managing the war, the draft, foreign relations, and planning a reconstruction of the Union, all at once." Hay almost always seemed to encounter a cheery, confident, and competent President. On April 25, 1861, "Lincoln seemed to be in a pleasant, hopeful mood. . . ." On October 17, 1861, Lincoln and Nicolay found a topic of discussion "vastly amusing." On July 11, 1863, "The President seemed in a specially good humor today. . . ." On July 19, 1863, "The Tycoon was in a very good humor. Early in the morning he scribbled this doggerel and gave it to me." On August 9, 1863, "Lincoln was in very fine spirits." On July 11, 1864, "The President is in a very good feather this evening." The next day, "The President seemed in a pleasant and confident humor today." Seldom in Hay's diary, in fact, is there evidence for Lincoln's depression. On November 23, 1863, Hay noted that Lincoln had been "a little despondent ab^t Grant" but cheered again with the news of Grant's advance on Chattanooga and Thomas's success. Lincoln's visit to the front on June 23, 1864, exhausted him but also left him "refreshed and cheered." And nowhere is there a more charming description of Lincoln than Hay's account of a midnight visit from him in the spring of 1864.

A little after midnight as I was writing those last lines, the President came into the office laughing, with a volume of Hood's works in his hands, to show Nico and me the little caricature "An Unfortunate Bee-ing," seemingly utterly unconscious that he with his short shirt hanging above his long legs & setting out behind like the tail feathers of an enormous ostrich was infinitely funnier than anything in the book he was laughing at. What a man it is! Occupied all day with matters of vast moment, deeply anxious about the fate of the greatest army of the world, with his own fame & future hanging on the events of the passing hour, he yet has such a wealth of simple bonhommie & good fellowship that he gets out of bed & perambulates the house in his shirt to find us that we may share with him the fun of one of poor Hood's queer little conceits.[31]

Hay's testimony is reliable and contemporary, and no one worked more closely with Lincoln for a longer period of time and kept a diary. Hay is observant, articulate, and witty. His regular entries in his diary capture the bustling activities of the White House but also Lincoln's calm, reassuring leadership. Hay at first seemed ambivalent toward Lincoln, referring jocularly to him as "The Tycoon" (thirty-eight times), "the Ancient" (twice), or "the old man" (once). But by the middle of the war Hay became deeply devoted to Lincoln and his style. "There is no man in the country," Hay wrote in 1863, "so wise, so gentle and so firm. I believe the hand of God placed him where he is."[32] But Hay seldom referred to Lincoln's melancholy and never noted a work inhibition on Lincoln's part. In Hay's diaries Lincoln emerges as a warm, inspiring, very hard-working, subtly competent administrator, a statesman, and a military strategist.

How, one asks, could Lincoln have combined such effective leadership with recurring, often devastating depression? The theologian Elton Trueblood has noted that "Lincoln's was the kind of mind which did not reach its true magnitude except in experiences of sorrow and strain."[33] Still, his vulnerabilities remained throughout his life. But his competence, his easy, confident style, his warmth and kindness, all suggest a large measure of transcendence of his debilitating conflicts. The Freudian model helps explain what made him so susceptible to separation, loss, death, and disturbances in the maintenance of his self-esteem. But the classical psychoanalytic model falls short of providing clues to his transcendence. One needs a way of understanding what provides cohesion, integrity, flexibility, growth, and change within the personality. Here the work of Heinz Kohut can be enormously helpful, especially his thoughts on the cohesiveness of the self. The criteria Kohut enumerates for evaluating psychological growth toward health are ultimately simple and obvious: humor, empathy, creativeness, and wisdom.[34] For Lincoln, these become the vehicles for his therapeutic transcendence of the core conflicts within his personality.

[213]

Humor needs no definition. Freud once wrote a whole book on why a joke "works," but Kohut's interest is more the psychological flexibility inherent in someone who can tolerate the regression and the self-reflection in joking itself. Humor in this sense excludes biting sarcasm or joking that takes someone else as the butt. Part of the appeal of Lincoln's humor was the self-deprecation of so many of his jokes. He loved to tell of a stranger who once came up to him on the circuit and said, "excuse me, sir, but I have an article in my possession which belongs to you." "How is that?" Lincoln asked with some' surprise. The stranger took a knife out of his pocket and said it had been given to him some years ago with the order "that I was to keep it until I found a man *uglier* than myself. I have carried it from that time to this. Allow me *now* to say, sir, that I think *you* are fairly entitled to the property."[35] Another favorite anecdote, which ridiculed his own modest habits, told of a friendly Kentuckian he once rode with in a carriage. The man offered Lincoln a chew of tobacco, then a cigar, and finally a sip of brandy from a flask. Each offer Lincoln politely declined. As they were parting the Kentuckian said good-humoredly: "See here, stranger, you're a clever but strange companion. I may never see you again, and I don't want to offend you, but I want to say this: my experience has taught me that a man who has no vices has damned few virtues. Good-day."[36]

Lincoln had a delicious sense of irony. Herndon once told him expansively of his impression of Niagara Falls with its "mad rush of water, the roar, the rapids, and the rainbow." He asked Lincoln for his opinion of Niagara Falls, and Lincoln replied: "The thing that struck me most forcibly when I saw the Falls was, where in the world did all that water come from?"[37] In fact, Lincoln had written rather extensive notes to himself on Niagara Falls after visiting them in 1849. "It calls up the indefinite past. When Columbus first sought this continent—when Christ suffered on the cross—when Moses led Israel through the Red Sea—nay, even, when Adam first came from the hand of his Maker—then as now, Niagara was roaring here. . . ."[38]

A week before his death, Lincoln visited the Confederate capital, Richmond, after its capture by federal troops. In the party was the French aristocrat, Adolphe de Chambrun, who described in a letter to his wife how a band came up to the Presidential steamer to play a few tunes. Afterward Lincoln asked them to play the *Marseillaise* (which was forbidden in the Third Republic). Lincoln turned to Chambrun with a twinkle in his eye, "You have to come to America to hear it."[39]

Lincoln told his friend Ward Hill Lamon that he "lived by his humor, and would have died without it." When he told a story, the fun danced in his eyes and played over every feature. The mirth "seemed to diffuse itself all over him, like a spontaneous tickle."[40] In the White House, Francis Carpenter once came across Lincoln telling a story to Nicolay and Hay late in the evening, "laughing and talking with the hilarity of a schoolboy."[41] Herndon remarked on how much Lincoln enjoyed his own telling of stories: "His little gray eyes sparkled; a smile seemed to gather up, curtain like, the corners of his mouth; his frame quivered with suppressed excitement; and, when the point—or 'nub' of the story, as he called it—came, no one's laugh was heartier than his."[42] Lincoln had a dread of people who could not appreciate humor and said once of a cabinet member (probably the dour Edwin Stanton) that "it required a surgical operation to get a joke into his head."[43]

He told all kinds of jokes in every conceivable context. In fact, his fame as a storyteller spread far and wide. "Men quoted his sayings, repeated his jokes, and in remote places he was known as a story-teller before he was heard of either as lawyer or politician."[44] As President, Lincoln often related the story of the Irishman who had foresworn liquor but told the bartender he was not averse to having a spot added to his lemonade, "so long as it's unbeknownst to me." David Donald feels this anecdote expressed the way Lincoln wrapped his pragmatism, even opportunism, in a cloak of passivity.[45] His humor was generally "clean" and the kind of American tall tale that would not have been out of place in a "ladies drawing room."[46] But not always. His bawdy humor was a special delight for the small group of lawyers following the eighth circuit. Moses Hampton wrote him on March 30, 1848, asking for a favor in a lighthearted vein: "Do you remember the story of the old Virginian stropping his razor on a certain *member* of a young negro's body which you told... ?"[47] Herndon, who was a bit of a stuffed shirt and a great reader of "heavy" texts, once asked Lincoln if he believed in heredity. Lincoln mused for a moment and replied, yes, he had no doubt that personality traits were passed from one generation to another. For example, old so-and-so from his New Salem days had fathered five boys. Well, Lincoln continued, "I know that ——— suffered terribly in the old days from chronic diarrhea, and you know for a fact that every one of the boys has turned out to be a perfect shitass!"[48]

Lincoln's bawdy humor was, in fact, decidedly anal. He once handed a bailiff in a Springfield court the following piece of foolery:

He said he was riding *bass-ackwards* on a *jass-ack*, through a *patton-cotch*, on a pair of *baddle-sags*, stuffed full of *binger-gred*, when the animal *steered* at a *scump*, and the *lirrup-streather* broke, and throwed him in the *forner* of the *kence* and broke his *pishing-fole*. He said he would not have minded it much, but he fell right in a great *tow-curd*; in fact, he said it give him a right smart *sick of fitness*—he had the *molera-corbus* pretty bad. He said, about *bray dake* he came to himself, ran home, seized up a *stick of wood* and split the *axe* to make a light, rushed into the house, and found the *door* sick abed, and his *wife* standing open. But thank goodness she is getting right *hat* and *farty* again."[49]

Another story that Herndon says he heard Lincoln tell "often and often" described a man of audacity. At a party "not far from here" (which, of course, puts it anywhere) a fine table was set and everyone was having a grand time. Among the guests was our man of audacity who was confident, self-possessed, and never off his guard. After some dancing, promenading, flirting, and so forth, dinner was served and the man of audacity was placed at the head of the table to carve. With everyone surrounding the table the man whetted the blade and set to work. But he expended too much energy, for he let go a large fart. Everyone heard it and was shocked. Silence reigned. But the audacious man was cool and self-possessed. He calmly took off his coat, rolled up his sleeves, put his coat deliberately on a chair, spat on his hands and rubbed them together, squared his shoulders and picked up his knife, all without a smile or a movement of the muscles in his face. "Now, by God," he said, starting to carve the turkey again, "I'll see if I can't cut up this turkey without farting."[50]

Lincoln's humor, even his vulgar jokes, had a purpose. If it was "merely a ribald recital" he had no use for it.[51] Often the purpose was political. In 1848, for example, Lincoln gave a pro-Taylor speech in the United States House of Representatives during his one term as a Congressman. Lincoln's goal in the speech was to debunk the spurious military record of Taylor's opponent, General Cass. To accomplish that, he recalled his own record:

> By the way, Mr. Speaker, did you know that I am a military hero? Yes sir; in the days of the Black Hawk war, I fought, bled, and came away. Speaking of Gen: Cass' career, reminds me of my own. I was not at Stillman's defeat, but I was about as near it, as Cass was to Hulls surrender; and, like him, I did not break my sword, for I had none to break; but I bent a musket pretty badly on one occasion. If Cass broke his sword, the idea is, he broke it in de[s]peration; I bent the musket by accident. If Gen: Cass went in advance of me in picking huckleberries, I guess I surpassed him in charges upon the wild onions. If he saw any live, fighting indians, it was more than I did; but I had a good many bloody struggles with the musquetoes; and, although I never fainted from loss of blood, I can truly say I was often hungry. Mr. Speaker, if I should ever conclude to doff whatever our democratic friends may suppose there is of black cockade federalism about me, and thereupon, they shall take me up as their candidate for the Presidency, I protest they shall not make fun of me, as they have of General Cass, by attempting to write me into a military hero.[52]

The device of lacing political speeches with anecdotes became a Lincoln hallmark.[53] In the early years of his career some found this trait offensive. On November 23, 1839, Springfield's Democratic paper, the *Register*, chided Lincoln for his "assumed clownishness" and warned that "this game of buffoonery convinces the mind of no man, and is utterly lost on the majority of his audience. We seriously advise Mr. Lincoln to correct this clownish fault before it grows upon him."[54] In time, however, even the *Register* noted in reporting a Lincoln speech on October 6, 1854, that he began with jokes, "the character of which will be understood by all who know him, by simply saying they were Lincolnisms."[55] He joked endlessly with law clients, obviously putting them at ease, sometimes repeating a story several times in the course of one day. Each time he laughed harder at his own jokes. Even Herndon, who had to listen to these stories over and over, was forced to laugh because he "thought it funny that Mr. Lincoln enjoyed a story so repeatedly told."[56] In the White House, Lincoln used anecdotes cleverly to ward off supplicants or angry politicians demanding action on some crucial measure. Charles Sumner, who had no sense of humor, found conversation with Lincoln "a constant puzzle" and asked Carl Schurz "with an air of innocent bewilderment," whether Schurz knew what the President meant.[57]

Lincoln's was a raucous, infectious, charming humor, a bubbling over of story, joke, anecdote, and tale that became a part of his every action and experience. It defined his style in law, politics, and in personal relationships. Nothing escaped, not even his famous tendency to pardon soldiers for desertion, cowardice, or failure to perform adequately in the army. A number of witnesses have described Lincoln's acts of pardon in saccharine terms, noting his sad eyes and melancholy appearance (for example, Carpenter). But two of Hay's diary entries are also worth pondering. On July 18, 1863, Lincoln told Hay he was averse to using the death penalty for desertion and cowardice. "He said it would frighten the poor devils too terribly, to shoot them." He also told Hay the government should let alone a boy who had escaped after his conviction for desertion; "We will condemn him as they used to sell hogs in Indiana, as they run."[58] And despite his deep commitment to the necessity of fighting the Civil War, Lincoln recognized that politics dictates the support of any country's war. To illustrate the point, he once told Seward of a politician he knew in Illinois (Justin Butterfield) who was asked why he supported the Mexican War when it was known he opposed it. "I opposed one war," Butterfield replied, "that was enough for me. I am now perpetually in favor of war, pestilence and famine."[59]

If humor was a central, it was also a necessary part of Lincoln's personality. Henry C. Whitney, his friend on the circuit, quoted him as saying, "I laugh because I must not weep—that's all, that's all."[60] The actual origin of the line is Lord Byron's *Don Juan*, a poem Lincoln knew well: "and if I laugh at any mortal thing, tis that I may not weep."[61] To laugh to keep from weeping expresses beautifully the dynamic relationship between Lincoln's humor and his depression. Contemporary observers were quite aware of the connection. Harriet Beecher Stowe felt Lincoln possessed "a never-failing fund of patience" that lay buried beneath his deep melancholy and periodically rose to the surface in some "droll, quaint saying, or story, that forced a laugh, even from himself."[62] David Davis, the judge on the eighth circuit and a dear friend of Lincoln and his campaign manager in 1860, said Lincoln's stories were intended primarily "to whistle off sadness."[63] Herndon stressed the rapid alternation of Lincoln's moods from gloom to joy—and back.[64] Chambrun also noted this alternation of mood. "He willingly laughed either at what was being said or at what he himself was saying. Then, suddenly, he would retire himself and close his eyes, while his face expressed a melancholy as indescribable as it was deep. After a few moments, as though by an effort of the will, he would shake off his mysterious weight and his generous and open disposition again reasserted itself. I have counted, in one evening, more than twenty of such alternations of mood."[65] And everyone noted his hearty laugh and sparkling eyes. "That laugh," noted Carpenter, "has been the President's life-preserver."[66]

Humor in this sense served therapeutic purposes for Lincoln, though it also relaxed his clients, helped keep political opponents in their place, won many friends and much influence, and facilitated his leadership as President. Humor seemed to provide a kind of vitality for Lincoln, a zest that kept his depression at bay. More hypothetically, it also seems that the effectiveness of his humor helped him to tolerate the regressive pulls of depression and thus to stop fearing his melancholy, as he probably did in his childhood and certainly did in his youth. Humor never completely eliminated his depression—he was gloomy to the end. But it helped ease his radical shifts in mood and gave him confidence that he himself need not disintegrate in his depression. Thus a gloomy patient at the start of analysis might wrap himself in a shroud of desperate isolation to avoid experiencing the pulls of the transference. Years later at the termination of analysis this same patient might still get depressed, but if things had worked out tolerably well he would be able to shift easily into other moods and see a quiet humor in his earlier fears.

Lincoln's humor itself changed as he matured and confronted increasingly complex responsibilities and challenges. In general he avoided cruel satire and biting sarcasm. But as a young man, when he himself was more confused and needy, his humor at times lost its empathic glow. As a youth in Indiana he wrote a long, angry satire, the "Chronicles of Reuben" (discussed in chapter 2), to get back at the Grigsbys, his sister's in-laws, who he felt were indirectly responsible for her death in childbirth in 1828. The poem describes in mock-Biblical style a wedding-night confusion after the joint wedding of Reuben's two sons. The wrong parties end up in bed together.[67] Then in the early 1840s Lincoln helped Mary Todd and Julia Jayne write the "Rebecca Letters" (see page 71), a cruel satire of the blustering James Shields, which was somehow psychologically associated with his broken engagement. Lincoln wrote one of the three tales (and, from a literary point of view, the best one), but he willingly assumed responsibility for all three when Shields demanded to know the author. To Lincoln's horror Shields challenged him to a duel. Lincoln reportedly suggested as weapons that they use cow-dung at five paces.[68] Shields was not amused, and the two had to proceed with all the silly rituals of seconds exchanging notes, challenges, and counter-challenges. Actual battle was prevented at the last minute, but Lincoln never forgave himself for getting into such a situation and refused ever to talk about it; nor did he develop a repertoire of duel jokes.[69] Still, even in this serious and, for Lincoln, shameful experience, he managed some humor: his final choice of weapons was broadswords at ten paces (about thirty feet).

"It really hurts me very much," Lincoln said during his debates with Stephen Douglas in 1858, "to suppose that I have wronged anybody on earth."[70] Such sentiments expressed Lincoln's need for support and esteem from those around him. But they also capture his sensitivity to others and his empathic relatedness to those figures from whom he sought esteem. "He was modest, quiet and unobtrusive in his manner," wrote Whitney of Lincoln before 1860, but also "sympathetic and cordial in social contract.... His sad countenance aroused universal sympathy, his *bonhomie*, geniality and humor drew all men involuntarily to him...."[71] Judge Holt, who implemented Lincoln's wartime reprieves for soldiers, called him "without exception the most tender-hearted man I ever knew."[72] Such characterizations contain an element of ambiguity, however, for someone with a "tender" heart is also "soft-hearted," a pushover. Lincoln, on the contrary, rose above the petty jealousies and compulsive ritualizations of our culture to deal honestly and empathically with personal and political issues. There is no reason to question his genuine feeling for the thousands of terrified young soldiers who proved to be cowards. He managed, however, to cover his kindness politically, by allowing the Secretary of War, Edwin Stanton, virtually free reign in repealing his reprieves. "I want to oblige everybody when I can," Lincoln once said, "and Stanton and I have an understanding that if I send on an order to him which cannot be consistently granted, he is to refuse it. This he sometimes does."[73]

Perhaps the most famous example of Lincoln's empathy was his letter to Mrs. Lydia Bixby on November 21, 1864. "I have been shown," he began, "... that you are the mother of five sons who have died gloriously on the field of battle." Lincoln notes how "weak and fruitless" any words from him must be to comfort her on the loss. "But I cannot refrain from tendering to you the consolation that may be found in the thanks of the Republic they died to save." In conclusion Lincoln essentially joins in prayer with Mrs. Bixby to help her mourn such a terrible loss: "I pray that our Heavenly Father may assuage the anguish of your bereavement, and leave you only the cherished memory of the loved and lost, and the solemn pride that must be yours, to have laid so costly a sacrifice upon the altar of Freedom. Yours, very sincerely and respectfully, A. Lincoln."[74] The invocation of God here and the rather extravagant imagery of the "altar of Freedom" is a good example of Lincoln slipping into the kind of language and metaphor that he suspected would prove most understandable to his reader. In the same way, he could move easily between folksy, sometimes vulgar humor with illiterate clients on the circuit and

A photograph of Lincoln, taken not long before his death. It captures visually the lines in the Second Inaugural Address: "With malice toward none; with charity for all." *National Portrait Gallery, Smithsonian Institution*

exalted, noble statements on the ultimate meaning of the war that spoke quite consciously to history. No one had finer tuning to his audiences.

It is also the case that Lincoln's fleeting experience with paranoia in the 1850s expressed primarily his own empathic sensitivity to the vulnerabilities in the group self. Certainly there was no basis for that sensitivity in his earlier experience, and once the war began—and the crisis passed—it all but disappeared as part of his public or private self. One of the wonders of Lincoln's style was the way it changed and adapted to new environments. The Presidency nourished Lincoln's strengths and gave him renewed confidence. His depression ebbed. He took complete charge of his cabinet and greater control of military affairs. He brushed aside the unrelenting criticism. And he carefully shaped his own heroic image. It was not simply that he was ambitious to the point of arrogance; Lincoln nourished a heroic style as the one best suited for a country emerging from a terrible civil war. The shaping of that style drew on his greatest empathic strengths. He knew better than anyone the deep yearnings for greatness in a war-torn nation. The style he developed fitted exactly.

Empathy also carries within it forgiveness. Lincoln, it can be fairly said, never held a grudge. Like most lawyers, he could leave a bitter courtroom battle without an ounce of enmity. He never seemed to feel petty anger toward anyone, tolerating even Mary's lifelong hatreds. Where possible he simply adjusted his behavior to meet her demands, while refusing to identify with her feelings. For example, he yielded to her dislike of his law partner Herndon by never having him in his home; but for all those years (1844–61) he also never questioned the permanence of their partnership. The most important example of Lincoln's forgiveness is in the public rather than the private sphere—his attitude toward southern responsibility for causing the war. "Both parties deprecated war," he noted in his Second Inaugural Address, "but one of them would *make* war rather than let the nation survive; and the other would *accept* war rather than let it perish. And the war came." Neither side anticipated the scale of war that resulted or that the "*cause* of the conflict might cease with, or even before, the conflict itself should cease." Both sides read the same Bible and pray to the same God; ". . . but let us judge not that we be not judged. The prayers of both could not be answered; that of neither has been answered fully."[75]

One of the wonders of Lincoln's creative impulse is that, superficially, it seems to have come from nowhere. As a child he read intently, but he had relatively few books at his disposal and the few "blab" schools he attended were hardly model institutions of learning. Many close to Lincoln were struck by how "desultory" his reading was,[76] even when he was an adult. Herndon said: "Beyond a limited acquaintance with Shakespeare, Byron, and Burns, Mr. Lincoln, comparatively speaking, had no knowledge of literature. He was familiar with the Bible . . . [but] he never in his life sat down and read a book through."[77]

Lincoln says he began reading law in 1834 with the encouragement of John T. Stuart. A contemporary later noted "He borrowed all the Law Books he could . . . get hold of. . . ."[78] It is not clear what else he read in those years, but it would seem he must have read something, although the oral history accounts record only his reading law books.[79] Herndon has left us a vivid description of Lincoln stretched out on his couch, reading aloud from the newspaper "to catch the sound with both senses."[80] The daily newspaper was the most important literary item in Lincoln's life.[81] He absorbed newspapers and everything they had to say about contemporary political affairs. Sarah Lincoln told Herndon how her stepson began reading newspapers closely in Indiana in the later 1820s. In New Salem Lincoln was largely interested in becoming postmaster because it gave him the opportunity to read the incoming newspapers free of charge. In Springfield he took an avid interest in the affairs of the *Journal,* writing many stories for it over the years and becoming close friends with the editor. He even owned a share of a German-language newspaper. The notebook that he carried with him to the debates with Douglas in 1858 consisted largely of clippings of newspapers. He even joked about his fascination with newspapers. He told John E. Rosette, an attorney in Springfield, once about the purchase of a new newspaper: "When the paper was brought to my house, my wife said to me, 'Now are you going to take another worthless little paper?' "[82]

The notion that Lincoln's simple literary tastes barely went beyond the newspaper (except, of course, for the Bible) draws largely on our mythical conception that Lincoln's genius was somehow imparted directly from God. In fact, he was quite a bookish fellow (in this, Randall has it wrong).[83] Roy P. Basler, Lincoln scholar and editor of the *Collected Works*, examined some of the textbooks Lincoln used as a boy and felt that he "probably had a more thorough training in formal rhetoric than the average college graduate of the present."[84] That, of course, says something about both Lincoln and our contemporary college graduates. What he read, from Parson Weems's *Life of Washington* to the Bible and the newspaper, he completely absorbed, often memorizing whole passages. He was able to recite long poems and knew much of his beloved Shakespeare by heart.

Nothing is more striking about Lincoln's creative style than the Biblical tone to his prose. At times he seems to be another Old Testament prophet. Elton Trueblood, a theologian, has given us the most complete discussion of this aspect of Lincoln's thought. The Gettysburg Address, for example, with its heavy use of monosyllables, reads like the Twenty-third Psalm, which Lincoln could recite from memory.[85] Of the 265 words in the Gettysburg Address,[86] 194 are of one syllable; the Twenty-third Psalm, with 118 words, has 92 of one syllable. By the time of his maturity, Lincoln had absorbed not only the contents of the Bible but its style and unique use of language. In the house divided speech Lincoln noted the superiority of a living dog to a dead lion, a reference to Ecclesiastes 9:4.[87] Even in personal letters Lincoln evoked the Bible. He wrote to Ward Hill Lamon: "as to the inclination of some Republicans to favor Douglas that is one of the chances I have to run and which I intend to run with patience." This phrasing evokes the beginning of the twelfth chapter of Hebrews in an "oblique and subtle" way.[88]

The Bible, however important, was not alone in shaping Lincoln's style of creativity. Two literary critics, William K. Wimsatt and Cleanth Brooks, make the astute point that Lincoln was

Lincoln reading to his son Tad on February 9, 1864. *Ostendorf Collection*

profoundly influenced by the oratorical tradition that began with the Greek sophists. This "Ciceronian ideal" is that "of rational man reaching his noblest attainment in the expression of an eloquent wisdom. Necessary steps in the attainment of this ideal are careful drill in the poets followed by a program of encyclopedic scope directed to the forensic end of political power."[89] Basler has noted the technical devices that characterize Lincoln's rhetoric—repetition, grammatical parallelism, and antithesis.[90] Lincoln strove always for emphasis and simplicity. The Gettysburg Address repeats "we" ten times, "here" eight times, and nearly half of all the words in the speech are repetitions.[91] Lincoln tended to read everything aloud—law, papers, and poetry—much to the annoyance of Herndon. His explanation was that he remembered it better when he heard *and* read it.[92] Lincoln wanted to hear what he read also because he knew his important, matured thoughts would be spoken.

The word, creatively used, is an instrument of enormous power. As a boy Lincoln tested his father by talking first to strangers. After church he stood on a stump and mimicked the preacher's sermon. Later, as a young man, he struck out in anger with the satirical poem "The Chronicles of Reuben," and again with his "Rebecca Letters." In time he learned to direct his power with words more productively. In his law practice he was simple, direct, and forceful; and his law practice brought him an entirely respectable life. But the most important achievement of his creative use of the word was the securing of political power. At first he groped, as in the awkward Young Men's Lyceum speech in 1838, which is confused in places: "Thus, then, by the operation of this mobocratic spirit, which all must admit, is now abroad in the land, the strongest bulwark of any Government and particularly of those constituted like ours, may effectually be broken down and destroyed—I mean the *attachment* of the People."[93] As he matured, however, Lincoln sharpened his skills. His long struggle with Stephen Douglas from 1854 to 1860 forced him to find clearer, simpler, more effective ways of saying the same thing repeatedly. With Lincoln each repetition became more eloquent. By the time of his inauguration in 1861, Lincoln could turn a phrase that mobilized a nation. Consider, for example, these two drafts for the closing paragraph of his First Inaugural Address that William Seward presented to Lincoln.

However unusual it may be at such a time to speak of sections or to sections, yet in view of the misconceptions and agitations which have strained the ties of brotherhood so far, I hope it will not be deemed a departure from propriety, whatever it may be from custom, to say that if in the criminations and misconstructions which too often imbue our political contests, any man south of this capital has been led to believe that I regard with a less friendly eye his rights, his interests, or his domestic safety and happiness, or those of his State, than I do those of any other portion of my country, or that I would invade or disturb any legal right or domestic institution in the South, he mistakes both my principles and feelings, and does not know me. I aspire to come in the spirit, however far below the ability and wisdom, of Washington, of Madison, of Jackson, and of Clay. In that spirit I here declare that in my administration I shall know no rule but the Constitution, no guide but the laws, and no sentiment but that of equal devotion to my whole country, east, west, north, and south.

I close. We are not, we must not be, aliens or enemies, but fellow-countrymen and brethren. Although passion has strained our bonds of affection too hardly, they must not, I am sure they will not, be broken. The mystic chords which, proceeding from so many battlefields and so many patriot graves, pass through all the hearts and all hearths in this broad continent of ours, will yet again harmonize in their ancient music when breathed upon by the guardian angel of the nation.

And compare them with the final draft Lincoln developed from them.

I am loth to close. We are not enemies. Though passions may have strained, it must not break our bonds of affection. The mystic chords of memory, stretching from every battlefield, and patriot grave, to every living heart and hearthstone, all over this broad land, will yet swell the chorus of the Union, when again touched, as surely they will be, by the better angels of our nature.[94]

No writer appealed more to Lincoln than Shakespeare. Some of the plays—*King Lear, Richard III, Henry VIII, The Merry Wives of Windsor, Hamlet,* and, his favorite, *Macbeth*—he knew virtually by heart.[95] He was fond of talking with James H. Hackett, the actor, of the subtle meanings of different characters and passages.[96] John Hay noted on December 13, 1863, that a conversation between Lincoln and Hackett "at first took a professional turn, the Tycoon showing a very intimate knowledge of those plays of Shakespeare where Falstaff figures."[97] Hay also noted a few days later that Lincoln went to Ford's theater with him, Nicolay, and Swett to see Hackett in *Henry IV*. Lincoln thoroughly enjoyed the performance, though he disputed Hackett's interpretation of one line.[98] It seems clear that Lincoln turned repeatedly to Shakespeare for the depth of his insight into human motivation, the cleverness of his wit, and, perhaps, most basically of all, for the aesthetic appeal of his language. Lincoln continually sought to chasten and perfect his style; in Shakespeare, and probably nowhere else, he found a master whose own creativity provided a model.[99]

What several recent commentators have found interesting psychologically about Lincoln's fascination with Shakespeare was his attraction to the plays in which ambitious and envious men actually kill their brothers and other members of their families to reach and keep power. These men—Macbeth, Hamlet, and the various princes and kings in the histories—reflect on their guilt but still carry forward plans of aggression and death. In *Hamlet*, Lincoln was struck most of all by Claudius's soliloquy, "O, my offence is rank," which he felt surpassed Hamlet's "To be or not to be."[100] Nowhere, however, are the issues of guilt and ambition clearer than in *Macbeth*, which was Lincoln's favorite play. "I think nothing equals *Macbeth*," Lincoln told Hackett. "It is wonderful."[101] Lincoln turned to *Macbeth* often but once most dramatically at the very end of his life. Richmond was liberated, the war all but over. Lincoln had traveled by steamer to visit the Confederate's fallen capital. He stared "a long while" at the battlefields "absorbed in thought," Chambrun reported to his wife the next day. And he read *Macbeth*. On Sunday, April 9, "Mr. Lincoln read aloud to us for several hours. Most of the passages he selected were from Shakespeare, especially *Macbeth*. The lines after the murder of Duncan, when the new king falls a prey to moral torment, were dramatically dwelt on. Now and then he paused to expatiate on how exact a picture Shakespeare here gives of a murderer's mind when, the dark deed achieved, its perpetrator already envies his victim's calm sleep. He read the scene over twice."[102]

Lincoln's fascination with these themes in Shakespeare suggests a large measure of unconscious guilt. This has prompted some to interpret Lincoln's plans for a rapid and gentle reconstruction of the Union as a kind of absolution for his responsibility in first causing the war. Don Fehrenbacher develops a rather larger view of Lincoln's apparent guilt ("apparent" Fehrenbacher remarks justly, for there is no direct evidence Lincoln felt guilty about anything). "Yet his responsibilities as President must have weighed as heavily as the guilt of any assassin, and the latest casuality lists must have seemed like accusations." And Fehrenbacher concludes dramatically: "It is not altogether unlikely that in the gloom of some sleepless night he too beheld blood upon his hands or found a prayer faltering on his lips.[103]

Even more recently, George B. Forgie interprets Lincoln's attraction to plays like *Macbeth* in terms of Lincoln's murderous hate and jealousy of Douglas in the 1850s during their titanic struggle for power. Lincoln only achieved power by finally slaying his opponent. This political victory, which meant the symbolic death of Douglas (who in fact died shortly after Lincoln's inauguration), seemed to bring with it large doses of guilt the war soon absorbed and enlarged. Lincoln's identification with conscience-stricken murderers in some of Shakespeare's plays, Forgie argues, derived from this guilt.[104] If Fehrenbacher draws attention to the events of the war itself as the basis for Lincoln's guilt, Forgie argues for the formative political struggles of the 1850s as the arena in which Lincoln's guilt was molded.

Guilt, however, is rooted psychologically and developmentally in childhood experiences. As a basic affect, guilt will later attach itself to many different derivative experiences. Events in the present, in other words, provide the material for our guilty thoughts, but the repressed, unconscious experiences from childhood generate the guilt itself. Both Fehrenbacher and Forgie miss this point. The war and the struggle with Douglas were perhaps the kind of psychologically expressive experiences that prompted the appearance of Lincoln's guilt. But they hardly created it. For one thing, the essential evidence is Lincoln's strong attraction to certain aspects of Shakespeare's writings. But Lincoln, as contemporaries unanimously agreed, was "a close and appreciative reader of many of the plays during his mature years in Springfield." Furthermore, he probably first encountered Shakespeare as a child in passages selected for grammar books such as one we know he used, William Scott's *Lessons in Elocution*. The famous soliloquies and other familiar passages were used for illustration in books like Scott's. It is likely Lincoln first memorized these disjointed parts of Shakespeare and later, as an adult, fitted them into the complete plays.[105]

Roy Basler has taken a more fruitful approach to Lincoln's fascination with Shakespeare's plays. Lincoln's lifelong devotion to Shakespeare, Basler argues, assumed new meaning during the war, for Lincoln came to see himself as a poetic figure imposed on the nation. He aimed to "identify himself, by words and in relationship to his contemporaries, as a representative, symbolic identity."[106] During the war Lincoln became a kind of Shakespearian figure, a tragic and symbolic hero, as much by his actions as by his words. And, further, as Basler suggests, Lincoln quite consciously created his image, shaping it as opportunity arose "with his mind's eye on the ultimate scene of the ultimate act." That Lincoln also seemed like an Old Testament prophet by no means contradicts this point. The apocalyptic vision, as Edmund Wilson once noted, imposed itself.[107]

Conclusion

INCOLN'S quest for union took many shapes. At first, the issues were purely personal and often conflicted; at the end, the public realm swallowed up the enlarged self. In between— where this study concentrates—public and private concerns blended in creative ways.

The story of Lincoln's personality and character has its own special interest. The personal lives of few historical figures have, in fact, attracted so much attention. In that story, generations of Americans have tried to find themselves. There was adversity in the poverty and lack of opportunity. There was conflict with the father, with sexuality and intimacy, within the self. There was sadness in the struggle with death and a lifelong pattern of depression. There was determination and hard work. There was unaccountable skill as the young boy defined his separateness from his rural environment and the man grew in stature after each defeat. There was wonderful humor. There was empathy. There was creativity.

Childhood themes merged with adult concerns of love and work. The young man juggled many roles before finding cohesion and integrity in his identity as a lawyer and politician. He worked hard at loving, first in courtship, then in a deeply satisfying but complicated relationship with his wife, Mary. Over the course of a decade he tried to find a viable role as husband and father. But his closeness alternated with inner demands for being apart, separate, and idealized. Mary in turn gave much, perhaps most of all the confirmation that he could love genuinely and father children. But their close relationship and enclosed home held their own divisions. Their intimacy, one might say, was always potentially explosive.

After 1854 Lincoln discovered, remarkably enough, that his private concerns found reflection in the country as a whole. His own ambivalent quest for union—with his dead mother, his bride, his alienated father—gave meaning to the nation's turbulence as it hurtled toward civil war. It took time for Lincoln to bridge the two exactly. He needed the right metaphor. In the idea of a house divided, Lincoln found a way of creatively enlarging his private concerns to fill the public space. When he found it, there was resonance.

Until the Presidency, however, Lincoln hardly spoke for the nation. He defined the issues of union—and disunion—but until late in the 1850s he was in many respects only a midwestern politician dwarfed by Stephen Douglas in his own state, even in his own town. In retrospect the extent to which Lincoln had his finger on the pulse of the nation after 1854 is much clearer. Lincoln expressed then the deep and underlying issues for everyone in the troubled country. It was a confusing time, when suspiciousness slipped into paranoia, when few were touched, as Lincoln put it in his First Inaugural Address, by the better angels of their nature.

Lincoln the President rose to new heights as he led the North toward victory and, as soon as that was secured, began to lay the groundwork for healing the wounds of war. He died, of course, before Reconstruction, which makes it futile to speculate what he might have done. But it is not frivolous to guess that he purposely shaped his heroic image to fit a nation longing for unity and greatness. The image he shaped dissolved struggles over father, fatherhood, and founders. It put him in touch with God. And it gave America its greatest hero.

NOTES

Preface and Acknowledgments

1. Charles B. Strozier, "Disciplined Subjectivity and the Psychohistorian: A Critical Look at the Work of Erik Erikson," *The Psychohistory Review* 5 (1976): 28-31. Disciplined subjectivity as the working method of psychohistory builds on the psychoanalytic notion of empathy. See Heinz Kohut, "Introspection, Empathy, and Psychoanalysis: An Examination of the Relationship between Mode of Operation and Theory," *The Search for the Self: Selected Writings of Heinz Kohut, 1950-1978,* ed. Paul H. Ornstein, 2 vols. (New York: International Universities Press, 1978), 1:205-32. It is worth pointing out that not everyone in psychohistory agrees with my own emphasis on "disciplined subjectivity." See Fred Weinstein and Gerald Platt, *Psychoanalytic Sociology: An Essay on the Interpretation of Historical Data and the Phenomenon of Collective Behavior* (Baltimore: Johns Hopkins University Press, 1973), p. 1.

2. William H. Herndon and Jesse W. Weik, *Life of Lincoln,* ed. Paul M. Angle (Cleveland: World Publishing, 1930), p. 1. Note also Herndon to Weik, January 22, 1887, and Herndon to Truman H. Bartlett, September 22, 1887, Herndon/Weik Collection, microfilm, Illinois State Historical Library; hereafter cited as Herndon/Weik Collection. The most important material in the Herndon/Weik Collection, as well as Herndon's correspondence with Weik, has been published in Emmanuel Hertz, ed., *The Hidden Lincoln* (New York: Viking Press, 1938). Over the years I have used both the microfilm copies of the manuscripts and the Hertz book, which unfortunately modernizes the spelling and syntax and is generally a sloppy edition of these papers. In cases where I cite material I have checked the manuscript (on microfilm), but for the convenience of the reader I will give both the manuscript reference and the Hertz page on which the published version of the manuscript occurs. Some of the material in Hertz consists of letters Herndon wrote to Ward Hill Lamon. This collection is housed in the Lamon Collection, The Huntington Library, Huntington, California; hereafter cited as Lamon Collection. Although I indicate which letters are contained in the Huntington Library, I never had enough money to travel to California and examine these letters in the original.

3. Herndon and Weik, *Lincoln,* pp. 1-2.

4. David Donald, *Lincoln's Herndon: A Biography* (New York: Alfred A. Knopf, 1948), p. 343

5. David Donald, *Lincoln Reconsidered: Essays on the Civil War Era* ((New York: Alfred A. Knopf, 1956), p. 304.

6. Ibid., p. 305.

7. Donald, *Lincoln's Herndon,* p. 347.

8. Herndon and Weik, *Lincoln,* p. xl.

9. See chapter 2, p. 40, for the discussion of the Drake letter.

10. Albert J. Beveridge, *Abraham Lincoln, 1809-1858,* 2 vols. (Boston: Houghton Mifflin, 1928), 1:49.

11. Roy P. Basler, *The Lincoln Legend: A Study in Changing Conceptions* (Boston: Houghton Mifflin, 1935), pp. 25-26.

12. Seminar at Sangamon State University in Springfield, Illinois, April 16, 1979.

Chapter 1

1. William H. Herndon and Jesse W. Weik, *Life of Lincoln,* ed. Paul M. Angle (Cleveland: World Publishing, 1930), pp. 2-3. Note also three Herndon letters to Ward Hill

Notes

Lamon (all in Lamon Collection), February 28, 1869 (Hertz, p. 59); February 25, 1870 (Hertz, pp. 62–69); and March 6, 1870 (Hertz, pp. 69–72).

2. Roy P. Basler, ed., *The Collected Works of Abraham Lincoln*, 8 vols. (New Brunswick, N.J.: Rutgers University Press, 1953), 4:59–61. For Leonard Swett's comments, see Allen Thorndike Rice, *Reminiscences of Abraham Lincoln by Distinguished Men of His Time* (New York: North American Review, 1889), p. 457.

3. Louis A. Warren, *Lincoln's Parentage and Childhood: A History of the Kentucky Lincolns Supported by Documentary Evidence* (New York: Century, 1926); William E. Barton, *The Life of Abraham Lincoln*, 2 vols. (Indianapolis: Bobbs-Merrill, 1925) and *The Lineage of Lincoln* (Indianapolis: Bobbs-Merrill, 1929).

4. Carl Sandburg, *Abraham Lincoln: The Prairie Years*, 2 vols. (New York: Harcourt Brace, 1926), 1:11–12.

5. David Donald, *Lincoln's Herndon: A Biography* (New York: Alfred A. Knopf, 1948), p. 357.

6. Benjamin P. Thomas, *Abraham Lincoln: A Biography* (New York: Alfred A. Knopf, 1952), p. 6; Stephen B. Oates, *With Malice toward None: The Life of Abraham Lincoln* (New York: Harper and Row, 1977), p. 6.

7. Herbert Guttman, *The Black Family in Slavery and Freedom, 1725–1915* (New York: Pantheon Books, 1976). Compare Alex Haley, *Roots* (Garden City, N.Y.: Doubleday, 1976).

8. Catherine Beecher, *Treatise on Domestic Economy, for the use of Young Ladies At Home, and At School* (Boston: T. H. Webb, 1842); Barbara Welter, "The Cult of True Womanhood: 1820–1860," *The American Family in Social-Historical Perspective*, ed. Michael Gordon, 2nd ed. (New York: St. Martin's Press, 1978), pp. 313–34; Nancy F. Cott, "Notes toward an Interpretation of Antebellum Childrearing," *The Psychohistory Review* 6 (1978):4–20; Nancy F. Cott and Elizabeth H. Pleck, eds., *A Heritage of Her Own: Toward a New Social History of American Women* (New York: Simon and Schuster, 1979); Carl Degler, *At Odds: Women and the Family in America, From the Revolution to the Present* (New York: Oxford University Press, 1980).

9. Kathryn Kish Sklar, "Victorian Women and Domestic Life: Mary Todd Lincoln, Elizabeth Cady Stanton and Harriet Beecher Stowe," *The Public and Private Lincoln: Contemporary Perspectives*, ed. Cullom Davis et al. (Carbondale: Southern Illinois University Press, 1979), pp. 20–37.

10. Charles Friend to Herndon, August 20, 1889, Herndon/Weik Collection (Hertz, p. 342).

11. Barton, *Lincoln*, p. 20.

12. Albert Beveridge, *Abraham Lincoln, 1809–1858*, 2 vols. (New York: Houghton Mifflin, 1928), 1:15.

13. Herndon to Ward Hill Lamon, February 25, 1870, Lamon Collection (Hertz, pp. 63–64).

14. Herndon to Ward Hill Lamon, March 15, 1870, Lamon Collection (Hertz, p. 79).

15. Herndon to Jesse Weik, January 19, 1888, Herndon/Weik Collection (Hertz, p. 138). Compare a similar account of Herndon's in a letter to Jesse Weik, September 30, 1887, Herndon/Weik Collection (Hertz, pp. 205–7). Herndon stuck by his Enloe thesis, despite the contradictory testimonial from Enloe's nephew, Charles Friend; see Friend to Herndon, July 30, 1889, Herndon/Weik Collection (Hertz, pp. 340–41).

16. Donald, *Lincoln's Herndon*, p. 357.

17. Herndon to Ward Hill Lamon, March 6, 1870, Lamon Collection (Hertz, p. 74).

18. Herndon to Ward Hill Lamon, February 25, 1870, Lamon Collection (Hertz, p. 63).

19. Sandburg, *Lincoln*, 1:13.

20. *Collected Works*, 4:61.

21. John Hanks's statement to Herndon, n. d., Herndon/Weik Collection (Hertz, p. 345). Compare Nat Grigsby to Herndon, September 12, 1865, Herndon/Weik Collection (Hertz, pp. 353–54).

22. William Woods's statement to Herndon, September 15, 1865, Herndon/Weik Collection (Hertz, p. 364).

23. Dennis F. Hanks to Herndon, June 13, 1865, Herndon/Weik Collection (Hertz, p. 276).

Notes

24. Herndon to Jesse Weik, January 19, 1886, Herndon/Weik Collection (Hertz, p. 139).

25. Sandburg, *Lincoln* 1:26. Dennis Hanks reported that "Lincoln's mother [Nancy] learned him to read the Bible...." See Dennis F. Hanks's statement to Herndon, June 13, 1865, Herndon/Weik Collection (Hertz, p. 276).

26. David Elton Trueblood, *Abraham Lincoln: Theologian of American Anguish* (New York: Harper and Row, 1973), p. 50.

27. Herndon to Truman H. Bartlett, October 1887, Herndon/Weik Collection (Hertz, p. 208).

28. Beveridge, *Lincoln*, 1:15.

29. Barton, *Lincoln*, p. 14.

30. Oates, *With Malice toward None*, p. 5.

31. This specific connection between the quality of the infantile empathic environment and the shape of the adult personality was first noted by Heinz Kohut, "Forms and Transformations of Narcissism," *The Search for the Self: Selected Writings of Heinz Kohut, 1950–1978*, ed. Paul H. Ornstein, 2 vols. (New York: International Universities Press, 1978), 1:427–60.

32. *Collected Works*, 1:118.

33. Dennis F. Hanks to Herndon, June 13, 1865, Herndon/Weik Collection (Hertz, p. 275).

34. Herndon to Ward Hill Lamon, February 25, 1870, Lamon Collection (Hertz, p. 63); Charles Friend to Herndon, July 30, 1889, Herndon/Weik Collection (Hertz p. 341); Herndon's notes to himself, n.d., Herndon/Weik Collection (Hertz, pp. 393–94).

35. Herndon's notes to himself, n.d., Herndon/Weik Collection (Hertz, p. 393).

36. Herndon to Jesse Weik, January 1, 1886, Herndon/Weik Collection (Hertz pp. 118–19).

37. Herndon's notes to himself, n.d., Herndon/Weik Collection (Hertz, p. 393). For years Herndon wrestled with the issue of the exact timing of castration but never doubted the reality of the event. He never seemed to note the distinction between castration and induced sterility from mumps. See Herndon to Truman H. Bartlett, September 30, 1887, Herndon/Weik Collection (Hertz, pp. 205–7).

38. Nat Grigsby's statement to Herndon, September 12, 1865, Herndon/Weik Collection (Hertz, p. 355).

39. Josiah G. Holland, *The Life of Abraham Lincoln* (Springfield, Mass.: Gurdon Bill, 1866), pp. 22–23, 28.

40. Ward Hill Lamon, *The Life of Abraham Lincoln: From His Birth to His Inauguration as President* (Boston: James E. Osgood, 1872), p. 75.

41. Herndon and Weik, *Lincoln*, p. 12.

42. Beveridge, *Lincoln*, 1:5.

43. Warren, *Lincoln's Parentage*, p. 47; Harry E. Pratt, *The Personal Finances of Abraham Lincoln* (Springfield, Ill.: Abraham Lincoln Association, 1943), p. 4.

44. Herndon's note on his visit to the Lincoln farm in Kentucky, September 14, 1865, Herndon/Weik Collection (Hertz, p. 359).

45. Warren, *Lincoln's Parentage*, pp. 122–23.

46. Herndon and Weik, *Lincoln*, p. 13.

47. Thomas, *Lincoln*, p. 5.

48. Oates, *With Malice toward None*, p. 6.

49. *Collected Works*, 1:280.

50. William E. Barton, *The Lineage of Lincoln* (Indianapolis: Bobbs-Merrill, 1929), p. 83.

51. Thomas, *Lincoln*, p. 134.

52. *Collected Works*, 4:61.

53. Ibid., 1:456.

54. Lincoln retained a disdain for the symbols of ignorance generally. He once asked Herndon to handle a letter from Louis W. Chandler because he was "bored more than enough about it; not the least of which annoyance is his cursed, unreadable, and ungodly handwriting." *Collected Works*, 1:445.

55. Dennis F. Hanks's statement to Herndon, June 13, 1865, Herndon/Weik Collection (Hertz, p. 280).

56. Ibid. (Hertz, p. 278).

57. Sarah Lincoln's statement to Herndon, September 8, 1865, Herndon/Weik Collection (Hertz, p. 351).

58. Dennis F. Hanks's statement to Herndon, June 13, 1865, Herndon/Weik Collection (Hertz, p. 278).

59. Beveridge, *Lincoln* 1:3.

60. Ibid., 1:51.

61. Ibid., 1:45.

62. John Hanks's statement to Herndon, n.d., Herndon/Weik Collection (Hertz, p. 346).

63. Sarah Lincoln's statement to Herndon, September 8, 1865, Herndon/Weik Collection (Hertz, p. 350).

64. Alexis de Tocqueville, *Democracy in America*, ed. Richard D. Heffner (New York: New American Library, 1956), pp. 243–47.

65. *Collected Works*, 4:61; Warren, *Lincoln's Parentage*, p. 154.

66. *Collected Works*, 2:94.

67. Ibid., 3:511; 4:61.

68. Ibid., 4:62.

69. Beveridge, *Lincoln* 1:36–37. Note also the discussion of this issue in Oates, *With Malice Toward None*, p. 6 and Benjamin Quarles, *Lincoln and the Negro* (New York: Oxford University Press, 1962), p. 16.

70. Beveridge, *Lincoln*, 1:33.

71. Dennis F. Hanks to Herndon, June 13, 1865, Herndon/Weik Collection (Hertz, p. 275).

72. *Collected Works*, 4:62.

73. Ibid.

74. Dennis F. Hanks to Herndon, June 13, 1865, Herndon/Weik Collection (Hertz, p. 278).

75. Ibid. (Hertz, p. 280).

76. Ibid.

77. Roy P. Basler, "Lincoln's Development as a Writer," *A Touchstone for Greatness: Essays, Addresses, and Occasional Pieces about Abraham Lincoln* (Westport, Conn.: Greenwood Press, 1973), p. 57.

78. John Hanks's statement to Herndon, n.d., Herndon/Weik Collection (Hertz, p. 347).

79. Sarah Lincoln's statement to Herndon, September 8, 1865, Herndon/Weik Collection (Hertz, p. 350).

80. Ibid. (Hertz, p. 351).

81. Herndon and Weik, *Lincoln*, p. 38.

82. Herndon to Weik, December 29, 1885, Herndon/Weik Collection (Hertz, p. 116); Donald, *Herndon*, p. 128; Herndon and Weik, *Lincoln*, pp. 258, 268, 272.

83. Sarah Lincoln's statement to Herndon, September 8, 1865, Herndon/Weik Collection (Hertz, pp. 351–52). Compare Matilda Moore's statement to Herndon on the same day, Herndon/Weik Collection (not published in Hertz).

84. Sarah Lincoln's statement to Herndon, September 8, 1865, Herndon/Weik Collection (Hertz, p. 351).

85. Herndon to Weik, November 12, 1885, Herndon/Weik Collection (Hertz, p. 99); Herndon to Cyrus O. Poole, January 5, 1886, Herndon/Weik Collection (Hertz p. 120).

86. Herndon to Weik, November 12, 1885, Herndon/Weik Collection (Hertz, p. 99).

87. Louis A. Warren, *Lincoln's Youth: Indiana Years, Seven to Twenty-one, 1816–1830* (New York: Appleton-Century-Crofts, 1959), p. 84.

88. Herndon's notes to himself, n.d., Herndon/Weik Collection (Hertz, pp. 422–24). In the book he wrote with Weik, the "thigh" became the "ankle"; see Herndon and Weik, *Lincoln*, p. 31. Oddly, Matilda in her one written statement says "foot"; see Matilda Moore's statement to Herndon, September 8, 1865, Herndon/Weik Collection (not published in Hertz). The best one can say with certainty, it seems, is that the ax cut Matilda somewhere in the lower half of her body. I have chosen the "thigh" version not to be scurrilous but because it is the most complete account. Weik probably censored Herndon for the book, though the conflict between Herndon's notes and Matilda's statement is un-

Notes

explained. Herndon perhaps missed the sexual meaning of the story because he focused too intently on the theme of honesty, an aspect of the story given emphasis by the ax that connects Lincoln to Washington and the cherry tree (personal communication, John Patterson, Springfield, Illinois).

89. Dennis F. Hanks to Herndon, June 13, 1865, Herndon/Weik Collection (Hertz, pp. 280–81).

90. Sarah Lincoln to Herndon, September 8, 1865, Herndon/Weik Collection (Hertz, p. 353).

91. *Collected Works*, 4:62.

92. Sarah Lincoln to Herndon, September 8, 1865, Herndon/Weik Collection (Hertz, p. 352).

93. Lamon, *Lincoln*, p. 463.

94. Joshua Fry Speed, *Reminiscences of Abraham Lincoln and Notes of a Visit to California: Two Lectures* (Louisville: John P. Morton, 1884), pp. 11–17.

95. Justin G. Turner and Linda Levitt Turner, eds., *Mary Todd Lincoln: Her Life and Letters* (New York: Alfred A. Knopf, 1972), pp. 464–65.

96. Sandburg, *Lincoln*, 1:50.

97. In Freud's early papers on hysteria he reported with absolute conviction that early childhood sexual trauma (by which he meant seduction by the parent of the opposite sex) lay behind every adult case of hysteria; see Sigmund Freud, "Heredity and the Aetiology of the Neuroses" (1896), *The Standard Edition of the Complete Psychological Works of Sigmund Freud*, ed. James Strachey, 23 vols. (London: Hogarth Press, 1962), 3:153, "Further Remarks on the Neuro-Psychoses of Defence" (1886), 3:163, and "The Aetiology of Hysteria" (1896), 3:199. By the fall of 1897 Freud realized his infantile seduction theory was implausible; see Sigmund Freud to Wilhelm Fliess, September 21, 1897, *The Origins of Psycho-Analysis: Letters to Wilhelm Fliess, Drafts and Notes: 1877–1902*, ed. Marie Bonaparte, Anna Freud, and Ernst Kris, trans. Eric Mosbacher and James Strachey (New York: Basic Books, 1954), pp. 215–16. What mattered, clearly, was fantasy rather than reality. That idea led to the theory of infantile sexuality; see "Three Essays on the Theory of Sexuality" (1905), *Standard Edition*, 7:125–245.

98. Sigmund Freud, "Screen Memories" (1899), *Standard Edition*, 3:301–22.

99. One must be highly selective in discussing this literature for it is enormous. The orienting theoretical statement on mourning and loss generally remains the first: Sigmund Freud, "Mourning and Melancholia" (1917 [1915]), *Standard Edition*, 14:239–58. George Pollock extended Freud's insights to include the adaptive aspects of mourning; see George Pollock, "Mourning and Adaptation," *International Journal of Psychoanalysis* 42 (1961):341–61. Pollock has also worked on the specific meanings of childhood parental loss; see "Childhood, Parent, and Sibling Loss in Adult Patients," *Archives of General Psychiatry* 7 (1962):295–305; and "Mourning and Childhood Loss," *Bulletin of the Association of Psychoanalytic Medicine* 5 (1966):51–54. Note also Jeanne Lample-de-Groot, "Mourning in a 6-Year Old Girl," *Psychoanalytic Study of the Child* 31 (1976):273–81; Joshua M. Perman, "The Search for the Mother: Narcissistic Regression as a Pathway of Mourning in Childhood," *Psychoanalytic Quarterly* 48 (1979): 448–64 (note Perman's excellent bibliography for additional references). The third volume of John Bowlby's impressive *Attachment and Loss* has recently appeared: *Loss: Sadness and Depression* (New York: Basic Books, 1980). For insight into the relationship between childhood parental loss and adult suicide, see T. L. Dorpat, "Suicide, Loss, and Mourning," *Life-Threatening Behavior* 3 (1973):213–24. Heinz Kohut's work provides a different perspective on these issues; see *The Analysis of the Self: A Systematic Approach to the Psychoanalytic Treatment of Narcissistic Personality Disorders* (New York: International Universities Press, 1971); *The Restoration of the Self* (New York: International Universities Press, 1977); and *The Search for the Self*. The most useful source, however, for interpreting mourning and loss specifically from a self-psychological point of view are the cases of Mr. E and Mr. M in *The Psychology of the Self: A Casebook, written with the Collaboration of Heinz Kohut*, ed. Arnold Goldberg (New York: International Universities Press, 1978), pp. 263–96, 121–64.

100. Paul Dry first brought this interpretation of the turkey story to my attention; see Paul Dry, "With Charity for All: A Study of Lincoln's Political Moratorium and Re-Emergence" (undergraduate thesis, Harvard University, 1966).

Notes

101. *Collected Works*, 4:62.
102. The turkey story seems part of family legend. Dennis F. Hanks added the detail of his mother loading the gun: "Lincoln saw a wild turkey near the camp on the second day after landing [in Indiana], and Mrs. Lincoln, Abe's good mother, loaded the gun. Abe poked the gun through the crack of the camp and accidentally killed one, which he brought to the camp house." Dennis F. Hanks to Herndon, June 13, 1885, Herndon/Weik Collection (Hertz, p. 278).
103. The turkey scene, even symbolically interpreted, could relate to current events in Lincoln's life. But, like dreams, such tales also (and always) have a link to childhood events. It is that aspect of the story that is most relevant for the purposes of this chapter.
104. *Collected Works*, 4:62.
105. Mary S. Vineyard to Herndon, July 22, 1866, Herndon/Weik Collection (Hertz, pp. 302–3).
106. J. D. Wickizer to Herndon, November 25, 1866, Herndon/Weik Collection (Hertz, p. 320).
107. Herndon to Jesse Weik, December 1, 1888, Herndon/Weik Collection (Hertz, p. 227); see also Herndon and Weik, *Lincoln*, p. 58.
108. Nat Grigsby to Herndon, September 12, 1865, Herndon/Weik Collection (Hertz, p. 355).
109. *Collected Works*, 4:64.
110. Herndon and Weik, *Lincoln*, p. 23.
111. *Collected Works*, 1:378.
112. Ibid., 1:367–70; 1:378–79; 1:386–89.
113. Beveridge, *Lincoln*, 1:39.
114. *Collected Works*, 1:388–89.

Chapter 2

1. W[illiam] D[ean] Howells, *Life of Abraham Lincoln* (Springfield, Ill.: Abraham Lincoln Association, 1938), pp. 32–33. Minutes from the New Salem Debating Society no longer exist, but the Illinois State Historical Library does have the minutes from the debating society in Petersburg. Membership in the societies overlap, and the range of topics discussed was quite similar. One can therefore infer the nature of the New Salem Debating Society with some confidence from these records.
2. Russell Godby told William Herndon in 1865 that he once hired Lincoln to do some farm work but to his surprise found him sitting on a woodpile reading a book. Godby asked Lincoln what he was reading: "I'm not reading," he answered, "I'm studying." "Great God Almighty!" Godby exclaimed and walked on. See William H. Herndon and Jesse W. Weik, *Life of Lincoln*, ed. Paul M. Angle (Cleveland: World Publishing, 1930), p. 92. One should note, however, the literary quality of Charles James Fox Clarke's letters to his mother and brother from the village in the 1830s. See Charles R. Clarke, "Sketch of Charles James Fox Clarke with Letters to His Mother," *Journal of the Illinois State Historical Society* 22 (January 1930):559–81. Jack Kelso quoted Shakespeare and Burns, with or without encouragement, and Mentor Graham was sufficiently educated to assist Lincoln when he needed to learn some mathematics quickly. Finally, Dr. Allen, as mentioned above, was a graduate of Dartmouth.
3. The best source on New Salem and Lincoln's life there is Benjamin P. Thomas, *Lincoln's New Salem: Its History, Its Influence on Lincoln, Its Lincoln Legends, and the Story of Its Restoration*, new and rev. ed. (1834; Chicago and Lincoln's New Salem: Lincoln's New Salem Enterprises, 1973). Most of the New Salem legends originate in Herndon and Weik, *Lincoln*. The Clarke letters are among the few pieces of documentary evidence that exist on the village. Thomas effectively utililizes other contemporary sources such as newspapers.
4. After 1831 Thomas Lincoln and his wife, Sarah, lived in Coles County, Illinois, some seventy miles from Springfield.
5. Roy P. Basler, ed., *The Collected Works of Abraham Lincoln*, 8 vols. (New Brunswick, N.J.: Rutgers University Press, 1953), 2:96–97.
6. Thomas, *Lincoln's New Salem*, pp. 81–82.

Notes

7. *Collected Works*, 1:510.

8. " 'I was out of work,' he [Lincoln] said to me [Herndon] once, 'and there being no danger of more fighting, I could do nothing better than enlist again.' " Herndon and Weik, *Lincoln*, p. 82.

9. *Collected Works*, 4:65.

10. Ibid., 4:64.

11. Ibid., 4:65.

12. Ibid.

13. Thomas, *Lincoln's New Salem*, pp. 102–3.

14. Harry E. Pratt, *The Personal Finances of Abraham Lincoln* (Springfield, Ill.: Abraham Lincoln Association, 1943), p. 13.

15. Thomas, *Lincoln's New Salem*, pp. 111–12.

16. *Collected Works*, 4:65.

17. Thomas, *Lincoln's New Salem*, pp. 95–96.

18. Ibid., p. 98. Note also Howells, *Life of Lincoln*, pp. 32–33.

19. Thomas, *Lincoln's New Salem*, pp. 96–97.

20. *Collected Works*, 1:25.

21. Thomas, *Lincoln's New Salem*, p. 101.

22. *Collected Works*, 3:16.

23. Ibid., 4:65.

24. Ibid.

25. After Lincoln's death, Dummer told Herndon that "Lincoln used to come to our office—Stuart's and mine—in Springfield from New Salem and borrow law books." Herndon and Weik, *Lincoln*, p. 145n.

26. Paul Simon, *Lincoln's Preparation for Greatness: The Illinois Legislative Years* (Norman: University of Oklahoma Press, 1965), pp. 277–78.

27. Ibid., pp. 232–36.

28. The most extensive thoughts on identity are in the writings of Erik Erikson. Note especially *Childhood and Society*, 2nd ed. (New York: W. W. Norton, 1963); *Identity: Youth and Crisis* (New York: W. W. Norton, 1968); *Insight and Responsibility* (New York: W. W. Norton, 1964); and *Young Man Luther* (New York: W. W. Norton, 1958).

29. Kenneth Kenniston, "Youth as a Stage of Life," *Youth and Dissent* (New York: Harcourt Brace Jovanovich, 1960), pp. 3–21.

30. Heinz Kohut, discussion of "On the Adolescent Process as a Transformation of the Self" in Ernest S. Wolf, John E. Gedo, David M. Terman, *The Search for the Self: Selected Writings of Heinz Kohut, 1950–1978*, ed. Paul H. Ornstein, 2 vols. (New York: International Universities Press, 1978), 2:659–62. See also Kohut, *The Analysis of the Self: A Systemic Approach to the Psychoanalytic Treatment of Narcissistic Personality Disorders* (New York: International Universities Press, 1971), pp. 43–44, 55, 70, 76–77, 119, 139, 261, 312–13, 321; and *The Restoration of the Self* (New York: International Universities Press, 1977), pp. 5, 6, 131, 272.

31. Herndon and Weik, *Lincoln*, p. 105.

32. James G. Randall, *Lincoln the President: Springfield to Gettysburg*, 2 vols. (Gloucester, Mass.: Eyre and Spottiswoode, 1945), 2:321–42. James Hurt, "All the Living and the Dead: Lincoln's Imagery," *American Literature* 52 (1980):360, argues that the Rutledge story may have originated to explain Lincoln's depression.

33. Benjamin P. Thomas, *Abraham Lincoln: A Biography* (New York: Alfred A. Knopf, 1952), p. 56.

34. *Collected Works*, 1:78–79.

35. Ibid., 1:94–95.

36. Mary S. Vineyard [Owens] to Herndon, May 22, 1865, Herndon/Weik Collection (Hertz, p. 303); Herndon quoted the entire letter in his book; see Herndon and Weik, *Lincoln*, p. 119.

37. *Collected Works*, 1:118.

38. Ibid., 1:119.

39. James C. Conkling to Mercy Levering, September 21, 1840, Illinois State Historical Library.

40. Justin G. Turner and Linda Levitt Turner, eds., *Mary Todd Lincoln: Her Life and Letters* (New York: Alfred A. Knopf, 1972), p. 21.

41. *Collected Works*, 1:78.

42. Herndon and Weik, *Lincoln*, pp. 163–82.

43. Ruth Painter Randall, *The Courtship of Mr. Lincoln* (Boston: Little, Brown, 1957). Note also Randall's earlier book, *Mary Lincoln: Biography of a Marriage* (Boston: Little, Brown, 1953).

44. Randall, *Mary Lincoln*, pp. 47–51, 64, 70–71; Randall, *The Courtship*, pp. 117–18.

45. Randall, *The Courtship*, p. 125.

46. Randall, *Mary Lincoln*, p. 64.

47. Except, perhaps, by the women he loved.

48. Edmund Wilson, *Patriotic Gore: Studies in the Literature of the American Civil War* (New York: Oxford University Press, 1962), pp. 118–19.

49. Herndon and Weik, *Lincoln*, p. 304.

50. Ibid., p. 163.

51. Herndon to Ward Hill Lamon, February 25, 1870, Lamon Collection (Hertz, p. 68).

52. Ninian Wirt Edwards's statement to Herndon, September 27, 1887, Herndon/Weik Collection (Hertz, p. 374).

53. Herndon to Jesse Weik, January, 1891, Herndon/Weik Collection (Hertz, pp. 259–60).

54. Milton H. Shutes, *Lincoln's Emotional Life* (Philadelphia: Dorrance, 1957), pp. 68–69.

55. Erikson, *Childhood and Society*, p. 263.

56. Ibid., p. 264.

57. Joshua Fry Speed, *Reminiscences of Abraham Lincoln and Notes of a Visit to California: Two Lectures* (Louisville: John P. Morton, 1884), pp. 16–17.

58. Joshua F. Speed, "Incidents in the Early Life of A. Lincoln," memorandum to Herndon, n.d. [after 1865], Joshua Speed Collection, Illinois State Historical Library.

59. Herndon to Ward Hill Lamon, February 25, 1870, Lamon Collection (Hertz, pp. 65–66). This personal letter is consistent with Herndon's treatment in Herndon and Weik, *Lincoln*, pp. 150–51 and with Speed's memorandum to Herndon, n.d. Herndon/Weik Collection. All commentators who have worked with this evidence agree that Lincoln therefore slept with Speed from 1837 to late December, 1840. Note Randall, *The Courtship*, p. 122; and Gary Lee Williams, "James and Joshua Speed: Lincoln's Kentucky Friends" (Ph.D. diss., Duke University, 1971), pp. 15–29. I agree with this reconstruction of events. However, it should be noted that Herndon contradicted himself in two letters to Jesse Weik. In Herndon to Weik, Springfield, January 15, 1886, Herndon/Weik Collection (Hertz, p. 134), Herndon wrote: "Lincoln came to this city in 1837, and Joshua F. Speed gratuitously took him into his room, gave him bed and house room, etc. William Butler was a man of some wealth for the time . . . he took Lincoln to his house, gave him a bed, sleeping room, and boarded him from 1837 to 1842, when Lincoln got married to Miss Todd." The next day Herndon wrote again to Weik: "I intended to say that, in the Butler note, Butler gratuitously, freely, and without charge boarded Lincoln from 1837 to 1842, when Lincoln got married." In these letters to Weik, Herndon was of course contradicting his own dating elsewhere as well as all the other evidence. The explanation seems to me to be, first, Herndon's concern in those two letters to Weik was with Butler, not the establishment of accurate dates, and since it was long after the event, he probably was simply confused; and second, Lincoln probably did stay with Butler after January, 1841, that is, after he left Speed's store. In other words, Lincoln stayed from 1837 to December, 1840, with Speed and from sometime in early 1841 to November, 1842, with Butler. Herndon simply collapsed the two in his 1886 letters to Weik, even though elsewhere he correctly dated Lincoln's stay with Speed. The importance of this question will become obvious later in my discussion.

60. Herndon and Weik, *Lincoln*, pp. 150–51.

61. Randall, *The Courtship*, pp. 11–17.

62. Speed, *Reminiscences of Lincoln*, p. 23.

63. Ward Hill Lamon, *The Life of Abraham Lincoln: From His Birth to His Inauguration as President* (Boston: James E. Osgood, 1872), p. 483.

64. Herndon to Jesse Weik, January 22, 1887, Herndon/Weik Collection (Hertz, p. 159).

Notes

65. *Collected Works*, 1:269.

66. Herndon wrote that "on the love question alone Lincoln opened to Speed possibly the whole." Herndon to Jesse Weik, January 22, 1887, Herndon/Weik Collection (Hertz, p. 159).

67. Randall, *The Courtship*, variously characterizes Speed as "the frequent lover" (p. 42); as having a "pleasing personality" (p. 12); as "apt to fall in love with practically every pretty girl he encountered" (p. 12); as having a "handsome Byronic face" (p. 12); and as "that Don Juan of Springfield, Joshua Speed" (p. 43).

68. To call Speed "frequent lover" and a "Don Juan" confuses mild flirtations with sexually consummated relationships. All the evidence indicates the former. Note Mary Todd to Mercy Ann Levering, Springfield, December 15, 1840, in Turner and Turner, *Mary Todd Lincoln*, p. 20; Lincoln to Speed, January 3, 1842 in *Collected Works*, 1:266; and the two references to Sarah Rickard in Lincoln to Speed, February 3, 1842, in *Collected Works*, 1:268, and Lincoln to Speed, March 27, 1842, in *Collected Works*, 1:282. As I argue here, Speed seemed to have the same kind of sexual conflicts as Lincoln, which in part explains their friendship.

69. Speed memorandum to Herndon, November 30, 1866, Herndon/Weik Collection (not published in Hertz).

70. The argument here is nicely complemented by the fascinating article by Carroll Smith-Rosenberg, "The Female World of Love and Ritual: Relations between Women in Nineteenth-Century America," *Signs: Journal of Women in Culture and Society* 1 (Autumn 1975):1–29.

71. Paton Yoder, *Taverns and Travelers: Inns of the Early Midwest* (Bloomington: Indiana University Press, 1969), pp. 146–47.

72. William G. Greene's statement to Herndon, n.d., Herndon/Weik Collection (not published in Hertz).

73. Henry Clay Whitney, *Life on the Circuit with Lincoln*, introduction and notes by Paul M. Angle (Caldwell, Idaho: Caxton Printers, 1940), pp. 62–63.

74. S. A. Crawford to Herndon, January 4, 1866, Herndon/Weik Collection (Hertz, p. 287).

75. Speed wrote Herndon on September 17, 1866: "I sold out to Hurst 1 Jany 1841. And came to Ky in the spring," Herndon/Weik Collection (not published in Hertz). Also note the weekly announcements in the *Sangamo Journal*, beginning January 8, 1841: "The co-partnership heretofore existing between Jas. Bell and Joshua F. Speed is this day dissolved by mutual consent ... January 1, 1841." A separate announcement noted the formation of the partnership of Bell and Charles R. Hurst, as of January 1, 1841.

76. Mary Todd wrote to Mercy Ann Levering in June, 1841: "Mr. Speed, our former most constant guest has been in Kentucky for some weeks past, will be here next month, on a visit perhaps, as he has some idea of deserting Illinois, his mother is anxious he should superintend her affairs, he takes a friend's privilege, of occasionally favouring me with a letter, in his last he spoke of his great desire of once more inhabiting this region & of his possibility of soon returning—." Turner and Turner, *Mary Todd Lincoln*, p. 27.

77. Erikson, *Insight and Responsibility*, p. 70.

78. *Collected Works*, 1:228–29.

79. Ibid., 1:282.

80. Speed, *Reminiscences of Lincoln*, p. 39.

81. *Collected Works*, 1:229n.

82. Herndon to Isaac Arnold, November 20, 1866, Herndon/Weik Collection (Hertz, p. 37).

83. Simon, *Lincoln's Preparation for Greatness*, p. 239.

84. Anson G. Henry to his wife, February 18 (?), 1863, Illinois State Historical Library.

85. *Collected Works*, 2:31, 46, 68–69.

86. See letters of Anson G. Henry to his wife, February 17, 1863; April 12, 1863; December 18, 28, and 30, 1864; January 2, 9, 16, 1864; February 8, 1864; March 9, 13, 21, 1864, Illinois State Historical Library.

87. Mary Todd to Mercy Ann Levering, June 1841. Turner and Turner, *Mary Todd Lincoln*, p. 27.

88. See Lincoln's thank-you note to Speed's half-sister Mary, *Collected Works,* 1:259–61.

89. Ibid., 1:266.

90. Ibid., 1:269.

91. Ibid., 1:280.

92. Ibid., 1:265–66.

93. Ibid., 1:267.

94. Ibid., 1:268.

95. Ibid., 1:280.

96. Ibid., 1:270.

97. John Hanks's statement to Herndon, n.d., Herndon/Weik Collection (Hertz, p. 350); Sarah Lincoln's statement to Herndon, September 8, 1865, Herndon/Weik Collection (Hertz, p. 352).

98. Herndon to Jesse Weik, January 5, 1889, Herndon/Weik Collection (Hertz, p.233).

99. Ibid., 1:303.

100. Ibid., 1:282.

101. Ibid., 1:289.

102. Ibid., 1:319.

103. Ibid., 1:389–91.

104. Ibid., 2:320–23.

105. Herndon and Weik, *Lincoln,* pp. 385–86.

106. *Collected Works,* 1:389–91.

107. Ibid., 2:17.

Chapter 3

1. Erik Erikson, *Gandhi's Truth: On the Origins of Militant Nonviolence* (New York: Norton, 1968), p. 123.

2. Sarah Lincoln's statement to Herndon, September 8, 1865, Herndon/Weik Collection (Hertz, p. 352).

3. Charles H. Coleman, *Abraham Lincoln and Coles County, Illinois* (New Brunswick, N.J.: Scarecrow Press, 1955), p. 25.

4. Roy P. Basler, ed., *The Collected Works of Abraham Lincoln,* 8 vols. (New Brunswick, N.J.: Rutgers University Press, 1953), 1:261.

5. Coleman, *Lincoln and Coles County,* pp. 24, 37.

6. Herndon to Jesse Weik, December 1, 1885, Herndon/Weik Collection (Hertz, p. 109).

7. *Collected Works,* 1:282.

8. Harry E. Pratt, *The Personal Finances of Abraham Lincoln* (Springfield, Ill.: Abraham Lincoln Association, 1943), pp. 73–75.

9. John D. Johnston for Thomas Lincoln to Abraham Lincoln, December 7, 1848, quoted in Coleman, *Lincoln and Coles County,* p. 73.

10. *Collected Works,* 2:15.

11. Ibid., 2:96–97.

12. Earl Schenck Miers, ed., *Lincoln Day by Day: A Chronology, 1809–1865,* 3 vols., (Washington: Lincoln Sesquicentennial Commission, 1960), 2:46–47.

13. Personal communication, Frank J. Williams, a lawyer, a close student of Lincoln, and the President of the Lincoln Group of Boston.

14. Ward Hill Lamon, *The Life of Abraham Lincoln: From His Birth to His Inauguration as President* (Boston: James E. Osgood, 1872), p. 463.

15. Justin G. Turner and Linda Levitt Turner, eds., *Mary Todd Lincoln: Her Life and Letters* (New York: Alfred A. Knopf, 1972), pp. 464–65.

16. Coleman, *Lincoln and Coles County,* p. 139.

17. George B. Forgie, *Patricide in the House Divided: A Psychological Interpretation of Lincoln and His Age* (New York: Norton, 1979), pp. 35–53.

18. Henry Clay, "The American System," *The American Whigs,* ed. Daniel Walker Howe (New York: John Wiley and Sons, 1973), p. 34–35.

19. Rush Welter, *The Mind of America, 1820–1850* (New York: Columbia University

Notes

Press, 1975), pp. 190–218. See also David Donald, *Liberty and Union* (Lexington, Mass.: D. C. Heath, 1978), pp. 3–51.

20. Forgie, *Patricide in the House Divided.*

21. All the following references to the Lyceum speech are in *Collected Works,* 1:108–15.

22. George W. Fredrickson, "The Search for Order and Community," *The Public and Private Lincoln: Contemporary Perspectives,* ed. Cullom Davis et al. (Carbondale: Southern Illinois University Press, 1979), pp. 86–98.

23. *Collected Works,* 1:385–86.

24. Herndon to Jesse Weik, February 5, 1887, Herndon/Weik Collection (Hertz, p. 165).

25. *Collected Works,* 1:279.

26. Edmund Wilson, *Patriotic Gore: Studies in the Literature of the American Civil War* (New York: Oxford University Press, 1962), p. 108. See also George B. Forgie, *Patricide in the House Divided* and James Hurt, "All the Living and the Dead: Lincoln's Imagery," *American Literature* 52 (1980):364–70.

27. *Collected Works,* 2:276.

28. Ibid., 3:522–50.

29. Herbert Mitgang, ed., *Abraham Lincoln, A Press Report: His Life and Times from the Original Newspaper Documents of the Union, the Confederacy and Europe,* (Chicago: Quadrangle Books, 1971), p. 158.

30. *Collected Works,* 4:190.

31. Mitgang, *A Press Report,* p. 225.

32. *Collected Works,* 7:17–18.

33. Ibid., 8:155.

34. Elton Trueblood, *Abraham Lincoln: Theologian of American Anguish* (New York: Harper and Row, 1973), p. 75.

35. Mitgang, *A Press Report,* p. 378.

36. *Collected Works,* 8:332–33.

Chapter 4

1. Elizabeth Norris to Emilie Todd Helm, January 12, 1895, Illinois State Historical Library.

2. Herndon to Jesse Weik, January 16, 1886, Herndon/Weik Collection (Hertz, p. 137).

3. Katherine Helm, *The True Story of Mary, Wife of Lincoln* (New York: Harper and Brothers, 1928), p. 81.

4. Justin G. Turner and Linda Levitt Turner, eds., *Mary Todd Lincoln: Her Life and Letters* (New York: Alfred A. Knopf, 1972), p. 15.

5. Ibid., pp. 20–21.

6. Ibid., p. 15.

7. Ibid., p. 22.

8. Mrs. John T. Stuart in Chicago *Tribune,* December 2, 1900, Louis A. Warren Library and Museum, Fort Wayne, Indiana.

9. Ruth Painter Randall, *Mary Lincoln: Biography of a Marriage* (Boston: Little, Brown, 1953), p. 77.

10. E. H. Merryman, "A Story of the Early Days in Springfield—And A Poem," *Journal of the Illinois State History Society* 16 (1923):141–46.

11. Turner and Turner, *Mary Todd Lincoln,* p. 25.

12. Ibid., p. 27.

13. Norris to Helm, January 12, 1895, Illinois State Historical Library.

14. See chapter 9, p. 220.

15. Helm, *The True Story,* p. 53.

16. Randall, *Mary Lincoln,* pp. 23–24.

17. Dennis Hanks interview, St. Louis *Globe-Democrat,* January 4, 1887, Louis A. Warren Library and Museum, Fort Wayne, Indiana.

18. Randall, *Mary Lincoln,* pp. 28–29.

19. Elizabeth Keckley, *Behind the Scenes; Or Thirty Years a Slave and Four Years in the White House* (New York: G. W. Carleton, 1868), pp. 228–29.

20. William H. Townsend, *Lincoln and the Bluegrass: Slavery and Civil War in Kentucky* (Lexington: University of Kentucky Press, 1955), pp. 26–59.

21. Ibid., p. 27.

22. Ibid., p. 48.

23. Turner and Turner, *Mary Todd Lincoln*, p. 37.

24. Randall, *Mary Lincoln*, p. 22.

25. Norris to Helm, January 12, 1895, Illinois State Historical Library.

26. Ibid.

27. Ibid.

28. Ibid.; compare Randall, *Mary Lincoln*, p. 31.

29. Herndon to Jesse Weik, January 16, 1886, Herndon/Weik Collection (Hertz, p. 137).

30. Randall, *Mary Lincoln*, pp. 81–82.

31. Turner and Turner, *Mary Todd Lincoln*, p. 523.

32. Randall, *Mary Lincoln*, p. 93.

33. Helm, *The True Story*, p. 140.

34. Anson G. Henry to his wife, February 18(?), 1863, Illinois State Historical Library.

35. Robert Todd asked Lincoln to handle some of his legal matters in Illinois and, later, to probate his will.

36. Turner and Turner, *Mary Todd Lincoln*, p. 536.

37. Harry E. Pratt, *The Personal Finances of Abraham Lincoln* (Springfield, Ill.: Abraham Lincoln Association, 1943), pp. 63–66.

38. Randall, *Mary Lincoln*, pp. 95–96.

39. Turner and Turner, *Mary Todd Lincoln*, p. 293. Herndon of course amply supported Mary's point. See Herndon to Jesse Weik, February 9, 1887, and to Truman Bartlett, September 22, 1887, Herndon/Weik Collection (Hertz, pp. 169 and 204). See also William H. Herndon and Jesse W. Weik, *Life of Lincoln*, ed. Paul M. Angle (Cleveland: World Publishing, 1930), p. 342.

40. Herndon to Jesse Weik, January 23, 1886, Herndon/Weik Collection (Hertz, p. 141).

41. Roy P. Basler, ed., *The Collected Works of Abraham Lincoln*, 8 vols. (New Brunswick, N.J.: Rutgers University Press, 1953), 2:391.

42. Turner and Turner, *Mary Todd Lincoln*, p. 53.

43. Earl Schenck Miers, ed., *Lincoln Day by Day: A Chronology, 1809–1865*, 3 vols. (Washington: Lincoln Sesquicentennial Association, 1960), 2:244.

44. James Gourley's statement to Herndon, n.d., Herndon/Weik Collection (Hertz, p. 383).

45. Herndon to Jesse Weik, February 9, 1889, Herndon/Weik Collection (Hertz, p. 240).

46. Herndon to Jesse Weik, January 8, 1886, Herndon/Weik Collection (Hertz, p. 129).

47. Herndon to Jesse Weik, January 16, 1886, Herndon/Weik Collection (Hertz, p. 137).

48. Herndon to Isaac N. Arnold, November 20, 1865, Herndon/Weik Collection (Hertz, p. 37).

49. Herndon to Jesse Weik, December 1, 1885, Herndon/Weik Collection (Hertz, p. 109).

50. Herndon and Weik, *Lincoln*, p. 166.

51. David Donald, *Lincoln's Herndon: A Biography* (New York: Alfred A. Knopf, 1948), pp. 151–53.

52. Nathaniel W. Brandon to Herndon, August 3, 1865, Herndon/Weik Collection (Hertz, p. 284); Herndon to Jesse Weik, January 5, 1889, Herndon/Weik Collection (Hertz, p. 233).

53. Herndon to Jesse Weik, January 23, 1890, Herndon/Weik Collection (Hertz, p. 248).

Notes

54. Edmund Wilson, *Patriotic Gore: Studies in the Literature of the American Civil War* (New York: Oxford University Press, 1962), p. 130.

55. *Collected Works*, 1:466.

56. Herndon to Jesse Weik, January, 1887, Herndon/Weik Collection (Hertz, pp. 160–62). Compare Randall's view of the story, *Mary Lincoln*, pp. 123–25.

57. James Gourley's statement to Herndon, n.d., Herndon/Weik Collection (Hertz, p. 384).

58. *New York Times*, February 6, 1938, Louis A. Warren Library and Museum, Fort Wayne, Indiana.

59. Herndon to Jesse Weik, January 23, 1886, Herndon/Weik Collection (Hertz, pp. 140–41).

60. Herndon to Jesse Weik, January 11, 1886, Herndon/Weik Collection (Hertz, pp. 133–34).

61. Chicago *Tribune*, January 1, 1921, Louis A. Warren Library and Museum, Fort Wayne, Indiana.

62. Frank Fuller, *A Day with the Lincoln Family* (New York, n.d.), pamphlet, Illinois State Historical Library.

63. Ward Hill Lamon, *The Life of Abraham Lincoln: From His Birth to His Inauguration as President* (Boston: James E. Osgood, 1872), p. 482.

64. Herndon to Jesse Weik, February 5, 1887, Herndon/Weik Collection (Hertz, p. 166).

65. Turner and Turner, *Mary Todd Lincoln*, p. 251. Note also that in a letter written in 1860 Lincoln commented on his son, Robert, who "promises very well, considering we never controlled him much." *Collected Works*, 4:82.

66. Herndon to Chauncey F. Black, September 17, 1853, Herndon/Weik Collection (Hertz, p. 42).

67. Turner and Turner, *Mary Todd Lincoln*, pp. 60–61.

68. Herndon to Jesse Weik, January 8, 1886, Herndon/Weik Collection (Hertz, p. 128). See also Lamon, *Lincoln*, pp. 472–73.

69. *Collected Works*, 1:477.

70. Ibid., 1:466.

71. Ibid., 1:391.

72. Randall, *Mary Lincoln*, p. 118.

73. Ibid., pp. 139–42; Miers, *Lincoln Day by Day*, 2:27.

74. Octavia Roberts, *Lincoln in Illinois* (Boston: Houghton Mifflin, 1918), p. 67; Randall, *Mary Lincoln*, p. 141.

75. Turner and Turner, *Mary Todd Lincoln*, p. 632.

76. Ibid., pp. 57–58.

77. Ibid., p. 59.

78. Ibid., p. 64.

79. Ibid., pp. 632–34.

80. James Gourley's statement to Herndon, n.d., Herndon/Weik Collection (Hertz, p. 383).

81. Turner and Turner, *Mary Todd Lincoln*, p. 42; Henry Villard, *Lincoln on the Eve of '61*, ed. Harold G. Villard and Oswald Garrison Villard (New York: Alfred A. Knopf, 1941), p. 63.

82. *Collected Works*, 1:495.

83. Turner and Turner, *Mary Todd Lincoln*, p. 475.

84. Kathryn Kish Sklar, "Victorian Women and Domestic Life: Mary Todd Lincoln, Elizabeth Cady Stanton, and Harriet Beecher Stowe," *The Public and Private Lincoln: Contemporary Perspectives*, ed. Cullom Davis et al. (Carbondale: Southern Illinois University Press, 1979), pp. 30–31.

85. Turner and Turner, *Mary Todd Lincoln*, pp. 46–47.

86. Ibid., pp. 48–49.

87. Ibid., p. 56.

88. Isaac N. Arnold, *The Life of Abraham Lincoln* (Chicago: Jansen, McClurg, 1885), p. 83; compare Randall, *Mary Lincoln*, p. 158.

89. Henry Villard, *Lincoln on the Eve of '61*, p. 63.

91. Gustave P. Koerner, *Memories of Gustave Koerner; Life Sketches Written at the Suggestion of His Children*, ed. Thomas J. McCormack 2 vols. (Cedar Rapids, Iowa: Torch Press, 1909), 2:66–67.

92. Turner and Turner, *Mary Todd Lincoln*, p. 66.

93. Walter Barlow Stevens, *A Reporter's Lincoln* (St. Louis: Missouri Historical Society, 1916), p. 48.

94. Randall, *Mary Lincoln*, pp. 30–31; Roy P. Basler, "Lincoln, Blacks, and Women," *The Public and Private Lincoln*, pp. 38–56; Townsend, *Lincoln and the Bluegrass*, pp. 72–80.

95. Turner and Turner, *Mary Todd Lincoln*, p. 46.

96. *Collected Works*, 2:323.

97. John Hay, *Lincoln and the Civil War in the Diaries and Letters of John Hay*, ed. Tyler Dennett (Westport, Conn: Nego Universities Press, 1972), p. 41.

98. Hay, *Diaries*, p. 41.

99. Randall, *Mary Lincoln*, p. 258. Compare Anson G. Henry's view of Hay in the letter to his wife, March 13, 1865, Illinois State Historical Library.

100. Randall, *Mary Lincoln*, p. 258.

101. Noah Brooks, *Washington in Lincoln's Time* (New York: Century, 1896), p. 281.

102. Marquis Adolphe de Chambrun, *Impressions of Lincoln and the Civil War: A Foreigner's Account* (New York: Random House, 1952), p. 76; see also Turner and Turner, *Mary Todd Lincoln*, p. 176.

103. Turner and Turner, *Mary Todd Lincoln*, pp. 188–89.

104. De Chambrun, *Impressions*, pp. 21–23.

105. Turner and Turner, *Mary Todd Lincoln*, p. 79.

106. Keckley, *Behind the Scenes*, p. 128.

107. Randall, *Mary Lincoln*, p. 299.

108. Noyes W. Miner, *Mrs. Abraham: A Vindication*, n.d., manuscript, Illinois State Historical Library, pp. 2–3.

109. Keckley, *Behind the Scenes*, pp. 116–17.

110. Turner and Turner, *Mary Todd Lincoln*, p. 71.

111. Randall, *Mary Lincoln*, p. 193.

112. Turner and Turner, *Mary Todd Lincoln*, p. 140.

113. Ibid.

114. Ibid., pp. 97–98.

115. Keckley, *Behind the Scenes*, p. 131.

116. Basler, "Lincoln, Blacks, and Women," p. 43.

117. Turner and Turner, *Mary Todd Lincoln*, p. 447.

118. Ibid., p. 183.

119. *Collected Works*, 5:492.

120. Turner and Turner, *Mary Todd Lincoln*, p. 159.

121. *Collected Works*, 7:34.

122. Anson G. Henry to his wife, February 17, 1863, Illinois State Historical Library.

123. Randall, *Mary Lincoln*, pp. 372–75; Stephen B. Oates, *With Malice toward None: The Life of Abraham Lincoln* (New York, Harper and Row, 1977), p. 455; Adam Baday, *Grant in Peace: From Appomattox to Mount McGregor, A Personal Memoir* (Hartford, Conn.: S. S. Scranton, 1887), pp. 356–65.

124. Turner and Turner, *Mary Todd Lincoln*, p. 114.

125. Randall, *Mary Lincoln*, p. 382.

126. De Chambrun, *Impressions*, p. 84.

127. Anson G. Henry to his wife, February 17, 1863, Illinois State Historical Library.

128. Turner and Turner, *Mary Todd Lincoln*, pp. 127–28.

129. Ibid., pp. 130–31.

130. Ibid., p. 189.

131. Elizabeth Edwards to Julia Edwards, March 1, 1862, Illinois State Historical Library.

132. Elizabeth Edwards to Julia Edwards, March 2, 1862, Illinois State Historical Library.

133. Elizabeth Edwards to Julia Edwards, March 12, 1862, Illinois State Historical Library.

134. Elizabeth Edwards to Julia Edwards, April 1, 1862, Illinois State Historical Library.

135. Elizabeth Edwards to Julia Edwards, April 9, 1862, Illinois State Historical Library.

136. Elizabeth Edwards to Julia Edwards, April 19, 1862, Illinois State Historical Library.

137. Elizabeth Edwards to Julia Edwards, April 26, 1862, Illinois State Historical Library.

138. Keckley, *Behind the Scenes*, p. 117.

139. Ibid., p. 104.

140. Randall, *Mary Lincoln*, pp. 292–94.

141. Turner and Turner, *Mary Todd Lincoln*, p. 525.

142. Helm, *The True Story*, pp. 226–27.

143. Ibid., p. 226.

144. Keckley, *Behind the Scenes*, pp. 121–22.

145. *Collected Works*, 8:223.

146. Turner and Turner, *Mary Todd Lincoln*, pp. 125–26. Note also Randall, *Mary Lincoln*, pp. 264–65.

147. Ibid., pp. 161–62.

148. Randall, *Mary Lincoln*, pp. 259–68; Turner and Turner, *Mary Todd Lincoln*, p. 89.

149. Turner and Turner, *Mary Todd Lincoln*, p. 321.

150. Keckley, *Behind the Scenes*, p. 85.

151. Turner and Turner, *Mary Todd Lincoln*, p. 179.

152. Ibid., p. 180.

153. Hay, *Diaries*, p. 234.

154. De Chambrun, *Impressions*, p. 175.

155. Anson G. Henry to his wife, May 8, 1865, Illinois State Historical Library.

156. Anson G. Henry to John Williams, May 1, 1865, Illinois State Historical Library.

157. Turner and Turner, *Mary Todd Lincoln*, p. 315.

158. Ibid., pp. 303–4; Randall, *Mary Lincoln*, pp. 391–92.

159. Turner and Turner, *Mary Todd Lincoln*, pp. 228, 228–29, 236, 257, 258, 260, 263, 264, 269, 289, 298, 302, 311–12.

160. Ibid., p. 265.

161. Ibid., p. 268.

162. Ibid., p. 284.

163. Ibid., p. 319; see also pp. 393, 454–55.

164. Ibid., p. 270.

165. Ibid., p. 269–71.

166. Ibid., p. 316.

167. Ibid., p. 366.

168. Ibid., p. 460.

169. Chicago *Tribune* and Chicago *Inter-Ocean*, May 19, 1875, Illinois State Historical Library.

170. Randall, *Mary Lincoln*, p. 431.

171. Turner and Turner, *Mary Todd Lincoln*, pp. 265–66.

172. Ibid., p. 547.

173. Ibid., p. 261.

174. Ibid., p. 306.

175. Chicago *Tribune* and Chicago *Inter-Ocean*, May 19, 1875, Illinois State Historical Library.

176. Leonard Swett to David Davis, May 24, 1875, Illinois State Historical Library.

177. Chicago *Tribune* and Chicago *Inter-Ocean*, May 19, 1875, Illinois State Historical Library.

178. Leonard Swett to David Davis, May 24, 1875, Illinois State Historical Library.

179. Rodney A. Ross, "Mary Todd Lincoln, Patient at Bellevue Place, Batavia," *Journal of the Illinois State Historical Society* 63(1970):5–34.

180. Robert Lincoln to Elizabeth Edwards, January 17, 1876, vol. 3, p. 382 of Robert Lincoln's correspondence (46 vols.), Illinois State Historical Library.
181. Miner, *Mrs. Abraham Lincoln*, pp. 6–7.

Chapter 5

1. Roy P. Basler, ed., *The Collected Works of Abraham Lincoln*, 8 vols. (New Brunswick, N.J.: Rutgers University Press, 1953), 2:506.
2. Ibid., 1:448.
3. Ibid., 1:490–91, 497, 499.
4. Ibid., 1:496.
5. Ibid., 2:489.
6. Ibid., 4:190.
7. Ibid., 1:305.
8. James C. Conckling to his wife, April 18, 1843, Illinois State Historical Library.
9. Elizabeth Keckley, *Behind the Scenes; Or Thirty Years a Slave and Four Years in the White House* (New York: G. W. Carleton, 1868), p. 104.
10. Noah Brooks, *Washington in Lincoln's Time* (New York: Century, 1896), pp. 64–66.
11. Ruth Painter Randall, *Mary Lincoln: Biography of a Marriage* (Boston: Little, Brown, 1953), p. 316.
12. Herndon to Jesse Weik, February 5, 1887, Herndon/Weik Collection (Hertz, p. 166).
13. *Collected Works*, 2:15, 111, 112, 113.
14. Herndon to Jesse Weik, December 1, 1885, Herndon/Weik Collection (Hertz, p. 109). Weik in *The Real Lincoln: A Portrait* (Boston: Houghton Mifflin, 1922), p. 54, corrected Herndon's dates. See also Randall, *Mary Lincoln*, p. 134.
15. *Collected Works*, 2:194–95.
16. Ibid., 2:203–4.
17. Justin G. Turner and Linda Levitt Turner, eds., *Mary Todd Lincoln: Her Life in Letters* (New York: Alfred A. Knopf, 1972), p. 59.
18. Ibid., p. 55.
19. Randall, *Mary Lincoln*, p. 93.
20. Earl Schenck Miers, ed., *Lincoln Day by Day: A Chronology, 1809–1865*, 3 vols. (Washington: Lincoln Sesquicentennial Commission, 1960), 1:207, 2:77.
21. Henry Clay Whitney, *Life on the Circuit with Lincoln*, introduction and notes by Paul M. Angle (Caldwell, Idaho: Caxton Printers, 1940), p. 62.
22. Herndon to Jesse Weik, February 2, 1887, Herndon/Weik Collection (Hertz, p. 178).
23. William H. Herndon and Jesse W. Weik, *Life of Lincoln*, ed. Paul Angle (Cleveland: World Publishing, 1930), p. 249.
24. David Davis's letters to his wife, 1843–1860, Illinois State Historical Library.
25. Herndon to Wendell Philips, August 4, 1857, Blagdon Collection, Houghton Library, Harvard University.
26. See, for example, *Collected Works*, 2:394.
27. Ibid., 2:327.
28. Ibid., 3:344.
29. The fact that only few letters have survived does not, of course, prove he never wrote any. However, Mary seemed to save letters generally, and in her expansive old age she never referred to letters of any kind from Lincoln.
30. *Collected Works*, 1:465.
31. Ibid., 1:477.
32. Ibid., 1:496.
33. Ibid., 4:190.
34. Ward Hill Lamon, *The Life of Abraham Lincoln: From His Birth to His Inauguration as President* (Boston: James E. Osgood, 1872), p. 472.

Notes

35. Noyes M. Miner, *Mrs. Abraham Lincoln: A Vindication*, n.d., manuscript, Illinois State Historical Library, p. 9.
36. Mrs. George C. Beal, *New York Times*, February 6, 1938, Louis A. Warren Library and Museum, Fort Wayne, Indiana.
37. Unidentified newspaper clipping, Louis A. Warren Library and Museum, Fort Wayne, Indiana.
38. Frances Wallace newspaper interview, "Lincoln's Marriage," Springfield, September 2, 1895 (privately printed, 1917), Illinois State Historical Library.
39. David Donald, *Lincoln's Herndon: A Biography* (New York: Alfred A. Knopf, 1948), p. 191, explains the confused story of Herndon's 1866 interview with Mary. The barely legible notes themselves are in the Herndon/Weik Collection. For Herndon's published version of the interview, see *Mrs. Lincoln's Denial and What She Says*, Massachusetts Historical Library.
40. Herndon and Weik, *Lincoln*, p. 344. Note also Herndon to Jesse Weik, November 19, 1885, and February 18, 1887, Herndon/Weik Collection (Hertz, pp. 105, 176–77).
41. Herndon to Jesse Weik, January 8, 1886, Herndon/Weik Collection (Hertz, p. 129). See also Herndon to Jesse Weik, November 10, 1885 (Hertz, pp. 104–5).
42. Herndon to Jesse Weik, January 18, 1886, Herndon/Weik Collection (Hertz, p. 129).
43. *Collected Works*, 1:496.
44. Ibid., 1:319.
45. Ibid., 1:325.
46. Ibid., 1:328.
47. Ibid., 1:391.
48. Ibid., 1:466.
49. Walter Barlow Stevens, *A Reporter's Lincoln* (St. Louis: Missouri Historical Society, 1916), p. 72.
50. Robert Todd Lincoln, autobiographical statement for the 1864 *Harvard Class Book*, Harvard University Archives, p. 1.
51. Ibid., p. 3.
52. See notes 81, 82, 83, 84 in this chapter.
53. Robert Lincoln to James Schouler, December 27, 1907, correspondence of Robert Todd Lincoln, vol. 40, p. 468, Illinois State Historical Library.
54. John S. Goff, *Robert Todd Lincoln: A Man in His Own Right* (Norman: University of Oklahoma Press, 1968), pp. 30–33.
55. Robert Todd Lincoln to David H. Bates, June 22, 1907, correspondence of Robert Todd Lincoln, vol. 40, p. 145, Illinois State Historical Library.
56. Goff, *Robert Todd Lincoln*, p. 215.
57. Robert Todd Lincoln, autobiographical statement, pp. 1, 3.
58. Ibid., p. 99.
59. Robert Todd Lincoln to John Hanna, April 29, 1884, correspondence of Robert Todd Lincoln, vol. 11, p. 151, Illinois State Historical Library.
60. Goff, *Robert Todd Lincoln*, p. 223.
61. Ibid., p. 197.
62. Robert Todd Lincoln to Miss Harriett Henton, October 17, 1902, correspondence of Robert Todd Lincoln, vol. 36, p. 118, Illinois State Historical Library.
63. Robert Todd Lincoln, autobiographical statement, p. 1.
64. Robert Todd Lincoln to J. C. Jankins, March 6, 1884, correspondence of Robert Todd Lincoln, vol. 10, p. 526, Illinois State Historical Library.
65. David C. Mearns, *The Lincoln Papers*, 2 vols. (Garden City, N.Y.: Doubleday, 1948), 1:134.
66. Robert Todd Lincoln to W. Ewing Hill, July 28, 1887, correspondence of Robert Todd Lincoln, vol. 3, p. 983, Illinois State Historical Library.
67. Robert Todd Lincoln to Mrs. Wyatt Eaton, June 4, 1900, correspondence of Robert Todd Lincoln, vol. 34, p. 260, Illinois State Historical Library.
68. Robert Todd Lincoln to E. A. Buck, January 7, 1887, correspondence of Robert Todd Lincoln, vol. 3, p. 891, Illinois State Historical Library.
69. Robert Todd Lincoln to Hon. H. M. Teller, June 23, 1883, correspondence of Robert Todd Lincoln, vol. 9, p. 184, Illinois State Historical Library.

Notes

70. Robert Todd Lincoln to Isaac N. Arnold, January 28, 1883, correspondence of Robert Todd Lincoln, vol. 8, p. 273, Illinois State Historical Library.

71. Robert Todd Lincoln to William H. Reed, May 5, 1884, correspondence of Robert Todd Lincoln, vol. 11, p. 171, Illinois State Historical Library.

72. Robert Todd Lincoln to Joseph Deuell, January 9, 1900, correspondence of Robert Todd Lincoln, vol. 34, p. 115, Illinois State Historical Library.

73. Robert Todd Lincoln to J. W. Wartmann, June 5, 1882, correspondence of Robert Todd Lincoln, vol. 7, p. 4, Illinois State Historical Library.

74. Robert Todd Lincoln to Samuel H. Bishop, January 29, 1900, correspondence of Robert Todd Lincoln, vol. 34, pp. 148-49, Illinois State Historical Library.

75. Robert Todd Lincoln, autobiographical statement, p. 2.

76. Turner and Turner, *Mary Todd Lincoln*, p. 440.

77. Goff, *Robert Todd Lincoln*, p. 247.

78. Robert Todd Lincoln to Le Grand Van Valkenburgh, May 26, 1913, correspondence of Robert Todd Lincoln, Illinois State Historical Library.

79. Robert Todd Lincoln to J. H. Orne, June 1, 1875, cited in Katherine Helm, *The True Story of Mary, Wife of Lincoln* (New York: Harper and Brothers, 1928), pp. 295-96.

80. A number of Robert's letters dealing with his mother were not available for scholarly inspection at the time of writing this book. It is possible, therefore, this statement will have to be modified when the collection is opened.

81. Goff, *Robert Todd Lincoln*, p. 196.

82. Herndon to Jesse Weik, January 15, 1889; to Truman Bartlett, December 20, 1889; to Jesse Weik, March 7, 1890; and to Jesse Weik, February 7, 1891, Herndon/Weik Collection (Hertz, pp. 238, 244, 249, 260-61).

83. Turner and Turner, *Mary Todd Lincoln*, p. 463.

84. Chicago *Tribune*, January 1, 1921, Louis A. Warren Library and Museum, Fort Wayne, Indiana.

85. Elizabeth Todd Grimsley, "Six Months in the White House." Illinois State Historical Library.

86. Keckley, *Behind the Scenes*, p. 103.

87. Grimsley, "Six Months," p. 13, gives a nice example from the war of how close Lincoln was to Willie.

Chapter 6

1. Joshua Fry Speed, *Reminiscences of Abraham Lincoln and Notes of a Visit to California: Two Lectures* (Louisville: John P. Morton, 1884), pp. 20-21.

2. Roy P. Basler, ed., *The Collected Works of Abraham Lincoln*, 8 vols. (New Brunswick, N.J.: Rutgers University Press, 1953), 2:327. See also John J. Duff, *A. Lincoln, Prairie Lawyer* (New York: Holt, Rinehart, 1960), p. 16; and Albert A. Woldman, *Lawyer Lincoln* (Boston: Houghton Mifflin, 1936), pp. 22-23.

3. *Collected Works*, 4:121.

4. Ibid., 3:344.

5. Ibid., 3:535.

6. William H. Herndon and Jesse W. Weik, *Life of Lincoln*, ed. Paul M. Angle (Cleveland: World Publishing, 1930), pp. 271-72.

7. John P. Frank, *Lincoln as a Lawyer* (Urbana: University of Illinois, 1961), pp. 10-11.

8. Herndon notes on interview with David Davis, n.d., Herndon/Weik Collection (Hertz, p. 427).

9. Herndon and Weik, *Lincoln*, pp. 268f. See also Herndon's notes on his interview with David Davis, n.d., Herndon/Weik Collection (Hertz, p. 427).

10. Henry Clay Whitney, *Life on the Circuit with Lincoln*, introduction and notes by Paul M. Angle (Caldwell, Idaho: Caxton Printers, 1940), pp. 232-33.

11. Benjamin Quarles, *Lincoln and the Negro* (New York: Oxford University Press, 1962), pp. 23-24.

Notes

12. Herndon to Jesse Weik, January 11, 1886, Herndon/Weik Collection (Hertz, pp. 133–34).

13. Herndon to Wendell Philips, May 12, 1857, Blagdon Collection, Houghton Library, Harvard University.

14. Herndon and Weik, *Lincoln*, p. 255.

15. *Collected Works*, 2:80.

16. Ibid., 2:218–19.

17. Frank, *Lincoln*, p. 17.

18. *Collected Works*, 2:81–82.

19. Ibid., 2:81–82.

20. Herndon to Wendell Philips, April 7, 1857, Blagdon Collection, Houghton Library, Harvard University.

21. Frank, *Lincoln*, p. 16.

22. Ibid., pp. 19–20.

23. Whitney, *Life on the Circuit*; Frank, *Lincoln*, pp. 21–25.

24. Herndon and Weik, *Lincoln*, p. 248.

25. Ibid., p. 283.

26. Ward Hill Lamon, *The Life of Abraham Lincoln: From His Birth to His Inauguration as President* (Boston: James E. Osgood, 1872), p. 478.

27. Herndon to Jesse Weik, November 13, 1885, Herndon/Weik Collection (Hertz, p. 101).

28. *Collected Works*, 1:290.

29. "Lincolniana Notes," *Journal of the Illinois State Historical Society*, 53 (1960):70.

30. *Collected Works*, 2:332–33.

31. Ibid., 1:345.

32. Ibid., 1:204.

33. Ibid., 2:106.

34. Ibid., 2:191.

35. Frank, *Lincoln*, p. 25; Stephen B. Oates, *With Malice toward None: The Life of Abraham Lincoln* (New York: Harper and Row, 1977), p. 113. For Lincoln's brief, see *Collected Works*, 2:397–98.

36. *Collected Works*, 2:398n.

37. Frank, *Lincoln*, p. 42.

38. Ibid., pp. 44–96; *Collected Works*, 2:415–22.

39. Frank, *Lincoln*, p. 98.

40. Ibid., p. 98.

Chapter 7

1. There is an old view (which began with Herndon) that Congressman Lincoln honorably but stupidly opposed the Mexican War, lost the support of his central Illinois constituency, and was forcibly retired to circuit work in 1849. See William H. Herndon and Jesse W. Weik, *Life of Lincoln*, ed. Paul M. Angle (Cleveland: World Publishing, 1930), pp. 219–36; compare Roy P. Basler, ed., *The Collected Works of Abraham Lincoln*, 8 vols. (New Brunswick, N.J.: Rutgers University Press, 1953), 1:51, n. 9. Nearly every detail of this interpretation has been shown wrong. It was a good Whig position from Maine to Illinois to oppose the war, though the party was divided on the issue. See Mark Neely, "Lincoln and the Mexican War. An Argument by Analogy," *Civil War History* 24 (1978): 5–24; see also Brian C. Walton, "Elections of the 30th Congress," *Journal of Southern History* 35 (1969): 186–87. There is also no indication beyond Herndon's own complaint to Lincoln that Whigs back home in the district took offence at his opposition to the war, and if they did it failed to register in newspapers, letters, or diaries that have survived. Only the stridently Democratic press made that charge. See Gabor Boritt, "Lincoln's Opposition to the Mexican War," *Journal of the Illinois State Historical Society* 67 (1974): 79–100; compare, for example, the comments of the *Register* on January 21 and March 10, 1848, in Herbert Mitgang, ed., *Abraham Lincoln, A Press Report: His Life and Times from the Original Newspaper Documents of the Union, the Confederacy and Europe,* (Chicago: Quadrangle Books, 1971), pp. 55 and 57, with the same paper on October 27, 1848, in *Collected Works*, 2:11–13. Nor, finally, is it true Lincoln retired

Notes

from politics between 1849 and 1854, in the sense of having abandoned involvement in it altogether. He held no elective office but remained important in party affairs throughout the state.

2. *Collected Works*, 1:420–22.

3. John P. Frank, *Lincoln as a Lawyer* (Urbana: University of Illinois, 1961), pp. 105–110. Lincoln never entirely abandoned his fondness for interrogatories, though he learned to use them more effectively, for example, in the 1858 debates with Douglas. It is also worth noting that the use of interrogatories was quite common in this period and reflected the legal cast of politics.

4. *Collected Works*, 1:427.

5. Ibid., 1:446.

6. Ibid., 1:447; compare 1:457–58 and 1:473–74.

7. Ibid., 1:451–52.

8. See Boritt, "Lincoln's Opposition to the Mexican War," pp. 79–100.

9. *Collected Works*, 1:430–31.

10. Ibid., 1:439.

11. Stephen B. Oates, *With Malice toward None: The Life of Abraham Lincoln* (New York: Harper and Row, 1977), p. 87.

12. *Collected Works*, 1:465.

13. The connection between narcissistic injury and depression is well developed in self psychology. See Heinz Kohut, *The Analysis of the Self: A Systematic Approach to the Psychoanalytic Treatment of Narcissistic Personality Disorders* (New York: International Universities Press, 1971), pp. 17, 18n, 117–18; the discussion of Mr. C, pp. 249–50; Mr. K, pp. 257–59; and Miss F, p. 284. See also Kohut, *The Restoration of the Self* (New York: International Universities Press, 1977), p. 281; and Arnold Goldberg, ed., *The Psychology of the Self: A Casebook, written with the collaboration of Heinz Kohut* (New York: International Universities Press, 1978), pp. 263–96 (case of Mr. E).

14. *Collected Works*, 2:320.

15. Ibid., 1:260. I am indebted to a conversation with Arthur Zilversmith, February 12, 1980, for a clarification of Lincoln's early attitudes on slavery and race. See Arthur Zilversmith's presentation on the topic of Lincoln and race, February 12, 1980, Abraham Lincoln Colloquium, State Historical Library, Springfield, Illinois, that will appear in the forthcoming *Papers* of the Abraham Lincoln Association, vol. 2.

16. *Collected Works*, 1:260.

17. Herndon and Weik, *Lincoln*, p. 64, has Lincoln vowing in 1830, after witnessing the slave trade in New Orleans, to hit slavery hard if he ever had the chance. However, Herndon's source was John Hanks, who according to Lincoln himself, was not with him on that trip; see *Collected Works*, 4:62; and Benjamin Quarles, *Lincoln and the Negro* (New York: Oxford University Press, 1962), p. 18.

18. *Collected Works*, 1:74–75.

19. Ibid., 1:279.

20. Ibid., 1:347–48.

21. Oates, *With Malice toward None*, pp. 92–94.

22. *Collected Works*, 1:458.

23. Quarles, *Lincoln and the Negro*, pp. 29–30, points out that Lincoln's record on slavery as a Congressman was not altogether consistent. However, Quarles acknowledges Lincoln's seemingly proslavery votes could well have been only parliamentary maneuvers. Compare Paul Findley, *A. Lincoln: The Crucible of Congress* (New York: Crown Publishers, 1979), pp. 13–43.

24. *Collected Works*, 2:22n.

25. Ibid., 2:20n.

26. *Collected Works*, 1:484.

27. Ibid., 1:382; compare 1:337f.

28. Ibid., 1:480–90.

29. Ibid., 1:395–98.

30. The best monograph on this subject is Donald W. Riddle, *Lincoln Runs for Congress* (New Brunswick, N.J.: Rutgers University Press, 1948).

31. *Collected Works*, 1:350.

32. Ibid., 1:363.

Notes

33. Ibid., 1:354.
34. Ibid., 1:349, 350, 351, 352, 353, 355, 356, 359–60, 365–66.
35. Ibid., 1:463.
36. Ibid., 1:453–54.
37. Ibid., 1:449, 452, 453, 463, 467–68.
38. Ibid., 1:503.
39. Ibid., 2:1–5, 6–11.
40. George W. Fredrickson, "A Man but Not a Brother: Abraham Lincoln and Racial Equality," *The Journal of Southern History* 41(1975), p. 41.
41. *Collected Works*, 1:268–69; 2:82–91; and 2:121–132; 5:340–41.
42. Ibid., 2:132.
43. Ibid., 2:124.
44. Ibid., 1:507.
45. Ibid., 2:25. See, for background, Thomas Ewing, "Lincoln and the General Land Office, 1849," *Journal of the Illinois Historical Society* 25(1932): 138–53.
46. *Collected Works*, 2:14.
47. Ibid., 2:28–29.
48. Ibid., 2:41.
49. Ibid., 2:45.
50. Ibid., 2:43.
51. Ibid., 2:40–41.
52. Ibid., 2:43.
53. Ibid., 2:49.
54. Ibid., 2:44–45.
55. Ibid., 2:43–44.
56. Ibid., 2:48–49.
57. Ibid., 2:49–50.
58. Ibid., 2:50–51, 53–54.
59. Ibid., 2:53–54.
60. Ibid., 2:57.
61. Ibid., 2:61.
62. Ibid., 2:65.
63. Herndon and Weik, *Lincoln*, pp. 246–47.
64. Neely, "Lincoln and the Mexican War," p. 24.
65. *Collected Works*, 3:6; see also 2:472.
66. Ibid., 3:213.
67. Benjamin P. Thomas, *Abraham Lincoln: A Biography* (New York: Alfred A. Knopf, 1952), p. 125, characterizes Lincoln's role in Congress as diligent but unspectacular; Oates, *With Malice toward None*, pp. 87–97 is a favorable account; Findley, *A. Lincoln*, p. 216, says, "Lincoln came home from Congress politically strong. . . ."; Gabor Boritt, *Lincoln and the Economics of the American Dream* (Memphis: Memphis State University Press, 1978), pp. 135, 142, 150, is somewhat ambiguous.
68. Herndon and Weik, *Lincoln*, p. 246; note also Herndon to Jesse Weik, February 11, 1887, Herndon/Weik Collection (Hertz, p. 172).
69. *Collected Works*, 2:461–62.
70. Herndon and Weik, *Lincoln*, p. 325.
71. Don E. Fehrenbacher, *Prelude to Greatness: Lincoln in the 1850's* (Stanford University Press, 1962), p. 72.
72. Ibid., p. 73, summarizes the historiography of this issue.
73. Christopher Breiseth, "Lincoln, Douglas, and Springfield in the 1858 Campaign," *The Public and Private Lincoln*, pp. 101–20.
74. *Collected Works*, 2:320.
75. Ibid., 2:501.
76. Ibid., 2:255.
77. Ibid., 2:492.
78. Ibid., 2:482.
79. Ibid., 2:349–52.
80. Ibid., 2:266.
81. Ibid., 2:273.

82. Quarles, *Lincoln and the Negro*, p. 35.

83. Ibid., 2:437–42.

84. Boritt, *Lincoln and Economics*; Eric Foner, *Free Soil, Free Labor, Free Men: The Ideology of the Republican Party before the Civil War* (New York: Oxford University Press, 1970), p. 45; Quarles, *Lincoln and the Negro*, pp. 30–38.

85. The issue of Lincoln and race has been hotly debated since Lerone Bennett, "Was Abe Lincoln a White Supremacist?" *Ebony* 23 (1968): 35–38, 40, 42. Herbert Mitgang replied to Bennett quickly and self-assuredly, "Was Lincoln Just a Honkie?" *New York Times Magazine* (February 11, 1968): 34–35, 100–7. In fact, quite a lot of scholarship preceded Bennett's 1968 article. See, for example, Edward Magdol, "Owen Lovejoy's Role in the Campaign of 1858," *Journal of the Illinois Historical Society* 59(1959): 403–16; and especially Quarles, *Lincoln and the Negro* (1962); and Arvarh E. Strickland, "The Illinois Background of Lincoln's Attitude toward Slavery and the Negro," *Journal of the Illinois State Historical Society* 55(1963): 474–94. See also Leon Litwack, *North of Slavery: The Negro in the Free States, 1790–1860* (Chicago: University of Chicago Press, 1961); and Martin Duberman, ed., *The Antislavery Vanguard: New Essays on the Abolitionists* (Princeton: Princeton University Press, 1965). Since 1968 a number of important works have appeared on this issue. The best general study is Foner, *Free Soil;* a careful analysis is Fredrickson, "A Man but Not a Brother." Compare Stephen B. Oates, "Lincoln's Journey to Emancipation," *Our Fiery Trial* (Amherst: University of Massachusetts Press, 1979). The historiographical story is nicely summarized in Zilversmith's forthcoming "Lincoln and Race."

86. *Collected Works*, 3:145–46; see also 2:405, 498.

87. Kenneth M. Stampp, *The Imperiled Union: Essays on the Background of the Civil War* (New York: Oxford University Press, 1980), p. 128.

88. *Collected Works*, 2:256.

89. Ibid., 2:520.

90. Ibid., 2:405–6.

91. Frederick Douglass, "Oration in Memory of Abraham Lincoln, Delivered at the Unveiling of the Freedmen's Monument in Memory of Abraham Lincoln in Lincoln Park, Washington, D.C., April 14, 1876," *The Life and Writings of Frederick Douglass*, 8 vols., (New York: International Publishers, 1955), 4:312. Compare Breiseth, "Lincoln and Frederick Douglass: Another Debate," *Journal of the Illinois State Historical Society* 68(1975):9–26.

92. *Collected Works*, 2:255.

93. Ibid., 2:255–56.

94. Ibid., 2:132.

95. Ibid., 2:298–99; Earl Schenck Miers, ed., *Lincoln Day by Day: A Chronology, 1809–1865*, 3 vols., (Washington: Lincoln Sesquicentennial Commission, 1960), 2:114.

96. Fredrickson, "A Man but Not a Brother," p. 50, makes this point, repeating, without credit, Harry V. Jaffa, *Crisis of the House Divided: An Interpretation of the Lincoln-Douglas Debates* (Seattle: University of Washington Press, 1959), p. 61.

97. *Collected Works*, 2:274.

98. Ibid., 2:264.

99. Ibid.

100. Ibid., 2:222.

101. Ibid., 2:230.

102. See also ibid., 2:242, 244.

103. Herndon and Weik, *Lincoln*, p. 343.

104. James Gourley's statement to Herndon, Herndon/Weik Collection (Hertz, p. 384).

105. *Collected Works*, 1:315.

106. Albert Beveridge, *Abraham Lincoln, 1809–1858*, 2 vols. (New York: Houghton Mifflin, 1928), 2:575.

107. Ibid., 2:318.

Notes

Chapter 8

1. Roy P. Basler, ed., *The Collected Works of Abraham Lincoln*, 8 vols. (New Brunswick, N.J.: Rutgers University Press, 1953), 2:461–69.
2. Illinois State *Register*, June 19, 1858, p. 2.
3. *Collected Works*, 2:20–22.
4. For example, ibid., 3:20.
5. Ibid., 3:404.
6. Ibid., 4:263.
7. Almost all commentators on Lincoln and the 1850s agree with the observation. Don E. Fehrenbacher, *Prelude to Greatness: Lincoln in the 1850s* (Stanford: Stanford University Press, 1962), p. 80, noted that there is "no evidence of any organized movement in 1858 to push slavery into the free states, or of any disposition among members of the Supreme Court to attempt such folly." (For a complete discussion of the Dred Scott case, see Fehrenbacher, *The Dred Scott Case: Its Significance in American Law and Politics* [New York: Oxford University Press, 1978]). James G. Randall, *Lincoln the President: Springfield to Gettysburg*, 2 vols. (Gloucester, Mass.: Eyre and Spottiswoode, 1945), 1:108, termed Lincoln's conspiracy theory "quite fanciful and non-existant," Allen Nevins, *The Emergence of Lincoln*, 2 vols. (New York: Scribner's, 1950), 1:362, called Lincoln's theory a "partisan analysis" which "in the eyes of posterity, was pitched on a disappointingly low plane." And in David Donald's view, "These utterances [in the house divided speech] reveal more about the state of Lincoln's mind and the receptivity of the Northern audiences that cheered his speeches than they do about historical reality." David Donald, *Liberty and Union* (Lexington, Mass.: D. C. Heath, 1978), p. 71. There has been one major dissenter to this interpretation, Harry Jaffa, *Crisis of the House Divided: An Interpretation of the Lincoln-Douglas Debates* (Seattle: University of Washington Press, 1959), pp. 81, 277–78. Jaffa, however, marshalls evidence only regarding the Dred Scott decision. Lincoln's theory went well beyond that. Jaffa's interpretation has been echoed by George W. Fredrickson, "A Man but Not a Brother: Abraham Lincoln and Racial Equality," *The Journal of Southern History* 41 (1975), p. 45: ". . . it is important to recognize that the years after 1854 not only saw an effort to extend and nationalize slavery but also provided the occasion for a torrent of racist propaganda." In support of this assertion, Fredrickson footnotes his own *Black Image in the White Mind: The Debate on Afro-American Character and Destiny, 1817–1914* (New York: Harper Torchbooks, 1971), pp. 44–164; and Eugene H. Berwanger, *The Frontier Against Slavery* (Urbana: University of Illinois Press, 1967), pp. 123–37. These sources, however, only support Fredrickson's notion that there was a "torrent of racist propaganda." His idea that there was an effort to nationalize slavery remains unproven. Oddly enough, Richard Hofstadter, *The Paranoid Style in American Politics and Other Essays* (New York: Alfred A. Knopf, 1966), passes over Lincoln and the 1850s.
8. Frederick Douglass, "Oration in Memory of Abraham Lincoln, delivered at the Unveiling of the Freedmen's Monument in Memory of Abraham Lincoln in Lincoln Park, Washington, D.C., April 14, 1876," *The Life and Writings of Frederick Douglass*, 8 vols. (New York: International Publishers, 1955), 4:318.
9. *Collected Works*, 3:9.
10. Ibid., 3:16, 29, 145–46, 221–22, 248–49, 299–30.
11. See Christopher Breiseth, "Lincoln, Douglas, and Springfield," *The Public and Private Lincoln: Contemporary Perspectives*, ed. Cullom Davis et al. (Carbondale: Southern Illinois University Press, 1979), pp. 101–20.
12. David M. Potter, *The Impending Crisis, 1848–1861*, completed and edited by Don E. Fehrenbacher (New York: Harper and Row, 1976), p. 246. See also Kenneth M. Stampp, *An Imperiled Union: Essays on the Background of the Civil War* (New York: Oxford University Press, 1980), pp. 156–57.
13. Lawrence J. Friedman, "Antebellum American Abolitionism and the Problem of Violent Means," *The Psychohistory Review* 9(1980):26–32.
14. Bruce Catton, *This Hallowed Ground* (New York: Simon and Schuster, 1955), p. 23.
15. James Strachey, ed., *The Standard Edition of the Complete Psychological Works of Sigmund Freud*, 23 vols. (London: Hogarth Press, 1962), 10:153–320.

16. Ibid., 2:21–47.

17. Stampp, *An Imperiled Union*, pp. 242–43.

18. George Fitzhugh, *Cannibals All! Or Slaves without Masters*, ed. C. Vann Woodward (Cambridge: The Belknap Press of Harvard University Press, 1852), p. 252.

19. Ibid., p. 11.

20. *Collected Works*, 2:73.

21. Ibid., 2:91.

22. Lawrence J. Friedman, "Garrisonism Abolitionism and the Boston Clique: A Psychosocial Inquiry," *The Psychohistory Review* 7(1978):6–19.

23. Fitzhugh, *Cannibals All!*; see also Fitzhugh, *Sociology for the South or the Failure of Free Institutions* (New York: Burt Franklin, 1854).

24. Arnold Goldberg, ed., *The Psychology of the Self: A Casebook, Written with the Collaboration of Heinz Kohut* (New York: International University Press, 1978), p. 282.

25. Steven M. Stowe, "The 'Touchiness' of the Gentlemen Planter: The Sense of Esteem and Continuity in the Antebellum South," *The Psychohistory Review* 8(1979):6–15.

26. Fehrenbacher, *Prelude to Greatness*, p. 14.

27. Admissions records of the Jacksonville State Hospital, 1852–1860, Illinois State Archives.

28. Harriet Beecher Stowe, *Uncle Tom's Cabin* (New York: Collier Books, 1852), p. 104.

29. See chapter 4, pp. 90–91.

30. Potter, *The Impending Crisis*, p. 252.

31. Approximately 40 percent of the patients clearly indicated to the staff of the hospital at intake that they had been born abroad. However, for those whose place of origin is listed as an eastern state—a sizable number—many could well have been born abroad but lived in the East long enough to establish residency before moving to Illinois. For example, I suspect many Irish immigrants, named Massachusetts or New York as their place of origin.

32. Potter, *The Impending Crisis*, p. 254. Note David Bryon Davis, *The Slave Power Conspiracy and the Paranoid Style* (Baton Rouge: Louisiana State University Press, 1969).

33. Heinz Kohut, "Thoughts on Narcissism and Narcissistic Rage," *The Search for the Self: Selected Writings of Heinz Kohut, 1950–1978*, ed. Paul H. Orenstein, 2 vols. (New York: International Universities Press, 1978), 2:615–58. See also Charles B. Strozier, "Heinz Kohut and the Historical Imagination," *Advances in Self Psychology*, ed. Arnold Goldberg (New York: International Universities Press, 1980):397–406.

Chapter 9

1. Roy P. Basler, ed., *The Collected Works of Abraham Lincoln*, 8 vols. (New Brunswick, N.J.: Rutgers University Press, 1953) 1:265.

2. Herbert Mitgang, ed., *Abraham Lincoln, A Press Report: His Life and Times from the Original Newspaper Documents of the Union, the Confederacy and Europe* (Chicago: Quadrangle Books, 1971), p. 378.

3. Marquis Adolphe de Chambrun, *Impressions of Lincoln and the Civil War: A Foreigner's Account* (New York: Random House, 1952), pp. 21–22.

4. Ward Hill Lamon, *The Life of Abraham Lincoln: From His Birth to His Inauguration as President* (Boston: James E. Osgood, 1872), pp. 464, 470, 475.

5. Francis B. Carpenter, *Six Months at the White House with Abraham Lincoln: The Story of a Picture* (New York: Hurd and Houghton, 1867), p. 30.

6. Ibid., pp. 18, 82, 217.

7. Herndon to Cyrus D. Poole, September 5, 1886, Herndon/Weik Collection (Hertz, p. 12); William H. Herndon and Jesse W. Weik, *Life of Lincoln*, ed. Paul M. Angle (Cleveland: World Publishing, 1930), p. 473.

Notes

8. Henry Clay Whitney, *Life on the Circuit with Lincoln*, introduction and notes by Paul M. Angle (Caldwell, Idaho: Caxton Printers, 1940), p. 65.

9. Ibid., pp. 51–52.

10. *Collected Works*, 1:59.

11. Ibid., 1:78.

12. Carpenter, *The Story of a Picture*, pp. 44–46.

13. John Hay, *Lincoln and the Civil War in the Diaries and Letters of John Hay*, ed. Tyler Dennett (Westport, Conn.: Nego Universities Press, 1972), p. 30; compare p. 182.

14. Mitgang, *A Press Report*, p. 378.

15. Lamon, *Lincoln*, pp. 476–77.

16. *Collected Works*, 1:268.

17. Ibid., 4:64.

18. Whitney, *Life on the Circuit*, p. 51. In a footnote the editor of Whitney's book, Paul M. Angle, contrasts Whitney's account with that of William A. Grimshaw, who encountered a resolute Lincoln on the day of his defeat to Douglas. Angle's purpose seems to be to cast doubt on the authenticity of Whitney's account. However, it is quite possible Lincoln showed two different moods on the same day.

19. *Collected Works*, 1:95.

20. Ibid., 1:289.

21. Hay, *Diaries*, p. 11.

22. Orville Hickman Browning, *The Diary of Orville Hickman Browning*, 2 vols. (Springfield: Illinois State Historical Library, 1925), 1:489.

23. *Collected Works*, 1:8.

24. Carpenter, *The Story of a Picture*, p. 145.

25. Lamon, *Life of Lincoln*, p. 468.

26. *Collected Works*, 2:81.

27. Ibid., 4:64.

28. Note in this regard David Donald's chapter, "A. Lincoln, Politician," *Lincoln Reconsidered: Essays on the Civil War Era* (New York: Alfred A. Knopf, 1956), pp. 57–81.

29. Ibid., p. 88.

30. Don E. Fehrenbacher, *Prelude to Greatness: Lincoln in the 1850's* (Stanford: Stanford University Press, 1962), pp. 19–47.

31. Hay, *Diaries*, p. 179. The earlier quotes are from pages 76, 11, 29, 66, 69, 77, 204, and 125.

32. Ibid., 76.

33. David Elton Trueblood, *Abraham Lincoln: Theologian of American Anguish* (New York: Harper and Row, 1973), p. 9.

34. Heinz Kohut first formulated these criteria in "Forms and Transformations of Narcissism" (1966), *The Search for the Self: Selected Writings of Heinz Kohut, 1950–1978*, ed. Paul H. Ornstein, 2 vols. (New York: International Universities Press, 1978), 1:427–60. See also the discussion of Mr. M in *The Restoration of the Self* (New York: International Universities Press, 1977), pp. 1–62; and of Mr. E in *The Psychology of the Self: A Casebook*, ed. Arnold Goldberg (New York: International Universities Press, 1978), pp. 263–96. Such criteria without theoretical foundation are necessarily arbitrary; see, for example, Martin A. Sweeney, "The Personality of Lincoln the War President," *Social Studies* 65 (1974):164–67.

35. Carpenter, *The Story of a Picture*, pp. 148–49.

36. Herndon and Weik, *Lincoln*, p. 244.

37. Ibid., pp. 238–39.

38. *Collected Works*, 2:10–11.

39. De Chambrun, *Impressions*, p. 82.

40. Lamon, *Lincoln*, pp. 478–79.

41. Carpenter, *The Story of a Picture*, pp. 149–50.

42. Herndon and Weik, *Lincoln*, pp. 249–50.

43. Carpenter, *The Story of a Picture*, p. 278.

44. Herndon and Weik, *Lincoln*, p. 94. See also Paul Findley, *A. Lincoln: The Crucible of Congress* (New York: Crown Publishers, 1979), p. 67.

45. Donald, *Lincoln Reconsidered*, p. 70.

46. Carpenter, *The Story of a Picture*, pp. 80–81.

47. David C. Mearns, *The Lincoln Papers: The Story of the Collection with Selections to July 4, 1861*, 2 vols. (New York: Doubleday, 1948) 1:169.

48. Roy P. Basler, *A Touchstone for Greatness: Essays, Addresses, and Occasional Pieces about Abraham Lincoln* (Westport, Conn.: Greenwood Press, 1973), p. 21.

49. *Collected Works*, 8:420.

50. Herndon fragment, n.d., Herndon/Weik Collection (Hertz, pp. 398–99).

51. Herndon and Weik, *Lincoln*, p. 94.

52. *Collected Works*, 1:510.

53. Ibid., 1:508, 516. See also Mitgang, *A Press Portrait*, p. 26.

54. Mitgang, *A Press Portrait*, pp. 17–18.

55. Ibid., p. 71.

56. Herndon and Weik, *Lincoln*, p. 256.

57. Donald, *Lincoln Reconsidered*, pp. 115–16.

58. Hay, *Diaries*, p. 68.

59. Ibid., pp. 79–80.

60. Whitney, *Life on the Circuit*, pp. 146–47.

61. Lord Byron, *Don Juan*, Canto IV, stanza 4.

62. Mitgang, *A Press Portrait*, p. 378.

63. Lamon, *Lincoln*, pp. 478–79.

64. Herndon and Weik, *Lincoln*, p. 473.

65. De Chambrun, *Impressions*, p. 100. Note also Herndon to Jesse Weik, February 21, 1891, Herndon/Weik Collection (Hertz, p. 263), and December 22, 1888 (Hertz, p. 231); and to C. O. Poole, January 5, 1886, Herndon/Weik Collection (Hertz, p. 124).

66. Carpenter, *The Story of a Picture*, p. 150.

67. S. A. Crawford to Herndon, January 4, 1886, Herndon/Weik Collection (Hertz, pp. 285–87).

68. Mitgang, *A Press Portrait*, p. 35.

69. Justin G. Turner and Linda Levitt Turner, eds., *Mary Todd Lincoln: Her Life and Letters* (New York: Alfred A. Knopf, 1972), pp. 293, 299.

70. *Collected Works*, 3:254; compare 8:96.

71. Whitney, *Life on the Circuit*, p. 119.

72. Carpenter, *The Story of a Picture*, p. 33.

73. Donald, *Lincoln Reconsidered*, pp. 70–71.

74. *Collected Works*, 8:116–17.

75. Ibid., 8:332–33.

76. Whitney, *Life on the Circuit*, pp. 121–22.

77. Herndon and Weik, *Lincoln*, p. 258.

78. *Collected Works*, 4:62. See also William Greene to Herndon, May 29, 1865, Herndon/Weik Collection (not published in Hertz).

79. James T. Hickey has attempted to track down the books Lincoln may have read while in New Salem. However, Hickey could only verify for certain that the books were available for Lincoln; whether he read them is another question. See James T. Hickey, "Three R's in Lincoln's Education: Rogers, Riggin & Rankin," *Journal of the Illinois State Historical Society* 52(1959): 195–207.

80. Herndon to Jesse Weik, October 21, 1885, Herndon/Weik Collection (Hertz, p. 95).

81. Luther E. Robinson, *Abraham Lincoln as a Man of Letters* (New York: G. P. Putnam's Sons, 1923), p. 20; Daniel K. Lodge, *Abraham Lincoln: Master of Words* (New York: Appleton & Co., 1924), p. 7.

82. *Collected Works*, 2:390.

83. James G. Randall, *Lincoln the President: Springfield to Gettysburg*, 2 vols. (Gloucester, Mass.: Eyre and Spottiswoode, 1945), 1:3.

84. Roy P. Basler, "Abraham Lincoln's Rhetoric," *American Literature* 11(1939): 170–71; compare Basler, *Touchstone*, p. 56.

85. Sandburg, *The Prairie Years*, 1:416.

86. Trueblood, *Theologian*, p. 49. Basler, "Lincoln's Rhetoric," p. 173, counts 272 words in the Gettysburg Address; I count 268 words. Perhaps humanists should not deal with numbers.

Notes

87. Trueblood, *Theologian*, p. 56.

88. Ibid., p. 49.

89. William K. Wimsatt and Cleanth Brooks, *Literary Criticisms: A Short History* (New York: Vintage Books, 1972), p. 74.

90. Basler, "Lincoln's Rhetoric," (1939).

91. Ibid., p. 173.

92. Herndon to Jesse Weik, October 21, 1885, Herndon/Weik Collection (Hertz, p. 95).

93. *Collected Works*, 1:111.

94. John G. Nicolay and John Hay, *Abraham Lincoln: A History*, 10 vols. (New York: Century, 1890), 3:343-44.

95. *Collected Works*, 6:392. See also Lamon, *Lincoln*, pp. 477-78; and Carpenter, *The Story of a Picture*, pp. 49-52.

96. David C. Mearns, *Largely Lincoln* (New York: St. Martin's Press, 1961), pp. 126-27.

97. Hay, *Diaries*, p. 138.

98. Ibid., p. 139.

99. Don E. Fehrenbacher, "Lincoln and the Weight of Responsibility," *Journal of the Illinois State Historical Society* 68(1975): 48.

100. *Collected Works*, 6:392.

101. Ibid., 6:392.

102. De Chambrun, *Impressions*, p. 83.

103. Fehrenbacher, "Lincoln and the Weight of Responsibility," p. 53.

104. George B. Forgie, *Patricide in the House Divided: A Psychological Interpretation of Lincoln and His Age* (New York: Norton, 1979), pp. 243-50.

105. Basler, *Touchstone*, p. 206.

106. Ibid., p. 225.

107. Edmund Wilson, *Patriotic Gore: Studies in the Literature of the American Civil War* (New York: Oxford University Press, 1962), p. 106. For an odd, if interesting, approach to these issues, see A. Bronson Feldman, "Lincoln: The Creation of a Cult," *The Unconscious in History* (New York: Philosophical Library, 1959).

INDEX

Index

Index

Index